Creative Dialogue

Creative Dialogue ... al guide to dialogic learning for every teacher and parent. It presents practical ... ...hing children to be more thoughtful and creative, and to learn more effectively ... ...aking and listening in school and at home.

The book incl...

- practical wa... ... ...p dialogic learning in the classroom
- a guide to ... ...alk for thinking across the curriculum
- more than ... ...es for stimulating talk with children of all ages and abilities
- advice on ... ...ue to support assessment for learning
- ideas for ... ...listening skills and concentration.

Written t... ..., expert in teaching thinking, *Creative Dialogue* is essential reading for all who wisl... ...tand and develop dialogic learning in education today.

Robert F... ...as a Professor of Education at Brunel University and has written more than thirty book... ...aching, thinking and creativity.

Creative Dialogue

Talk for Thinking in the Classroom

Robert Fisher

Routledge
Taylor & Francis Group

LONDON AND NEW YORK

First published 2009
by Routledge
2 Park Square, Milton Park, Abingdon, Oxon OX14 4RN

Simultaneously published in the USA and Canada
by Routledge
270 Madison Avenue, New York, NY 10016

Routledge is an imprint of the Taylor & Francis Group, an informa business

Typeset in Bembo by
Keystroke, 28 High Street, Tettenhall, Wolverhampton
Printed and bound in Great Britain by
TJ International Ltd, Padstow, Cornwall

British Library Cataloguing in Publication Data
A catalogue record for this book is available from the British Library

Library of Congress Cataloging-in-Publication Data
Fisher, Robert, 1943–
Creative dialogue : talk for thinking in the classroom / Robert Fisher.
p. cm.
Includes index.
1. Communication in education. 2. Verbal behavior. 3. Teacher–student relationships.
4. Creative teaching. 5. Thought and thinking. I. Title.
LB1033.5.F565 2009
371.102'2–dc22   2009000187

ISBN10: 0–415–49726–4 (hbk)
ISBN10: 0–415–49727–2 (pbk)

ISBN13: 978–0–415–49726–8 (hbk)
ISBN13: 978–0–415–49727–5 (pbk)

Contents

Acknowledgements

The author thanks the many teachers and children who have contributed to his research into dialogic teaching and learning and, in particular, to Lizann O'Conor and Julie Winyard for their helpful advice on this book.

Every effort has been made to trace possible copyright holders but if any have been inadvertently overlooked acknowledgements will be made at the first opportunity.

Introduction

It's about being interested in what they think, not just whether they give the right answer.

(Teacher)

This book is written for anyone interested in teaching children how to think, to learn and to engage in creative dialogue. The message of the book is that the key to improving children's education is to improve the quality of dialogue between children and their teachers or carers. It argues that creative dialogue should feature in every lesson in school and be part of the daily experience of children at home. It is a message that reflects worldwide educational research into dialogic teaching and learning. The book identifies the principles of dialogic learning with children, and offers practical guidance to helping children of all ages and abilities learn through dialogue at home and in the classroom.

When a group of nine-year-olds were asked why dialogue with others was important, Andrea said: 'It helps you to think'. Dan replied: 'It helps to build your brain'. Pat added: 'It helps you learn more' (quoted in Fisher 2007a). Research shows that they are surely right. Human intelligence is primarily developed through speaking and listening. The quality of our lives depends on the quality of our thinking and on our ability to communicate and discuss what we think with others. Talk underpins literacy and children's ability to form relationships with others. It is the foundation of their verbal and emotional intelligence, and of success in learning and in life.

Dialogue is the primary means for developing intelligence in the human species. The large human brain evolved to enable individuals to negotiate through dialogue the complexities of social living. The capacity for dialogue was, and still remains, central to human flourishing. The vast majority of pieces of information that inform human lives have always been, and are today, not written but spoken, listened to and remembered. In much of education the insistence on the written as opposed to the oral has undervalued the fundamental importance of dialogue. How wrong are those educators and policy-makers who think that language education equates to and should be taught as 'literacy'. It is through the capacity to talk and listen that consciousness and understanding develop. Human consciousness originates in the motivation to share emotions, experiences, and activities with others. This 'dialogic' capacity is more fundamental than language, writing or tool use. It is through dialogue that children develop consciousness, learn control over their internal mental processes and develop the conceptual tools for thinking.

A child's self-awareness and ability to think creatively are first internalized from the dialogic bond formed between mother (or primary care-giver) and child (Hobson 2000). These dialogues begin pre-verbally, starting with peek-a-boo games in the cradle, opening up through dialogue a 'mental space' in which things become thinkable for the first time. A child's consciousness and repertoire of concepts is expanded through talk with significant others such as parents and peers. Children's dialogic experience before they enter school varies greatly in terms of potency and quality, putting some children at a disadvantage and empowering others with learning potential. This book is about how to empower the learning potential of children through dialogue.

The concept of 'dialogic teaching' builds upon a long tradition of theoretical and empirical research into the role of talk in learning and teaching. The fruits of this research have not always permeated into educational practice. Classroom research has found that children's experience of speaking and listening in the classroom is often not dialogic; nor does it necessarily lead to learning or stimulate cognitive response (Alexander 2006). Research shows that not all teachers fully exploit the potential of talk for learning in the classroom.

To help improve the capacity of children to learn through dialogue we need to make explicit the principles that underpin dialogic learning and, because educational practices can have profound effects on the brain in promoting or inhibiting habits of intelligent behaviour, we need to explore practical ways of developing dialogue with children. Many children are perceptive about the strengths and limitations of their teachers. When one child was asked whether her teacher was a good teacher she replied, 'No, because she never tells you what you don't already know.' Another complained: 'The teacher does all the talking. She's not interested in what we think.' A third commented: 'I dread getting things wrong so I keep quiet.' Children can also be perceptive about what they need. As one twelve-year-old put it: 'A teachers' job is not to make your work too easy, or too difficult. You need to be challenged and sometimes you make mistakes. If you don't make mistakes you don't learn.' Another said: 'A good teacher makes what you think matter.'

What this book is about

This book is about creative dialogue with children. It argues that not all speaking and listening is necessarily creative. Talking with and talk among children can be limited, repetitive and dull, but creative dialogue is about using talk to stimulate thinking and learning. Dialogues become creative when they are open-ended, allow for different opinions (including critical viewpoints) and stimulate new ideas.

In this introduction the principles of dialogic learning are discussed, as well as why children need dialogue, the different kinds of talk and special features of creative dialogue. Each chapter begins with a discussion of principles related to creative dialogue, and ends with examples of practical activities that may be used in the home or classroom and which illustrate the principles. The activities in each chapter are not offered as recipes but only as possible models for your own creative dialogues with children. Each chapter is a self-contained unit, thus allowing the reader to take any chosen route through the book. The index provides a guide to all the main topics explored in the book.

Chapter 1, 'Listening: learning to attend', discusses the necessary pre-conditions for good dialogue. It argues that learning to listen well is as important for teachers as for learners. It offers advice on helping children to become good listeners, including how to still the mind, focus attention, listen well and respond to what is heard, and suggests practical activities to help children listen, focus and attend.

Chapter 2, 'Questions for thinking', discusses the essential role of questions in sustaining creative dialogue. It discusses how to improve questioning, and how to help children ask better questions. The chapter ends with practical examples of how to stimulate creative questioning and talk with or among children.

Chapter 3, 'Creative talk for thinking', is about developing and sustaining the creative energy that characterises good talk. This energy needs to be stimulated by questions and challenges, making connections and seeing relationships, imagining what might be, exploring and reflecting critically on ideas, actions and outcomes. The key principles of talk for creative thinking are discussed as well as practical activities to stimulate creative dialogue.

Chapter 4, 'Critical talk for thinking', argues that children need to develop the skills of critical thinking to enrich their dialogue and help them identify and evaluate reasons; argue with care; assess the strength of evidence; give thoughtful reasons for opinions and actions; use inference, deduction and precise language to explain concepts and ideas, and use judgements based on criteria, reasons and evidence. The chapter ends with practical activities illustrating these points.

Chapter 5, 'Talking to learn across the curriculum', discusses some key principles of dialogic teaching and strategies to help children to know and understand key ideas and concepts; what skills and strategies to use to learn independently and as part of a group; how to use technology for learning and create their own learning and research plans in any subject, illustrated with practical activities to stimulate talking to learn across the curriculum.

Chapter 6, 'Talking together', explores children talking to think in pairs, trios or groups and shows how it can help children to better understand their learning tasks, including how to ask questions and solve problems with others, think more widely and deeply, learn collaboratively as part of a group and develop dialogic, social and cooperative skills, with some practical activities to stimulate children talking to think in groups.

Chapter 7, 'Extending talk for thinking', explores the practice of discussion in a community of enquiry to enable children to discuss philosophical issues in a large group, create their own agenda for dialogue, practice critical and creative thinking, develop social and emotional skills and practice the habits of intelligent behaviour, together with practical activities that can help promote a community of enquiry.

Chapter 8, 'Dialogic assessment', explores ways of engaging children in dialogic assessment of their learning. Dialogic assessment can help children to gain a better understanding of themselves as learners and of their learning needs. The key principles of dialogic assessment are discussed and fifteen practical activities illustrate how to practice elements of dialogic assessment.

Chapter 9, 'The dialogic future', discusses the need for children to think ahead, focus on creative futures, environmental challenges and possibility thinking. It discusses the limitations and the potential of technology.

The key principles of dialogic learning

The principles of dialogic learning that underpin this book are drawn from worldwide research, and in particular from three successful approaches to teaching through dialogue. These approaches are Piagetian approaches which aim to set pupils work one step ahead of their current level, Philosophy for Children programmes which update a 2000-year-old tradition of dialogic enquiry for classroom use, and Assessment for Learning strategies which embody dialogic principles in helping children assess their own learning. Three key principles are common to these approaches and are characteristic of successful lessons and learning conversations:

- dialogic challenge – dialogue that challenges thinking
- dialogic construction of meaning – dialogue that develops understanding
- dialogic review – dialogue that leads to self-awareness

Putting these key dialogic principles into practice is what this book is about.

Why children need dialogue

The following are some reasons why children need to be engaged in creative dialogue on a daily basis.

Dialogue and social success

We are preparing our children for an uncertain world. They will face a range of problems in an unpredictable future. Whatever the problems, they will need the skills and ability to work with others to find solutions. The ability to relate to others and to engage in creative dialogue will be a key to the future success of our children in both their public and private lives.

Dialogue and thinking

'The little girl had the making of a poet in her who, being told to be sure of her meaning before she spoke, said "How can I know what I think till I see what I say?" ' (Wallas, *The Art of Thought*, 1926). Dialogue forces children to translate their thoughts into words. It can expand children's thinking by creating thoughts that they would not have had before. As Paula, aged 10, said about discussion: 'You know it was good when you realise you have said things that you had never thought before.'

Dialogue and intelligence

Research has shown that a number of dialogic approaches can help raise levels of intelligence in children. This evidence is particularly strong in relation to cognitive acceleration programmes, philosophy for children and assessment for learning. These approaches share a number of similar features, including classroom dialogue, open-ended collaborative learning activities and self-assessment. Making thinking and learning more 'visible' through dialogue in classrooms is crucial to developing intelligence and learning for understanding.

Dialogue and creativity

The mind's power of invention enables us to create new ideas about the world. Thinking becomes creative through the use of imagination. Imagination may be thought of as the mind's plastic material, enabling us to conceive of things that are beyond the senses. Like clay it allows us to mould thoughts and ideas into new forms. But imagination can lie dormant unless engaged, expressed and practised through creative thought, talk and activity.

The following are some characteristics that make dialogue creative:

- many voices
- different viewpoints
- open-ended speculation
- shared understanding (even if it is agreement to a difference of opinion).

Dialogue and well-being

Dialogue contributes to human well-being. For many people childhood is not a carefree time. In an increasingly materialistic, competitive world children are subjected to many of the same stresses and strains as adults. They can become just as irritable, anxious and depressed. They are bombarded by an information overload of words, images and noise, surrounded by demanding and persuasive voices telling them what to think, value and buy. They are prey to the frustration and anger of others and often experience negative emotions more deeply and intensely than do adults. Many find it hard to articulate their problems. No wonder so many find concentrating in class difficult and are impulsive in their behaviour. Targets, tests and exams increase pressure in schools. We need to find natural ways for children to combat the pressures of modern living and better ways to focus children's minds on matters of importance.

Dialogue provides an opportunity for children to connect to others, to express feeling and emotion, to communicate needs and to answer worries. No wonder dialogue is the primary therapeutic tool in helping people to develop positive relationships with themselves and with others.

Dialogue and employability

Contemporary work and culture will present children with a range of dialogic demands. This can be illustrated by the sorts of skills employers are looking for. In one survey about 25 per cent of employers reported skill shortages in:

- communication
- customer handling

- team-working
- problem-solving.

(National Skills Task Force Research Report, 2000)

The ability to communicate, relate to, work and solve problems with others are essential if children are to maximise success in the workplace.

Dialogue and problem-solving

Classroom research shows that some groups solve problems better than others. In problem-solving tasks, groups that succeed best tend to:

- listen to each other
- be able to ask for help
- be willing to change their ideas.

Successful groups are more dialogic.

Dialogue and democracy

Dialogue is a crucial element in educating for democracy. Children are flooded with written and visual information. They need to be given a voice; a voice to question, to challenge, to construct and deconstruct the meanings around them. They need to exercise choice in making decisions that fulfil their needs. As Jason, aged 10, says: 'Everyone is telling you things and not getting you to think things through.' A dialogue that is genuinely interactive is an exercise in democratic citizenship. If a dialogue is to model democratic processes then what children say and think is as important as what teachers, parents or carers say.

What kind of talk is dialogue?

There are many kinds of talk that teachers, parents and carers use with children. These can be divided into five broad categories: telling, questioning, conversation, discussion and dialogue.

Telling – 'I tell you'

The need to tell children things is clear, since they lack knowledge and experience of the world, and without knowledge the world will remain in a state of 'buzzing blooming confusion'. The traditional approach to teaching was that of instruction and rote learning. The teachers told their students what they thought the students needed to know and the students were supposed to remember it. Facts, ideas, principles and procedures were implanted into children's heads by means of constant repetition. Teaching by exposition or lecturing, when well done, can be cognitively challenging and can form a basis for thinking and dialogue, but telling does not constitute dialogue nor does it teach anything about dialogue. It is part of what children need, and may provide the necessary groundwork for discussion.

Telling puts the teacher firmly in control of classroom events and of the ideas with which the lesson deals. No wonder that in classrooms where telling dominates there is a lack of deep learning, understanding, confidence and the capacity of children to engage in dialogue. Telling tends to persuade children that learning comes from what others say and not what you think and say for yourself. Few classrooms today rely on teachers simply telling children what to think and believe. Usually telling is augmented by the teacher's use of questions.

Questioning – 'Can you tell me . . .?'

Question-and-answer is a common technique to find out what children know and to build understanding. Questions like 'What was it called?', 'What is the answer?', 'What do you know about . . .?' are designed to focus attention, elicit a response and stimulate children to recall what they know. This technique is often combined with repetition, either of the question or of the child's answer, in order to highlight it or to encourage an alternative. Prompting is another feature of 'question-and-answer' sessions, where the teacher cues the right answer, as in the following example – Teacher: 'What kind of an animal is a frog? . . . An amph . . . an amphib . . . Yes an amphibian!' Sometimes the prompting takes the form of exhortation where the teacher encourages the child to 'think', to 'try', to 'remember', as when a teacher said: 'Oh come on, you know it, we did it yesterday, you got it right then, try to remember, what's wrong with you, everyone else knows . . . let me give you a clue. . . .'

Another common feature of teacher questioning is reformulation, where teachers paraphrase in their own words what the child has said either to make its meaning clearer or to make it easier to understand for others. These are all teacher-directed techniques. They are not sufficient for encouraging children to think for themselves. They encourage children to play the game 'guess what is in the teacher's mind'. They encourage children to think that learning is about 'getting the right answer' and not thinking things through, that it is about the questions that teachers ask and not about questions that children might ask. They are not about creative dialogue.

However, questioning may be used to scaffold and facilitate genuine dialogue. For more on ways that questioning can be used to stimulate creative dialogue see Chapter 2.

Conversation – 'Let's talk'

Conversation is merely friendly social talk, simply speaking and listening with others that needs no further purpose than that. One dictionary defines it as 'talk merely to avoid a silence'. It is often what happens when children are put into pairs and groups without any clear purpose or monitoring; their talk usually descends into mere conversation, gossip and anecdote. Conversation can be about deep matters and human concerns, but it is often more about relating to others through the casual interplay of ideas. That is why merely 'speaking and listening' is not enough for creative dialogue and does not guarantee learning. As one child said when challenged by a teacher: 'We were just talking, it was only a conversation . . . it didn't mean anything.'

In conversations speakers build positively but uncritically on what the other has said. They use talk to construct a 'common knowledge' by addition. Conversation is characterised by telling – I tell you something, you tell me something back – and by repetition, confirmation and elaboration. Conversation is a vital means of sharing personal experience. What children learn through conversation is incidental, with pieces of knowledge and odd snippets of information picked up by chance. Such 'learning conversations' are more effective if they involve questions that take the talk further. But conversations for learning are most effective when they take the form of discussions or dialogues.

Discussion – 'Let's discuss this . . .'

Discussion is a form of talk that is made systematic by having a focus or purpose. A discussion often involves argument or debate around a given topic. A discussion where there is no focus or subject matter is a conversation. A conversation where there is an agreed agenda or purpose is a discussion. As Melanie, aged 11, put it: 'You have to stick to the point otherwise you're not discussing it.'

A discussion often involves differences of opinion and the use of reasoned arguments. The subject matter of a discussion will determine how it is described (for example, a philosophical discussion will involve philosophical topics, a political discussion will involve political argument from differing viewpoints). A discussion is not a free-for-all or talking shop. There is an expectation in a discussion that knowledge and understanding will come from testing argument and evidence, analysing ideas and exploring values rather than just accepting what somebody says, as is common in a conversation. In a discussion you are expected to justify your point of view. As Tania, aged 8, said, 'You can't just say something, you must say why.'

Discussion can be characterised by disagreement and disputation. Where discussion becomes disputational there may be few attempts to pool ideas or to offer constructive criticism of suggestions. When discussion becomes disputational it is characterised by short exchanges consisting of assertions, challenges and counter-assertions. As Ben, aged 10, said: 'If you keep repeating the same thing you go round and round and no one gets anywhere.'

Dialogue – 'Let's think together . . .'

A dialogue has many characteristics of discussion but does not necessarily have a set agenda. A dialogue, unlike a monologue, involves two or more people listening to each other, sharing ideas and taking account of different viewpoints. A dialogue aims to be a meeting of minds. So there can be discussion, or an exchange of set viewpoints, without any real understanding or dialogue (as is often the case when politicians are brought together for a 'discussion' and each simply ends up reiterating their differing policies). In a dialogue, those involved are seeking to reach a common understanding, though not necessarily agreement. In a dialogue, participants build on each other's ideas and try to link them into coherent lines of thinking and enquiry.

A dialogue becomes creative when it allows for playful and divergent ideas. A creative dialogue is purposeful but it follows the thinking of the participants and does not necessarily keep to a set agenda. It is open to variation, innovation and unexpected lines of enquiry. It is generative and open-textured, and has the potential to move in a multiplicity of directions and reach unexpected conclusions. It becomes an opportunity, as Carla says, 'for taking out your feelings and showing them to someone'.

Examples illustrating these features of creative dialogues appear throughout this book taken from traditional stories featuring the legendary wise man and trickster the Mulla Nasruddin. Nasruddin stories are traditional teaching stories that have been handed down for generations throughout the Middle East. What is special about a Nasruddin story is that it may be understood at many levels. Each story illustrates a creative response to a human problem expressed through dialogue. They are meant to be jokes with a moral. They are not about the problems we face but are analogies that may enable us to see connections with our own lives and problems. They can be used to stimulate dialogue or discussion with children or be enjoyed as creative dialogues for their own sake. Here is an example:

> One day four boys approached Nasruddin and gave him a bagful of walnuts. 'Nasruddin, we can't divide these walnuts among us evenly. So would you help us, please?'
>
> Nasruddin asked, 'Do you want God's way of distribution or the human's way?'
>
> 'God's way,' the children answered. Nasruddin opened the bag and gave two handfuls of walnuts to one child, one handful to the other, only two walnuts to the third child and none to the fourth.
>
> 'What kind of sharing is this?' demanded the baffled children.
>
> 'Well, this is God's way,' he answered. 'He gives some people a lot, some people a little and nothing to others. If you had asked me for the human way I would have given the same amount to everyone.'

Facilitating dialogue is not easy. What we are aiming for is the highest form of human communication that it is possible to achieve. We are trying to facilitate interaction that is at the peak of nature's organising power. Nothing that we know of in the universe has the communicative capacity that humans have, but the ripest fruit is often the hardest to reach. You only achieve difficult ends by taking risks, and risk-taking sometimes results in failure. The important point is that communicative failures need only be temporary if others are there to give the dialogic support that may be needed.

Both discussion and dialogue facilitate exploratory talk, where partners engage critically and creatively with each other's ideas. Statements and suggestions are offered for joint consideration. These may be challenged and counter-challenged, but challenges are justified and alternative hypotheses are offered. Compared with conversation, in exploratory talk knowledge depends on reasoning rather than just telling.

Dialogic teaching is not just getting children to say what they think but is also challenging them to be creative and to think in new ways. Dialogue is creative because it is about improvising and making connections between ideas and concepts that you have not thought of connecting before.

Dialogue across differences: the development of empathy

Dialogue is needed to help develop understanding of others (empathy, or what Goleman calls 'social intelligence'). It should involve a reciprocal relationship in which not only the child but also the teacher or parent is challenged to think. Martin Buber, in his seminal work *I and Thou*, draws a distinction between the 'I–thou' type of relationship, characterised by mutual responsiveness, and 'I–it' relationships in which an active subject confronts and dominates a passive object. Bakhtin, in a similar vein, contrasts the 'authoritative' voice, which demands that we either accept or reject it, with the 'persuasive' voice that enters into us and stimulates our own answering words. In a genuine dialogue the authority should be shared; each is allowed a 'persuasive voice' and it is the differences in what the voices have to say that makes a dialogue creative.

Dialogue provides a space for thinking. The philosopher Heidegger distinguishes two kinds of thinking in dialogue, which he calls 'calculative' and 'reflective' thinking. Calculative thinking is narrowly focused on a specific end or result, whereas reflective thinking is characterised by thinking things through in an open-minded way. Dialogue that is a space for shared reflection is what Habermas calls an 'ideal speech situation'. It is ideal to the extent that it is underpinned by certain rules, including that of participants having equal rights to question the claims of others, and by the attitude of wanting to reach a shared understanding (see p. 151 for more on the ground rules for dialogue). Dialogue becomes creative when thinking is shared.

Many researchers, like Vygotsky, have argued that a child's capacity for verbal reasoning is best developed through dialogue with others. Vygotsky said that: 'all that is internal in the higher mental functions was at one time external', meaning that individual cognitive ability stems from some prior dialogic experience when similar cognitive tasks are performed with the help of others. He saw dialogue as fundamentally a cooperative enterprise aimed at ever-greater agreement. For him the ideal speech situation is one in which agreement is reached and misunderstandings are resolved. But for Bakhtin what is special about dialogue is the distinctiveness of the *other*. It is the very 'otherness' of each person, speaking from a different viewpoint, that makes dialogue productive. For him success in dialogue is not measured by consensus; the aim of dialogue is to reveal differences of opinion. Each voice which speaks should expect an answering voice that is different, and it is differences that make dialogue so potentially enriching.

Here then is a dilemma – do we seek a consensus or value diversity and difference of opinion in our dialogues with children? Perhaps a good dialogue should both respect the 'otherness' of the child and value differences of opinion while seeking to reach a common understanding. We may not succeed in creating an 'ideal speech situation' but we can aim to include more dialogue in our teaching of children and make our dialogue with them more creative by using talk to:

- probe
- challenge and
- spark their thinking.

Creative dialogue: the heart of personalised learning

The personalising of learning, which means putting the student or learner at the heart of the educative process, has always been the essence of effective teaching and of lifelong learning. At the heart of personalised education is self-expression through talk. As Peter, aged 8, put it: 'A good teacher is interested in what you are thinking.' Talk is the most effective means of finding out what children are thinking, feeling or learning. However, research shows that the quality of classroom talk has the power to enable or inhibit cognition and learning (Alexander 2006; Hattie 2008).

Education is about children as *persons* in all aspects of their humanity; not just as a bundle of specific gifts and talents, but as people in their wholeness including the physical, emotional, intellectual, social and economic aspects of their being. Persons are not merely the *functions* they fulfil, the skills and standards they can achieve, but are, more fundamentally, the *inner purposes* of their lives as human beings living among others. These purposes include self-expression, a sense of self-worth and self-knowledge, as well as social relationships with and knowledge of others (for an activity that invites dialogue on what a person is see p. 199).

We find out what makes us individual by being in communion with ourselves and with others. As Maria, aged 9, put it: 'It is not enough to just go round and round in your own thoughts, you need to get others to tell you what they think or how else are you going to get more thoughts?' Personalising learning through dialogue is about making all students special.

TABLE 1 Some differences between creative dialogue and traditional interaction

CREATIVE DIALOGUE	TRADITIONAL INTERACTION
Children's questions	Teacher's questions
Shared agenda	Teacher's agenda
Imaginative	Informative
Exploratory	Limited focus
Variation of viewpoint	One directing view
Reflective	Calculative
'I–thou' relationship	'I–it' relationship
Persuasive	Authoritative
Possible answers	Right answers
Cooperative enquiry	Competitive answer-giving
Personalised learning	Content-focused learning
Related to inner purposes	Related to functional outcomes

It recognises that as human beings they are both 'at potential' as well as 'at risk', and need practice in communicating what they think as well as in responding to the thinking of others. In short they learn best to become themselves through dialogue with others.

Table 1 sums up some of the differences that might distinguish creative dialogue from traditional teacher–pupil interaction. Traditional teacher–pupil interaction is a necessary feature of learning, but it is not sufficient, nor is it the best means for maximising the learning potential of children. Traditional teacher talk tends to place limits on learning, whereas research suggests that creative dialogue expands the possibilities of children's learning.

A Japanese proverb says: 'Don't learn it, just get used to it.' We need to get used to disturbing the current levels of children's thinking through talk that extends, challenges and surprises. We need to help children practise being creative through dialogue, to think for themselves, to develop the capacity to talk intelligently with others and to use dialogue to aid learning. Given the challenges children face today and the problems they will have to face in the future there can be no more important task for teachers than to improve children's capacity both to think for themselves and to benefit from the thinking of others by means of dialogue. As one teacher said about her work in engaging children in dialogue for learning: 'It's very hard, but it's by far the most satisfying part of teaching.'

1

Listening

Learning to attend

There was an old owl who lived in an oak
The more he heard the less he spoke,
The less he spoke the more he heard
Oh why can't we be like that wise old bird.
                    Old nursery rhyme

This chapter is about creating the optimum conditions for good dialogue. Human attention naturally wanders and children often find that concentration is not easily sustained. Listening well is a skill that has to be learned. Active listening engages the mind. To listen well, children need to learn how to focus and attend. The processes of active listening outlined in this chapter include:

1 Stilling the mind

2 Focusing attention

3 Listening well

4 Responding to what you hear

5 Learning to listen, focus and attend in practice.

The better children listen, the more their brains take in, and the more they will learn. Listening is one of the most important skills for effective learning. Children tend to remember the things they hear more easily than the things they read. The first half of this chapter is about helping children to become good listeners. The second half offers practical activities to help children learn to become active listeners.

Any good learning conversation requires a balance of attention and articulation. If in education we simply focus on the articulation of ideas we miss the other vital elements in the interaction of minds – that of listening, focusing and sustained attention. Dialogue requires attentive listening as much as the fluent use of words. However, like all of us, children do not listen at the same intensity all the time; rather they tend to listen in erratic spurts. Listening takes time – it is a slow process, whereas thinking is a very fast process. We think four times faster than anyone can talk and have lots of time to fill our heads with other thoughts, any of which can be distracting.

This can be a particular problem first thing in the morning when children's heads are full of other things, after the physical and emotional 'rough-and-tumble' of playtime, or after protracted periods of passive activity. At such times merely saying, 'sit down and pay attention', may not be enough. They need an activity that grabs and holds their attention.

Our attention system has evolved to recognise dramatic changes that signal danger and to ignore steady states of gradual change and subtle differences. Human attention is focused by sudden surprises. In talking with children we need to capture their attention from the very start, just as we would do in any lesson or at the start of any learning activity. As Chris, aged 10, put it: 'I like to listen when it's something new.'

What a good dialogue does is to help train children to hold and sustain attention. It also challenges children to focus attention on relevant memories, experience and knowledge and to shift attention to what others are saying. A good dialogue engages the receptive mind and a receptive mind depends on an attending ear.

Being able to direct attention helps children to fight off distraction. Directed attention is needed to help them to process information effectively and to sort the important from the unimportant among the vast quantities of stimuli they encounter on a daily basis. Dialogue can help children sustain attention when their thinking is challenged and where they have a range of possible responses that link to their personal concerns or engage them in ways of looking at the world that are their own. Open-ended dialogue offers them opportunities to share their thinking and attend to the thinking of others. To do this they need to shift and re-focus their attention. It is therefore worth discussing with children their own ability to focus attention and to listen well. Discuss with children what it means to be a good listener. Donna, aged 10, said: 'To be a good listener you need to think. If you're not thinking you're not really listening.'

Ask children to think about and discuss the difference between 'hearing' and 'listening'. Does being able to hear automatically mean they are listening? When they listen, the information they hear is processed by the conscious brain and enters short-term memory. The sounds their ears hear are not necessarily processed, since their brains may be engaged on other things. Much of what you can hear is not processed but is ignored by the brain. We can hear it but do not listen to it, so we are not aware of it.

We need to listen to a problem carefully before deciding what method to use to solve it. For example, tell your children this problem about runaway sheep:

> *A farmer has seventeen sheep in his pen. All but nine of them escape. How many are left?*
>
> **Ask them to find the answer to this problem. What is the answer?**

If a problem ends with 'how many are left?' it is common for people to think that the answer is reached by subtraction and therefore 17–9 leaves 8. But on carefully listening to (or reading) the problem it says that 'all but nine escaped', so of course nine were left. Subtraction is not the right method; careful listening (or reading) of the problem is.

A common problem about listening is that we often hear what we expect to hear. Listening is influenced by past experience, expectations and beliefs. The brain gets into habits of interpreting sounds in particular ways. If children have heard something before, they will tend to interpret it in the same way. Their past experience will influence what they think they hear. If someone whom they think is boring begins to speak, they will expect what they have to say to be boring and may switch off. If they believe what they are hearing is important, they will tend to listen carefully.

Memory is the daughter of attention. We cannot expect children to focus on or remember what they do unless we help to train their attention. A good idea therefore is to say to children: 'Listen carefully because I am going to make a mistake in the next x minutes and I want to see if you spot it.' Then of course you need to make a (deliberate) mistake. Some specific attention-training strategies are included on pp. 24–5. These involve actually hearing what is being said and not listening with one ear as you think about something else. To do this you must first try to eliminate distracting noise and thoughts, and to still the mind.

Stilling the mind

A Zen story tells of a professor who came to the Zen master Nan-in to learn about Zen. Nan-in poured the professor a cup of tea, and when the cup was full he kept pouring. The professor protested, 'Stop! The cup is overfull already.' Nan-in replied: 'Your mind is overfull like this cup. To learn about Zen you must first empty your cup.'

The optimum psychological state for engaging in dialogue is one of relaxed attention. Children will not be able to engage fully in dialogue (which involves critical and creative thinking) until they have quietened any distracting thoughts buzzing in their brains and calmed their emotions. Discuss with your children ways of calming down and stilling the mind. Give them the chance to make posters to display their own calming-down strategies and share their 'cueing' words (such as the rhyme below). This cue alerts the child to the need to use a calming-down strategy. Older children might devise their own mantra of calming-down words:

> Get your body calm and ready.
> Get your thinking cap on steady!

It is important that children are encouraged to use their favoured calming techniques each time the need arises. Ideas for calming down include:

- Tell yourself to STOP AND THINK!
- Give yourself thinking time.
- Tell yourself you can handle this!
- Say to yourself: 'Be calm . . . be calm . . . be calm.'
- Walk away from what bothers you.
- Count backwards from 10, 20, or 100.
- Tell someone else how you feel.

- Breathe deeply and slowly – in and out five times.

- Tense and relax your muscles.

- Go for a walk.

- Go into a quiet area to be by yourself.

- Feel your pulse.

- Picture yourself dealing with the situation calmly and strongly.

(With thanks to Kevin Hogston for suggesting many of these strategies which he uses with his children at Latchmere School.)

Do you have other strategies for calming down? Discuss which strategies you think work for you with a partner (see activity on p. 24).

One series of strategies for stilling the mind and focusing attention with a long tradition and gaining ground in schools is meditation, as I found as a new teacher more than thirty years ago when struggling with a tough inner-city class of ten-year-olds. To help them gain more control over their minds and bodies I experimented by starting each session with a period of meditation. I aimed at first for half a minute of absolute stillness and silence, listening to 'distant sounds'. I wanted the children to develop the ability to still their minds and focus with full concentration whenever they needed or wanted to. In time we established a regular minute's-worth of absolute stillness and silence, then longer. For many of those children it was the first time they had heard absolute silence. One child described the silence as 'spooky'. But this small investment of time I found had a marked effect in calming the class and focusing them ready for dialogue and learning.

Many years later I met an ex-pupil from this class, now a successful businessman. I asked what he remembered of his time in my class. After a pause he said: 'I always remember those times we sat there and did nothing.' It took me a while to realise that what had stayed in his memory were our experiments in meditation.

Meditation

> Man . . . is a meditative being.
>
> (Martin Heidegger)

Meditation provides a good preparation for creative dialogue. It builds upon the long tradition of meditative practice in spiritual, religious and humanistic settings and is supported by evidence of the practical benefits that meditation can bring. Meditative experience provides useful groundwork for discussing with children body/mind concepts such as consciousness, thinking and imagination, and has been found to be an ideal preparation for philosophical discussion (Haynes 2008). Teachers report benefits in increased levels of concentration, anger management and relaxation in their classrooms (Fisher 2006).

The word 'meditation', derived from the Latin *meditatio*, originally referred to all types of physical or intellectual exercise. Later it came to mean contemplation, as when Christians 'meditate' on the sufferings of Christ, or as in Descartes's *Meditations* to refer to philosophical thinking about the nature of reality. Meditation can simply be defined as a range of mental states relating to attention, which include states of consciousness, concentratation and contemplation.

By the late nineteenth century the word 'meditation' was used to to refer to religious or spiritual practices drawn from various Eastern religions. The word 'meditation' was never an exact translation of any single term or concept (such as the Sanskrit *dhyana, samadhi* or *pranayama*). Forms of meditative practices are to be found within almost all religions as well as some humanist and secular traditions, such as the martial arts. Many religious traditions see meditation as a way to access the divine 'life force' that lies within us, a source of energy that connects the personal to the universal.

Researchers agree that we are at the very beginning of understanding the effects meditation can have on a child's brain and body. Teachers often find that students who have meditated tend to listen more attentively and deeply and so remember and experience more in a learning situation, but there is a need for more research and experimentation to extend professional knowledge about the effects of meditation with children. This is not just something for experts in meditative practice, but is for all who have, in the Japanese phrase *soshin*, 'beginners' minds'. As a Zen saying puts it: 'In the beginner's mind there are many possibilities, but in the expert's there are few'. The practice of meditation with children is full of possibility – as a means for stilling the mind, encouraging mindfulness, and providing optimum conditions for generative thinking and creative talk.

Critics will argue that hard evidence for the long-term benefits of meditation with children is lacking. But to ask whether there is statistical evidence that a class of students who engage in regular meditation will, for example, outperform, on a range of academic and psychological measures, a similar class who do not, is surely to miss the point. We know that consciousness and concentration in children is often patchy and intermittent, and that their attention is easily distracted. We know that many children suffer stress and anxiety and other psychological barriers to learning. If we can help children to be more 'mindful' – to still their minds, to focus and sustain attention, to control their emotions, and to clear their minds ready for thinking, dialogue or other creative activity – then we should surely do so.

Through meditation the mind can be stilled, the body relaxed and the spirit nourished, creating the optimum conditions for learning. If you focus your attention on an object in stillness and silence, your mind gradually becomes calmer and more receptive. In principle, any object will do – a sound, a visual image such as a candle flame, or a physical sensation. Receptive meditation means having a point of focus, such as a picture, object, sound, word or image, and being receptive to whatever experience is arising. Another way to still the mind and focus attention is through listening to music (for more on music see p. 120). Some traditions use chants, mantras or prayers for this purpose. The aim of this practice is to become more open and receptive, to achieve a heightened consciousness of experience. Experiment to find out what works best for you and your children. We can all benefit from the practice of 'still thinking'. As Jamie, aged 10, put it: 'It's like a shower. It cleans your mind, so you can do your best thinking.'

Meditation is about the stilling of children's minds. The ability to still the mind is developed through practice over time with experience of different ways of sustaining and focusing attention before, during or after a learning dialogue. This practice of attention can include attention to thoughts, words and experiences. Meditation can help to 'open the brain' and prepare children's minds by focusing and energising them ready for the challenge of creative learning. It can help children become aware of the ever-shifting nature of our consciousness. It can help to still our flickering minds and sustain our focus on what really matters. As Josh, aged 10, said: 'It helps me remember who I am.'

Stilling the mind needs practice, and activities to help in this may be found on p. 24.

Focusing attention

Nasruddin climbed into an orchard and started to pick the apricots. Suddenly the gardener saw him. Nasruddin instantly climbed up a tree. 'What are you doing here?' asked the gardener.

'Singing,' said Nasruddin, 'I'm a nightingale.'

'All right, let me hear you sing.' Nasruddin made strange squawking noises.

The gardener laughed. 'I've never heard a nightingale like that before,' he said.

'Ah, you have not travelled much,' said Nasruddin, 'that was the song of a rare and exotic nightingale.'

To learn well you need to turn your full attention to what you are doing. Listening is hard work because it takes attention and energy. Think about a time when you had to sit for a long period trying to concentrate on a speaker. Did you find your mind wandering to other things? It is not always easy to focus your attention or tune into what you are hearing, so that the brain is actively processing the information being taken in by the ears. To focus your attention you need to reduce distractions from outside and from within your mind.

The first thing to try to ensure is that the physical conditions for listening and learning are right. If you are cold, hungry, tired, cramped or uncomfortable your attention will be distracted by these physical inconveniences. You need to be in the best physical state for learning. This includes having a good diet of natural foods, fruit and pure drinks (and generally there is no purer drink than plain water). Dehydration leads to inattention. Make sure you are not thirsty. You need to drink the equivalent of eight glasses of water a day to be at your best.

The optimum physical temperature should be at least 20 degrees. If it is too hot or too cold the body begins to experience stress. You will not be able to listen or concentrate so well in an overheated room. If you feel the room is too hot or airless try to change the physical conditions or have a break. The quality of air is also important. It is easier to concentrate when the air is fresh rather than polluted with smoke or dust.

Your attention tunes in and out naturally, without you realising it. It varies between focused and peripheral attention, between internal and external attention and relaxed or vigilant attention. The ideal for listening is focused vigilant external attention. The trouble is that we humans find this difficult to sustain. We have a natural 'rest–activity–rest–activity' cycle. At certain points of the day we are more attentive than others. When we are fully attending, blood flow and oxygen to the brain increase. We cannot keep up full attention for long, usually for only about twenty or thirty minutes, so try to build brain breaks into your periods of study. Listening and learning improve if you have breaks during learning sessions. Physical exercise during these breaks also helps boost the energy needed for subsequent attention.

Just as you can train your muscles to work better, so you can train your mind and your senses. You can practise at becoming better at listening and attending. See p. 25 for activities designed to help you increase your attention and perception of sounds.

Visualising

Visualising is a form of focusing the mind, for example, by being guided on an imaginative journey and perhaps towards a personal creative response (see p. 25 for an example of such a guided journey). This kind of guided imagination features in religious traditions such as Japanese Shingon Buddhism, and in the Christian teachings of St Ignatius Loyola who proposed a series of imaginative visualisations as a means of deepening spiritual awareness (see p. 66).

Reflective meditation

Reflective meditation involves contemplating and repeatedly turning your attention to a stimulus and being open to whatever arises from the experience, such as a thought, question or image. The focus could be on a word or concept or a set of words (such as a prayer or poem), or on a visual, sound or kinaesthetic experience, such as a walking meditation. Here the response is not controlled or guided but open (for activities, see p. 24).

Once they are paying attention, children need to learn to continue to listen well.

Listening well

To learn well children must listen well; they will tend to do this if they have a good reason to listen. The following 'LISTEN' list of skills needed to be good listeners was compiled by a group of teachers:

L   Look ahead to what you will hear
I   Indicate you are listening
S   Select key words and ideas
T   Take part
E   Enquire
N   Note

To LISTEN well includes many skills, and the practice of these skills begins with looking ahead to what you are going to listen to. What do you expect to hear? Try to anticipate what you might hear. This will help you to be mentally prepared and in the right frame of mind. Try to be on time so you are ready to listen. Try to link in your mind what you are going to hear with what you already know.

Discuss with children:

■ How do you show you are listening? You focus your attention on what you are listening to by looking at the speaker and responding to them. You listen better if your body is right. Your body language – the way you sit, where you look, what you do – often shows whether you are listening or not. Have you ever spoken to someone who looks away, or is fiddling with something while you are speaking? Are they really listening to you?

■ Can you pick out two or three themes or objectives that are the main ideas of the lesson or topic? Speakers will often signpost their key ideas by saying things like: 'These are the reasons why . . .', 'Remember that . . .', or 'The most important thing is . . .'. You cannot remember everything you hear but you can try to pick out the main or the most interesting ideas.

■ Do you think about what you are listening to? Key ideas are usually supported by the giving of examples, explanations and evidence. Have you heard this before? How does this link with what you already know? Think about what you are listening to – if nothing else it will help to keep you awake.

■ Do you take part? Sit where you can see and be seen. Focus your thinking on the speaker and be open to what they say. Be positive and prepared to be interested in the person and what they are saying. Respond to the speaker by nodding, smiling, frowning. This encourages the speaker (no one likes talking to blank faces). This again is using your body language to show that you are not only listening but responding to what the speaker is saying. You do this personalised listening not just out of courtesy for the speaker but for yourself, to help you to listen well and remember what is being said.

■ Do you enquire about what is being said by asking questions? Have some questions in mind. Think of some more while you are listening; for example, *Why is the person saying this? How does he or she know? What are the reasons? What is the evidence?* If you do not understand any points ask a question, or for an example to help you understand the point being made.

■ With older children ask whether they take notes. Taking notes is an easy way of concentrating on and remembering what you hear (for more on note-taking see p. 25).

Try to make it necessary for the children to listen. Tell them you are not going to repeat instructions or information. Avoid repeating what children say; get them to remind you what has been said. Encourage children to speak audibly so that everyone can hear. Try at regular intervals to speak very quietly. Demonstrate active listening through eye contact, asking questions, and non-verbal responses such as smiles and nods. Ask children to reflect on how they listened (for a further listening activity see p. 26).

Responding to what you hear

What sort of listener are you? Do you tend to daydream during lectures? Are you anxious that you do not remember all that others are telling you? Do you wonder whether you should just listen or make notes? The trouble with listening to a lecture or speaker is that to learn best you need to do three things simultaneously:

- attend to what is being said

- think about and make sense of what is being said

- note what you should remember.

Trying to do these things all at once is a difficult task. Your mind has to jump quickly from one task to another. You not only have to attend to the talk but listen intelligently as well. The trouble with listening intelligently is that from time to time you have to stop and think (make connections with ideas already in your mind). To help you remember the key points you need to make notes, either during the talk or afterwards.

In making notes of a talk do not try to write down everything you hear. Listening is your main task, but you also need to note what you hear to help you remember. When you make notes try to make them brief and only pick out the main ideas. Do this either during or straight after the talk.

As we have seen, there is no one best way to take notes. Some people scribble away during a lecture, others take occasional notes of the key points, some sketch diagrams or thinking maps. If you try to write everything down you will probably learn very little from the talk or lecture. The beginnings and ends are often good times to take down notes. At the beginning there will often be clues given about the topic or structure of the talk; at the end there may be some conclusions. It may be useful to copy down any examples or illustrations about the key points. The names of important people or books may be mentioned. Questions may occur to you that you want to ask or find out about. The practice of writing brief notes and deciding what is or is not important during the talk may be more important than the notes you end up with. The act of making notes keeps your mind focused, active and alert.

Notes need not be words. Encourage children to use drawings, sketches or mind-maps to help in noting information and help focus on what they need to remember. 'Barrier games' are a good way to practise this. Put a barrier between speaker and listener to encourage a focus on listening to the words being said. Here are some examples of barrier games:

- Put children either side of a screen. The speaker describes an object that the listener cannot see but has to draw. The listener can ask questions to achieve a better understanding of the hidden object they have to draw.

- Blindfold a child. Their partner has to guide them using words only through a maze (e.g. of furniture).

- Ask a child to face the wall and listen while a friend speaks in a disguised voice and see if the listener can identify the mystery speaker.

Remember: we always hear but we do not always listen. If we listened better we would learn more. Listening to others and noting what they say is just one aspect of the way we can learn from, with and through others. However, hearing what people say is not enough; active listening means to listen and think, and preferably to discuss with others what one has heard before jumping to conclusions, as this tale illustrates:

One cold, wintry night Nasruddin arrived at a roadside inn and was happy to see a roaring fire in the courtyard. However, when he drew near, he found that there were several villagers gathered a round the fire and he could not get close enough to it to get warm.

'What a day,' said Nasruddin loudly. 'What an unlucky day! I was carrying a bag of gold coins and I've lost it, I must have dropped it on the way here.'

'Why don't you go in search of it?' asked a man.

'It's too dark now,' said Nasruddin. 'I'll get up at the crack of dawn and go in search of it. The bag will be safe till then.'

'Don't be too sure,' warned the man. 'See, all the men who were crowded around the fire have left. They overheard you and they've all gone in search of the bag!'

'Quick,' said Nasruddin. 'Let's get a place near the fire and when it has warmed us I'll . . .'

'. . . go in search of the bag?' asked the man.

'No,' said Nasruddin. 'I'll tell you another fairy-tale!'

Learning to listen, focus and attend in practice

Creative dialogue with children depends on them listening and sustaining attention. The following activities can help children practise active listening, attending and responding which can be adapted and developed in different ways. The chapter ends with some questions for engaging children's thoughts about learning to listen – again expressing a central message of this book that good talk depends on good listening.

The listening-to-talk tasks presented here offer ways to prepare for dialogue through using the following strategies:

1 Posture

2 Breathing

3 Listen to near–silence

4 Calming and taking control

5 Focus on a sound or word

6 Use music for thinking

7 Use a visual focus: word or colour

8 Focus on a candle

9 Focus on smell, touch and taste

10 Play Kim's game

11 Visualise in your 'mind's eye'

12 Create a poster for good listening or calming down

13 Record what is said: remember the main ideas

1 Posture

Posture is an important element in most forms of meditation in creating the physical conditions for relaxed concentration. A primary teacher asks her class to imagine an invisible thread pulling them up straight. A secondary teacher tells his pupils to adopt the 'concentration position' they have learnt – sitting up, with head up, straight back and open chest to allow deep, regular breathing, relaxed and fully attentive.

■ Sit in the 'concentration position' – sit up, with head up, straight back and open chest to allow deep, regular breathing. Count your breaths. Breathe deeply – in and out – five times.

2 Breathing

Breath awareness – 'following the breath' – helps to still the mind. Common to breathing techniques is the practice of conscious breath control. This includes inhaling fully and slowly and exhaling fully and quickly, then reversing this, breathing in fully and quickly and breathing out slowly. Breathing should be through the nose. One teacher reported a child as saying, 'But Miss, I've never breathed through my nose before!'

■ One basic yoga technique is 'staircase breathing' – that is, breathing in as 'going up slowly', breathing out as 'coming down fast as a lift' which re-energises (and the reverse: go up fast, then down slowly to calm down).

■ Another technique drawn from yoga is 'butterfly breathing'. Tell the children: 'Interlace your fingers, tuck them under your chin. Breathe in. Let your elbows come up and your head tilt back. Breathe out slowly and let your elbows come back down.' This is a good way to calm a boisterous class so they are ready for dialogue.

3 Listen to near-silence

These two activities are aimed at sharpening your hearing and your concentration. They help to train you to listen more carefully.

■ *Listen to distant sounds*

Ask children to try to concentrate their listening to distant sounds for as long as they can. Start with half a minute, working up to one minute or more.

■ *Listen to soft words*

Ask children to tune into a sound source, such as your voice or a recorded sound. How low can the volume be for the children to still understand what is being said? Starting with no sound at all turn the sound up very slowly, stopping from time to time to remind them to listen carefully. Help them to practise listening carefully to hear softer sounds.

4 Calming and taking control

- Tense and relax your muscles. Be aware of every part of your body.

- Sit in silence, feeling your pulse.

- Calm yourself completely. Say to yourself, 'Be calm . . . be calm . . . be calm.'

5 Focus on a sound or word

- Concentrate by focusing on a sound . . . a sound effect such as the sea, a repeated musical sound or a calming piece of music (preferably without words).

- Concentrate by focusing on a word. Choose a word to chant with the children, preferably something calming like 'think', 'clear' or 'still'. Get the class to chant the word over and over again to clear and focus the mind.

6 Use music for thinking

As Rick, aged 10, said: 'Music helps to calm me down and helps me to be ready to listen.'

- *(Play some instrumental music)* Close your eyes and listen carefully to the music. What pictures do you see in your mind? Draw and discuss the ideas, images or patterns that you see.

- *(Play some slow or sad music)* Close your eyes and listen carefully to the music. Use words or drawings to describe your feelings, ideas or images.

- *(Play some music from a different culture)* What does it make you think or feel? Write down or draw and discuss your ideas.

7 Use a visual focus: word or colour

- Use a visual focus such as the word JOY (with a dot in the central letter) on a card or whiteboard.

- Focus the whole group on a colour or give a card of a particular colour to each child to focus on.

8 Focus on a candle

Concentration is achieved by focusing on a single point of perception, which might be an object such as a leaf, candle or stone, or a word, sound or picture. For the human mind used to flitting hither and thither, concentration is hard to maintain.

- Use a candle to focus attention, and create a pause to reflect on a question (e.g. What would you like to ask God? What would you like to find out?).

- Use an aromatherapy candle. Concentrate by focusing on the smell.

9 Focus on smell, touch and taste

■ Ask children to visualise an orange in their minds. Focus on the orange. Slowly peel the orange (in their minds) looking carefully at details. 'Eat' a segment of orange, focusing on smell, touch and taste.

10 Play Kim's game

One way to link listening with memory is to play concentration games such as Kim's game (Fisher 1997a).

■ Place various objects on a tray, or pictures on a board, and ask children to examine and meditate carefully on them. Remove the tray or pictures, then ask them to recall, with a partner, as many objects as possible.

■ Instead of seeing the objects, simply name a list of objects or other words, and see, after listening to the list, how many words can be remembered by pairs or groups of pupils.

11 Visualise in your 'mind's eye'

Visualising is a generative technique to focus the mind. It uses 'the inner eye' to create and explore special places in the mind. Guided use of the imagination is a useful technique which enables children to create what may be described as 'waking dreams'. These can be tightly controlled or offer freedom for the imagination to range around the subject suggested by the guide.

■ Start by getting the children to close their eyes and to listen to distant sounds. Then lead them on a journey in the imagination to a special place – for example, a circular pool of water, utterly still, without a ripple to disturb the surface.

12 Create a poster for good listening or calming down

In groups, children discuss strategies to encourage people to be good listeners or to calm down.

■ What does a good listener do? Design a poster together to help others to be good listeners.

■ What strategies can you think of for calming down? Design a poster together to help others to calm down.

13 Record what is said: remember the main ideas

Ask children to practise getting the main ideas from a talk by using a radio or TV programme. In many ways radio is easier than TV for listening to talk since it is more like someone chatting to you in person, while TV programmes often have distracting pictures.

1 Choose a radio (or TV) talk, interview or talk show (record it on CD or hard drive).

2 Play the recording and concentrate on what is being said.

3 At the end of the programme try to recall and discuss the main ideas. Then keep these in your mind or write them down, not during the programme but afterwards.

4 Play back the recording to see what you remembered and what you forgot.

5 Discuss with the children why they did or did not remember the key ideas and share these with other groups or pairs.

14 Listen again: record and discuss your dialogue

This activity involves making a sound recording of a discussion children have had, a talk or lesson. One of the advantages of recording what you hear is that you can check up later whether you have missed any main points or continue discussing a point you wish to take further. Here is what to do:

1 Children record their dialogue, talk or lesson.

2 They listen to and try to remember the content of the dialogue or talk as they record it.

3 They discuss and may make notes during, or straight after, the main points of the talk.

4 They play back the tape of the talk after finishing the notes.

5 They then listen to the tape and see what they remembered, or missed out.

6 Discuss this and add or alter their notes accordingly.

How good were they at listening, remembering and recording what they heard?

15 Questions to discuss about listening

- How is listening different from hearing?
- What do you need to do to listen well?
- Does it matter whether you are a good listener? Why?
- What do you feel when others do not listen to you?
- How do you show you are listening?
- How do you know you are listening well?
- How do you calm your mind?
- What helps you to concentrate?
- Does meditation help you to listen well?
- Why is it important to take notes of what you listen to?

2

Questions for Thinking

You need a question to get your mind going.

(Salome, aged 10)

> *The Sultan was unhappy because his subjects were untruthful. He had a gallows erected in front of the city gates and a herald announced: 'Whoever would enter the city must first answer the truth to a question which will be put to him by the captain of the guard.'*
> *Nasruddin who was outside the gates stepped forward.*
> *'Why have you come?' asked the captain, 'Tell the truth or you will be hanged.'*
> *'I have come to be hanged,' said Nasruddin.*
> *'I don't believe you,' said the captain.*
> *'Then you have to hang me for telling a lie,' said Nasruddin.*
> *'But if we hang you it will mean you have told the truth,' said the captain.*
> *'That is true,' said Nasruddin. So the captain had no option but to let him go.*

Asking questions lies at the heart of good teaching and learning, and plays an essential role in sustaining creative dialogue. This chapter explores these aspects of questions and questioning:

1 Why ask questions?

2 How do we improve our questioning?

3 How do we help children to ask questions, more questions and better questions?

4 Questions for thinking in practice.

Through the skilful use of questions, teachers can challenge children's thinking, develop their awareness of their own learning and enable them to ask their own questions and create their own agendas for research. However, there is a danger, even with skilful questioning, of following a pre-set agenda and not encouraging student initiative. Questions should open up a dialogue, with pupils being given time to discuss their learning with the teacher and with one another. The first part of this chapter focuses on questioning and is followed by examples of activities to stimulate creative questioning and talk with or among children.

Why ask questions?

People usually ask questions because they want to know something. Questioning is a means to focus attention, sustain dialogue, find out what others know and to get them thinking. Questions help us find out what children think and know, but they can also stop children making the effort to think. If they are always on the receiving end of questions children may not learn to question for themselves. So as well as asking questions we need to encourage children to ask questions, to enquire and to interrogate the world. We need to use questions to test what children know but also to stimulate their thinking, learning and questioning (see Figure 2.1).

We ask ourselves questions when we are preparing lessons, assessing pupils or evaluating our own performance as teachers. We develop children's learning and our own learning by asking questions. But perhaps teachers ask too many questions. Studies suggest that teachers who ask most questions are less likely to:

- receive questions from children
- promote elaborated answers from children
- encourage children to contribute spontaneously to dialogue.

The more children are questioned the less they learn to think for themselves. We should try therefore to ask fewer questions but better and more open questions – and use alternatives to questions to stimulate their thinking.

Questioning may be used at any of three stages during a learning task:

- *before* the task
- *during* a task
- *after* the task is completed.

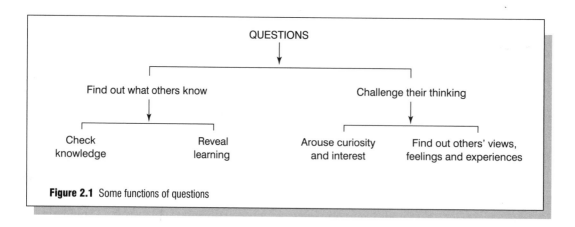

Figure 2.1 Some functions of questions

Before the task: planning stage

We can encourage thinking before doing – both at the cognitive (What we are we going to do?), and the metacognitive level (What do we need to think about?). Before a task we do this, for example, by discussing the learning objectives and making links to previous learning and previous ways of learning. Because metacognition is about what *the children themselves think* it is not enough to tell them what they have previously learnt and what the learning objectives are; we need to help them to think and express these in their own words. Questions that might help this process include:

- Have you learnt anything like this before?

- What do we need to think about/remember?

- What are we trying to learn today?

We begin by showing them what a plan or strategy for learning is, we model it for them by talking it through, they internalise the process and come to express it for themselves in their own words. It is through internalising and then adapting the model the teacher provides that metacognitive awareness of learning develops.

During the task: monitoring stage

We can stop and monitor our thinking during the task. This means not just talking about what we have done (though it might include this) but what we should be thinking about and how we should be learning. Because metacognition is about the 'me' in thinking, again we encourage children to reflect on and say what they should be thinking about what they are doing.

This monitoring or self-regulation of learning can be prompted by metacognitive questions, at first shared and hopefully internalised at an individual level (see Table 2.1).

TABLE 2.1 Metacognitive questions

AT THE SHARED LEVEL	AT THE INDIVIDUAL LEVEL
'How are you doing?'	'How am I doing?'
'What must you remember?'	'What must I remember?'
'What is the process/strategy involved?'	'What is the process/strategy?'
'What do you find difficult?'	'What do I find difficult?'
'What do you need to think about and do?'	'What do I need to think about/do?'
'What will happen if you do this?'	'What will happen if I do this?'
'Does it work/make sense?'	'Does it work/make sense?'

After the task: review stage

At the end of a task can come the review, plenary or debriefing stage. Review involves reflecting back on your own thinking and learning, aided by Socratic questions – that is, questions that lead children's thinking from concrete examples towards organising ideas. Plenary discussion can help this process. Thinking about thinking at this stage depends on:

- tasks being worth serious thought
- thinking and reasoning being valued
- time being given for discussion and review.

Leading a metacognitive discussion in a review or plenary session is a complex skill, characterised by open questions, lengthy pupil responses, reference to the 'big' concepts and connections to other subjects or strategies for learning.

How to improve our questioning

One day a scholar came to the court of Emperor Akbar and challenged Birbal to answer his questions and thus prove that he was as clever as people said he was.

He asked Birbal, 'Would you prefer to answer a hundred easy questions or just a single difficult one?'

Birbal had had a tiring day and was impatient to leave.

'Ask me one difficult question,' said Birbal.

'Well, then, tell me,' said the scholar, 'which came first into the world, the chicken or the egg?'

'The chicken,' replied Birbal.

'How do you know?' asked the scholar, with a note of triumph in his voice.

'We agreed that you would ask only one question,' said Birbal, 'and you have already asked it.'

Birbal and the emperor walked away, leaving the scholar speechless.

Teachers ask a lot of questions. Studies show that many teachers ask more than 300 questions a day. Most of the questions teachers ask are 'closed' in the sense of only requiring one answer, for example: 'What colour is it?'; 'What is it called?'; 'Where is it from?' Questions are 'open' when they have more than one possible right answer. Open questions are more complex and demand more than one-word answers.

Ask open questions

Poor questions limit children's thinking and opportunities for dialogue. Questions that are too closed or narrow are often the 'guess-what-the-teacher-is-thinking' type of question. When

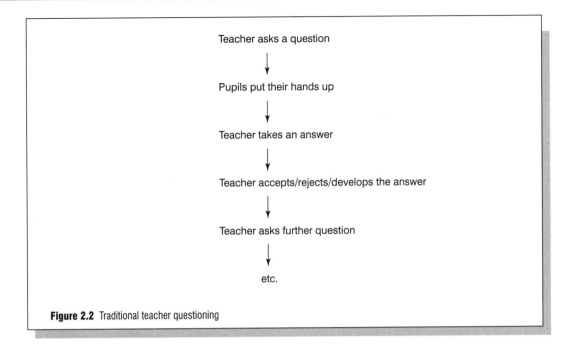

Teacher asks a question

↓

Pupils put their hands up

↓

Teacher takes an answer

↓

Teacher accepts/rejects/develops the answer

↓

Teacher asks further question

↓

etc.

Figure 2.2 Traditional teacher questioning

too easy they can be of the traditional stimulus–response–stimulus–response type: 'What is this . . .?'; 'What is that . . .?'; 'What is the other . . .?' This leads not to creative dialogue but to a kind of verbal tennis match, batting questions and answers back and forth. There is a place for this quick, closed, fact-finding, quiz-type questioning. A memory test can remind children what they know, and help them to remember. Children enjoy showing off what they know – when they do know the right answer. But there needs to be a balance between the closed 'quick-fix' questions, and open questions that really challenge children's thinking.

A good question, whether closed or open, should pose an intellectual challenge – provoking what Piaget called the 'cognitive conflict' which can help to challenge children's thinking. When 'cognitive challenge' is put into the context of dialogue, children's own questions as well as those of the teacher help move thinking to a more advanced level of development, helping to 'scaffold' new levels of learning.

A good question shines a light on both truth and mystery, but not all questions are good questions. One of the characteristics of a good 'open' question is that it avoids the trap of a 'yes' or 'no' response. When one teacher was getting her children to evaluate their work she asked, 'Are you pleased with the way it's worked out?' As she listened later to a tape of the discussion she realised her question required only a yes/no response; whereas, 'How well do you think it has turned out?' would have invited more.

Examples of open-ended questions include:

'What do you think . . .?'
'How do you know . . .?'
'Why do you think that . . .?'
'Do you have a reason . . .?'

'How can you be sure . . .?'

'Is this always so . . .?'

'Is there another way/reason/idea . . .?'

'What if . . .?' What if not . . .?'

'Where is there another example of this . . .?'

'What do you think happens next . . .?'

'Would you rather . . . or . . .?'

Ask increasingly challenging questions – Socratic questions

It is usual to begin questioning with easy, literal 'Do you know?' type questions, then to lead on to increasingly challenging open-ended questions, a method called Socratic, named after the Greek philosopher Socrates whose way of teaching was to help the learner reach a conclusion through response to a sequence of challenging and increasingly abstract questions (see Chapter 8 for more on this method). Questions become Socratic when they are genuine invitations to enquiry; for example, 'What do you think?' They differ from random open-ended questioning in that they follow a pattern, a progression of questions that probe reasons and assumptions and take the enquiry further. Socratic questions urge students to probe or 'dig deep', and to think clearly about the concepts they use to explain the world. A Socratic sequence of questions begins with a simple, literal question such as 'What is a butterfly?', through more analytical questions such as 'How does a butterfly differ from a bird?', and on to more abstract or conceptual questions such as 'So what defines an insect?'

Socratic questions are the kind that can add rigour to any dialogue. They help move discussion from unstructured talk and unsupported opinion to dialogue with purpose and direction. Research suggests that, in general, teachers should ask fewer but better questions. What are these 'better questions'? There is no fixed set of questions that are Socratic, but the following is a summary of questions that are open, Socratic and act as progressive invitations to move the dialogue forward. Leading a creative dialogue is like sailing a boat tacking into the wind, with the Socratic use of questions helping it to change course and move forward (Table 2.2).

Asking a good question is necessary but we need more to get the best out of a creative dialogue, for in a dialogue listening is as important as speaking.

Build in thinking time

Shifting the balance of questioning from teacher to learner lies at the heart of creative dialogue. Research suggests that teachers on average waited only one second after asking a question before either rephrasing the question or seeking an answer from another pupil (Black and Wiliam 1998). Increasing this 'wait time', listening and thinking time to five seconds can result in improved responses, such as children:

- giving longer answers
- being more willing to offer an answer

TABLE 2.2 Ask Socratic questions

Questions that seek clarification

What is . . .?	Asking for information
Can you explain that . . .?	Asking for an explanation
What does x mean . . .?	Seeking a definition
Can you give me an example of . . .?	Seeking examples
Does anyone have a question to ask . . .?	Initiating enquiring

Questions that probe reasons and evidence

Why do you think that . . .?	Forming an argument
How do we know that . . .?	Probing assumptions
What are your reasons . . .?	Seeking reasons
Do you have evidence . . .?	Asking for evidence
Can you give me an example/counter-example . . .?	Requesting counter-examples

Questions that explore alternative views

Can you put it another way . . .?	Restating a view
Is there another point of view . . .?	Inviting speculation
What if someone were to suggest that . . .?	Alternative views
What would someone who disagreed with you say . . .?	Counter-argument
What is the difference between those views/ideas . . .?	Distinctions

Questions that test implications and consequences

What follows (or what can we work out) from what you say . . .?	Implications
How does x differ from y . . .?	Analysing
What would be the consequences of that . . .?	Consequences
Is there a general rule for that . . .?	Generalising rules
How could you test to see if it was true . . .?	Testing for truth

Questions about the concept or key idea

What is the concept or key idea?	Abstracting/conceptualising
How would you now define . . .?	Defining
Where have we got to/who can summarise so far . . .?	Summarising
Are we any closer to answering the question/problem . . .?	Concluding
What do we still need to find out?	Extending the research

- being willing to ask more questions

- responding in more thoughtful and creative ways.

There are two aspects to thinking time – after the question and after the answer. The two elements of thinking time are:

1 allowing children time to think

2 the teacher thinking for a few seconds about the answer.

Allowing silence is a deliberate act by the teacher to encourage a more thoughtful response, as in this example:

> *Teacher*: What makes a good piece of writing?
> *Child 1*: When you write neatly.
> *Teacher*: Hmm . . . [pauses]
> *Child 1*: Like it's a good story . . . and it's easy to read.
> *Teacher*: Ahh . . . easy to read. What else?
> *Child 2*: Well it has to have a good beginning or you don't want to carry on . . . I mean it's got to be exciting . . . make you want to go on reading it.

Indicate the kind of answer you want

Answers are as important as questions. It is helpful to indicate to children the kind of answer you are hoping for, for example: 'give me a quick answer'; 'I want an answer in a proper sentence'; 'Say something no one else has said'; 'Say whether you agree or disagree'; 'Give me as many reasons as possible'.

Here is how one child, aged 7, responded to the question, 'Would you rather be a bird or a butterfly?' Her teacher does not just ask for an answer; she wants as many 'interesting' reasons as possible. She does not expect a good answer straight away. She says 'stop and think' before you give an answer 'so you really know what you want to say':

> I want to be a butterfly. I would like to be a peacock butterfly. I would like to be a butterfly because I like their pretty colours and I can go on holiday without paying and you can fly very fast and butterflies can flit about. Butterflies can sleep in flowers and sit on them. Butterflies can close their wings. Butterflies can't be caught easily. Butterflies are smaller than birds.

Mediate the questions: pause, prompt, probe and praise

A number of questioning skills have been identified in research into those that mediate creative dialogue through questioning. These skills include:

- sequencing a set of questions – moving from literal to higher order

- pitching appropriately – putting the questions clearly

- distributing questions around the class – to the shy as well as to the 'stars'

- prompting and probing – giving clues where necessary

- listening and responding in a positive way – inviting pupil questions

- challenging right as well as wrong answers

- using written questions effectively – key questions for further thinking.

Good teachers mediate the dialogue through being sensitive to individual needs. They mediate the discussion by personalising responses to support or challenge individual children as needed. A creative dialogue needs conducting, facilitating and monitoring. Different students need differing sorts of stimuli. Often the 'puzzled listener' role will be effective if it reflects genuine interest and attention to the student's answer.

Other strategies to support thinking and talking include '*pause, prompt, probe and praise*'.

- *Pausing*. Giving thinking time, and opportunities for rethinking and restating an idea – 'Can you explain/tell us again?' Sometimes minimal encouragement will prompt further response – 'Hmmm', 'Umm', 'Uh huh', 'Yes?', 'OK', 'I see', 'And?' Non-verbal reinforcement includes eye contact and facial signals (e.g. smiles and body gestures).

- *Prompting and probing*. Giving verbal encouragement, for example by 'reflecting back' to check whether we have understood what the student has said. Examples of probing questions include: 'Why do you think that . . .?'; 'How do you know . . .?'; 'What do you mean by . . .?'; 'What if . . .?'; 'Is it possible that . . .?'

- *Praising*. Giving positive feedback. Being specific and personal with praise – 'That's an interesting answer', 'Thanks for that answer' – can foster general participation by supporting the hesitant, rewarding risk-takers and valuing contributions.

Use dialogic alternatives to questions

It's good to talk about what you've done, what you got right and what you got wrong – which is sometimes a real mystery!

(Sarah, aged 11)

There is a danger in adopting a 'teacherly' role because we can dominate the talk by asking too many questions and imposing our own meaning. Teachers who ask too many questions tend to discourage students from giving elaborate or thoughtful answers. We move on from questioning to dialogue by using alternatives to questions.

It is not only questions that encourage thinking and talking things through. There are alternative strategies to questions that can prove more effective in stimulating thoughtful discussion. The following are some alternative strategies and examples that can actively encourage thinking and dialogue (see Table 2.3).

Different students need differing sorts of support during dialogue. Often the teacher's 'puzzled listener' role will be effective if it reflects genuine interest and attention to the learner's answer. 'I didn't quite understand . . .', as one teacher responded, only for the child to say, 'I didn't understand either.' In dialogic talk more extended answers are sought and the teacher

TABLE 2.3 Alternatives to routine questions

Withhold judgement	Respond in a non-evaluative fashion, ask others to respond
Invite pupils to elaborate	Say more about . . .
Cue alternative responses	There is no one right answer: What are the alternatives? Who's got a different point of view?
Challenge pupils to provide reasons	Give reasons why
Make a challenging statement	Supposing someone said . . .
Contribute your own thoughts/experience	I think that/remember when
Use 'think–pair–share'	Allow thinking time, discuss with partner, then group
Allow 'rehearsal' of response	Try out the answer, in your head and to partner
Invite student questions	Anyone like to ask Pat a question about that?
Use 'think alouds'	Model rhetorical questions – 'I don't quite understand'
Child to invite response	Ali, ask someone else what they think
Don't ask for show of hands	Expect everyone to respond

takes on a more challenging role on occasion – 'Try again and explain it clearly so that everyone can understand' – disagreeing or putting an opposing argument – 'I think the opposite might be true . . .' – and not rewarding children simply for making a response.

Dialogue involves sharing ideas, summarising the main points and then challenging children with further questions to extend their thinking. The task of promoting learning through dialogue is difficult; it is a delicate balance between letting discussion wander at random, and dominating it so that pupils do not feel free to say what they think. The crucial indicators of good dialogue are the ways in which:

- ■ thinking is challenged by teachers
- ■ pupils' responses show extended thinking.

Pupils must be encouraged to express arguments in fully formed sentences using such words as 'think' and 'because', and not merely give short one-word or one-phrase answers.

Planning questioning to promote thinking (Bloom's taxonomy)

There are many taxonomies of thinking but perhaps the most familiar is that of Bloom. According to Bloom's taxonomy, *analysis*, *synthesis* and *evaluation* demand more complex and 'higher' levels of thinking. Questions that ask for *knowledge*, *comprehension* and *application* demand less complex and thus 'lower' levels of thinking.

TABLE 2.4 Higher and lower levels of thinking (Bloom's taxonomy)

1	*Knowledge*	e.g. Who . . . What . . . Where . . . When . . . How . . .?
2	*Comprehension*	e.g. What do we mean by . . .? Explain . . .
3	*Application*	e.g. What other examples are there . . .?
4	*Analysis*	e.g. What is the evidence for parts or features of . . .?
5	*Synthesis*	e.g. How could we add to, improve, design, solve . . .?
6	*Evaluation*	e.g. What do you think about . . .? Criteria to assess success?

One effective questioning strategy is to ask questions which make increasing cognitive demands on students, to move from simple knowledge/recall questions, through questions that ask for comprehension/explanation, and application, then to analysis, synthesis and evaluation. Often this will mean moving from the 'what' and 'how' descriptive question, to the 'why' and 'what for?' questions that ask for a more complex response. A good question offers progressive and productive challenge to learning. It offers a model for the sorts of productive questions students can ask of themselves and of others.

Use creative questions for thinking

One of the purposes of questions is to help extend thinking in unexpected ways.

Asking the right questions can help stimulate curiosity, and new ways of thinking through dialogue. For many pupils school may be the only place where they experience and develop habits of creative talk.

Certain key questions can help focus the mind on new ways of thinking and stimulate more flexible thinking, regardless of what the issue or problem is. The following is a taxonomy of questions for stimulating creative ideas about any topic, grouped under the mnemonic CREATE:

■ *Combine?* Can you bring ideas together? What can you unite? Can you combine purposes, ideas?

■ *Rearrange?* Can you make another pattern, layout, sequence? Can parts be moved, changed, replaced?

- *Eliminate?* What to remove, omit, get rid of? Make smaller, shorter, or split up? Take away part or whole?

- *Adapt?* Can it be adapted? What else is this like? What ideas does it suggest? What else? Who else?

- *Try other uses?* Can it be put to other uses? Could it be put to other uses if changed? Can it be adapted?

- *Extend?* What to add? Add – time, frequency, value, ingredient, number, feature, person, process, approach?

For more on developing creativity through dialogue see Chapter 4.

An open-ended question allows for a possible range of answers, and hence encourages more flexible thinking, allows depth of discussion, tests the limits of knowledge rather than one item of knowledge, encourages better assessment of children's beliefs and the possibility to clear up misunderstandings, and may result in unanticipated and unexpected answers, new hypotheses and connections to previous knowledge. One way of doing this is simply to ask children to compare two words/ideas/objects/events/phenomena by asking, 'Is there a difference between . . . and . . . ?' When asked, 'Is there a difference between knowing something and believing something?' a child replied, 'Yes there is because – for example, I believe in Father Christmas, but I know he doesn't exist!' In the ensuing discussion another child came back to this comment and said: 'How do you *know* he doesn't exist?' In asking this he had made that important move in a dialogue from being one of the questioned to being a questioner.

Help children to ask questions

> I keep six honest serving men
> They taught me all I knew
> Their names are What and Why and When
> And How and Where and Who.
> > Rudyard Kipling

As Rudyard Kipling says, asking questions lies at the heart of good teaching and learning, but it is not always easy for students to ask questions. Evidence suggests that as they get older students ask fewer questions. As one student described it:

> Sometimes I want to ask something but I don't feel comfortable to ask because I know that they will all look at me. But if there are others asking it is easier. It starts to get usual and people will not look at me, because I am just doing what everyone else does.

If we want pupils to be active and adventurous thinkers we need to encourage them to ask questions and create a climate of peer support (for more on creating a community of enquiry see p. 149). When a class of ten-year-olds were starting the study of a country the children were put into groups to create questions on: '*What do we want to know about our country?*' The groups shared, displayed and discussed their questions. Further questions were added to this list by teacher and pupils during the project.

Questions worth thinking about are worth keeping. Display them and come back to them. Ask which out of a list of questions they think is the best or most interesting question. Find out what questions they would most like to have answered.

If children themselves identify what they want to know by asking a question, they are much more likely to value and remember the answer. Some questions will not be easy to answer. One teacher was asked: *'What is the difference between the ozone layer and the greenhouse effect?'* At the time she did not feel able to give a full answer, so she gathered a variety of responses from the children, displayed the question in the classroom, involved them in researching an answer and even got in an 'expert' to judge the different answers to the question.

A simple way to assess the ability of children to devise questions is to give them a picture of a person, or a common object such as a chair or a cup, and ask them to list as many questions about it as they can. Another way is to take a subject of current study and see how many questions children can create about the topic. A third way is to choose a text, such as part of a story or a poem and see how good they are at interrogating the text by asking them to create questions about it (see p. 45 for an activity).

A common way to start children thinking is to set a question that directly derives from the outcome of the last lesson (which may have come through wishing to assess something specific which they have been taught or to apply what they know to a new area). Children could make up their own quiz questions to ask the rest of the class based on the week's work/topic.

Teachers help children to learn by asking good questions and by encouraging students to ask their own questions. Children should have opportunities to generate questions and their ability to do so will improve with practice. In enquiring classrooms good questions, from teachers and children, are valued and displayed.

Albert Einstein once said: 'The important thing is not to stop questioning.' Questions, like good wine, can improve with keeping. Display them, savour them, come back to them. Find some more. Sort them into categories, for example:

■ questions we can answer

■ questions we can find the answer for

■ questions that cannot be answered.

Discuss with children the nature of questions. Give them a list of questions and ask which they think is the best or most interesting question. Discuss good and bad questions. Find out what questions they would like to have answered. Display the question of the day for children to see at the start of the day. Use think–pair–share. Give children time to think about the question (or draft responses), discuss with a partner then share and discuss as a whole group. Decide on someone to interview, for example, a visitor or a local VIP. Ask students to devise, share, evaluate and prioritise interview questions.

To engage more fruitfully in creative dialogue children need to learn how to ask:

■ more questions

■ better questions.

The first aspect of questioning to develop is the ability to ask many questions. When Isidor Rabi, the Nobel Prize-winning physicist, was asked the secret of his success he answered that when he came home from school his mother did not ask him 'What did you learn?', but, 'Did you ask a good question today?' We learn through asking questions. But unless you ask you may never find out, like the man who complained at the end of his life: 'I wanted to know more, but was always afraid to ask.'

The following sections are about helping children to practise and develop their questioning skills so as to be able to sustain dialogue.

Asking more questions

Nasruddin was famous not only for asking questions but for answering the questions he was asked with another question. One day one of his friends said to him, 'Tell me Nasruddin why do you always answer a question with another question?' Nasruddin answered, 'Do I?'

Ask children how many questions could be asked about any one object or experience. The answer of course is that we do not know, since the limit of questions will be the limits of the power of human thinking and we do not know what these limits are. We may not know the limits of our own thinking, but there are ways to test and improve them. Help children improve their questioning skills through practice.

Improving questioning is about improving the quantity and quality of the questions you can ask. If children practise asking more questions you will find you are able to ask more and learn more about any object or aspect of life. What kinds of questions could they ask about any object?

The following are some questions that children could ask about any object:

- *Physical features.* What is it? What is it made of? Is it made of natural or manufactured materials? Is it complete? Has it been altered, adapted or amended?

- *Construction.* Who made it? How was it made? Was it made by hand or machine?

- *Function.* Why was it made? What was it made for? How is it used?

- *Age.* Is it old or new? How old is it? How do we know?

- *Value.* Is it valuable? What is it worth?

- *Origin.* Where does it come from? Where was it made?

- *Design.* Is it well designed? What is good about the design? What could be improved?

The more you practice asking questions the more you will be able to think, learn and question any object or aspect of life. The trouble is that the older people get the fewer questions they tend to ask. Very young children are full of questions about the world, full of natural curiosity. As they get older many people lose this natural sense of curiosity and wonder at the world.

They are so used to being given answers that they lose the habit of asking questions. Try to get into the habit of asking questions, not any question for the sake of it, but ones that focus attention on what is most interesting, strange or puzzling about the topic in hand. Get into the habit of asking yourself 'I wonder why . . .?' Share your curiosity with others, have the courage to ask, to reveal your doubts and to be open about the things you do not know or understand.

It is through questioning that we check what we know and check what others know. To do this well, children need to ask many questions, and be helped to ask a wider range of questions.

Asking better questions

Why is grass always green?
What holds up the sky?
Why is hair upon my head?
Why, oh why, oh why?

Why does rain go down, not up?
Why is salt in every sea?
Why is there a sun and moon?
Why is there only one me?

Why do bees buzz and birds sing?
Why do nails grow on my toes?
How long is a piece of string?
Why is it no-one knows?

Why is night so full of dreams?
Why do we have one nose, two eyes?
Why do questions never end?
Why are there so many whys?

Robert Fisher, *First Poems for Thinking*, p. 70

Here are some common ways of asking factual questions (try to complete these examples for yourself on any chosen topic):

- ■ 'What . . .?'
- ■ 'Who . . .?'
- ■ 'Where . . .?'
- ■ 'When . . .?'
- ■ 'How . . .?'
- ■ 'Why . . .?'

Discuss with children differences between open and closed questions. Sometimes it is not easy to work out what is an open and what is a closed question. A question about the causes of things, for example, 'Why do cats purr?' is a closed question if it is thought that there is only one right answer, but it is open if we are going to allow other possible answers. There may be one right answer, but if we do not know what it is the question remains open. There may of course be many reasons why cats purr – for example: because they are happy, to communicate their feelings, because that is the way God made them and so on. So we must beware of thinking that the answer we have is the only answer. Look again at the poem 'Why?' printed above. Each line is a question. Ask children to work out which they think are open questions (with more than one possible right answer) and which are closed questions (with only one right answer).

See 'Question what you read' (p. 48).

> One day Nasruddin opened a booth with a sign above it saying, 'Two Questions On Any Subject Answered For Only 100 Silver Coins'. A man came saying he had two very urgent questions he wanted answered. He handed over his money to Nasruddin, saying, 'A hundred silver coins is rather expensive for two questions, isn't it?'
> 'Yes,' said Nasruddin. 'And the next question, please?'

Teacher: You have not given me the right answer.
Pupil: You have not asked me the right question.

The skill of questioning means not only being able to ask many questions and a wide range of questions but asking better questions. Discuss why some questions are better than others. What makes a poor question? A poor question is one that does not lead anywhere; that does not add to our knowledge or understanding. A poor question is one whose words have no useful purpose in the situation; for example, because the answer is so obvious – like the crying child being asked after her mother died, 'How do you feel?' Questions are poor when they are irrelevant to the situation, like the student who replied to the question, 'What is the answer?' with the question, 'When is lunch?' A question is a poor one when it gets too often repeated, like the person who asks repeatedly on a journey, 'Are we there yet?'

Not all questions are good questions. A good question gets to the heart of what you really want or need to find out. A good question has a purpose. A good question may be:

- A factual question, seeking information, for example by asking, 'What . . .?'

- A reasoning question, seeking an explanation, for example by asking, 'How . . .?' or 'Why . . .?'

- An open question, seeking better understanding, for example by asking, 'What do you think . . .?'

'Twenty questions' is a popular game for practising asking closed factual questions (remember: closed questions are those where there is only one right answer). For this you need two or more players. About six players are best although it can be played with any number. One (or more) of the players chooses an object, person or place. The others may ask up to twenty questions to try to find the answer. Only 'yes' or 'no' answers are allowed.

If we want pupils to be capable of engaging in their own research we need to encourage them to ask good questions. As they grow older children often grow out of the questioning habit. We need to fight this tendency and find strategies to foster curiosity and encourage the questioning child.

Discuss with children the nature of questions (see Question Quadrant below) and sort them, for example into:

- questions we can answer
- questions we can find the answer for
- questions that cannot be answered.

Give the children a list of questions and ask which they think is the best or most interesting question. Find out what questions they would like to have answered. Can they think of a question that can never be answered? Question a text or topic. Ask, for example: 'What do you not know or understand about it? What do you want to find out? What questions can you ask about it?'

Devise, write and display questions to stimulate thinking and discussion about objects, pictures or texts of interest in your classroom. Display a question or problem of the day. Use the 'think–pair–share' strategy. Give children time to think about the question (or draft responses), discuss with a partner, then share and discuss as a whole group. Collect any interesting or puzzling questions that arise in the classroom. Create a place to write, store or display your questions, such as in a box, on a board (or Wonder Wall) or in a special book. Set aside some time, such as at the end of the week, to choose and discuss a question or share out the questions for children to work on at home or swap with another class or group. Use computers, including email and website pages, to extend the opportunities for questioning, interaction and dialogue. Use the interactive whiteboard to allow children to engage with a focal question or to develop questions within a lesson.

Analyse questions: the Question Quadrant

The questions students ask can be sorted by their characteristics. A useful distinction is that between closed questions that only require one answer and open questions that have many possible answers. These can also be called factual (closed) or enquiry (open) questions. When applied to a text a closed question is a comprehension question where the answer is in the text. An open question may require the use of imagination or reading 'beyond the lines', and make an inference, speculation or hypothesis requiring the use of imagination.

The 'Question Quadrant' is a thinking 'tool' devised by Professor Phil Cam that is particularly effective in the context of Philosophy for Children when the children are asked to raise questions from a stimulus which could be a text, object or picture. Having listed their questions these can then be analysed using the Question Quadrant (Figure 2.3). Teachers report that the use of this tool improves the quality of children's enquiry questions. Philosophy for Children is a valuable pedagogy to improve the quality of critical thinking in your classroom (see Fisher 2008a).

When the children have raised questions about the stimulus, they can use the Question Quadrant to identify which are the open-ended philosophical questions. For an activity based on this approach see the task 'What kind of question is this?' on p. 50.

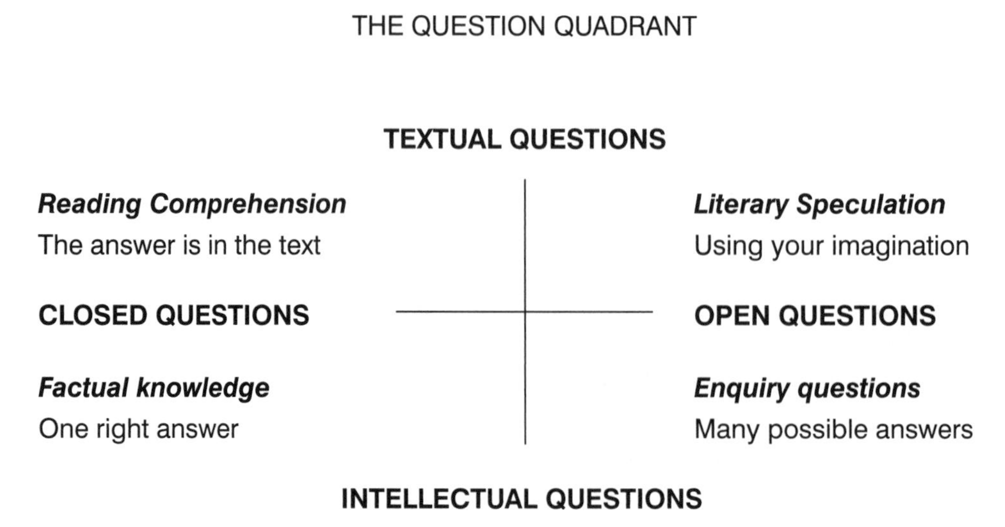

THE QUESTION QUADRANT

TEXTUAL QUESTIONS

Reading Comprehension
The answer is in the text

Literary Speculation
Using your imagination

CLOSED QUESTIONS ————+———— OPEN QUESTIONS

Factual knowledge
One right answer

Enquiry questions
Many possible answers

INTELLECTUAL QUESTIONS

Figure 2.3 Intellectual questions

Source: Adapted from Cam, P. (2006) *20 Thinking Tools*, ACER

Questions to assess learning

Display some questions to encourage pupils to assess and reflect on their own learning, such as: 'What have I learnt?'; 'What have I found hard?'; 'What do I need to learn next?' For more on questions to assess learning, see p. 190.

Questions for talk in practice

In stimulating creative dialogue with children try to make questioning visible by discussing the questions that might be asked. The following activities may be adapted and developed in different ways. The chapter ends with some questions for engaging children's thoughts about questioning – again expressing the central message of this book that if it is worth talking about it is worth asking better questions about.

The questions for talk tasks presented here offer ways to stimulate dialogue through using the following strategies:

1 Question of the day

2 Question of the week

3 Journalists' questions

4 Osborn's questions

5 Would you rather be . . .?

6 How many questions?

7 Twenty questions

8 Question what you read

9 Interview questions

10 I wonder why . . .?

11 Question an answer

12 Problem box

13 Question the world

14 What kind of question is this?

15 Talk about questions.

1 Question of the day

Ask individuals to think for themselves or to jot down their initial ideas in response to an idea-generating question such as, 'Can you love someone and hate someone at the same time?' Try to generate lots of responses, encourage thinking of alternatives and greater fluency of ideas. Question cues include:

■ How many kinds of . . . can you think of?

■ List all . . . that could be used for . . .

■ What might be the arguments for . . . (and against . . .)?

A written list of mind-stimulating questions is useful because it reminds us of approaches and possibilities that we might not otherwise think of.

2 Question of the week

At the beginning of the week a question is posted somewhere in the room. The question might be linked to the curriculum, or not, but must require the children to go away, think or research their answer. On Friday they can then discuss their responses to the question in groups before widening the discussion to the whole class.

3 Journalists' questions

These are the six key questions that journalism students are taught to answer somewhere in their news articles to make sure that they have covered the whole story. These questions encourage critical thinking about a topic from different angles.

1 *Who?* (Agent)   Who is involved? What are the people aspects of the problem?

2 *What?* (Event)   What happened? What was done and not done?

3 *When?* (Time)   When will, did, should this happen?

4 *Where?* (Scene)   Where did, will, should this occur or happen? Where else is a possibility?

5 *Why?* (Purpose)   Why was or is this done, avoided, permitted? Why should it be done, avoided, permitted?

6 *How?* (Method)   How did it, could it, should it happen/be changed/prevented? How did beginning lead to conclusion?

Ask children to imagine they are journalists investigating a current news story of their choice. Discuss with a partner the questions you would want to try to answer in the news story (use the 'journalists' questions' above to help in the discussion).

4 Osborn's questions

Alex Osborn's is a classic list of idea-generating questions (adapted below). Not all the questions apply to all topics, but some will stimulate thinking whatever the topic.

Other uses?	New ways to use it? Other uses if modified?
Adapt?	How to adapt? What is it like? What does it suggest?
Modify?	How to change – meaning, colour, motion, sound, form, shape?
Magnify?	What to add – time, shape, ingredient? Multiply? Exaggerate?
Minify?	What to subtract – smaller, shorter, omit, split up?
Substitute?	What to substitute? Who/what else instead? Try other approach?
Rearrange?	Change components? Try other pattern, layout, sequence?
Reverse?	Try opposites? Turn it backwards, upside down, reverse?
Combine?	Try to blend, combine units, purposes, ideas?

1 Choose any common object such as a chair, a toy or a tool that you do not usually think about.

2 Take each each of the questions in the list above and apply to the object in question to think about it in a different way.

3 See how many different ideas you can generate.

Remember there is more than one way of thinking about something if you ask yourself the right questions.

5 Would you rather be . . .?

Discuss with a partner which you would rather be. Give as many reasons as you can for your choice.

Would you rather be . . .

- a bird or a butterfly?
- a child or an adult?

- rich or happy?
- a boy or a girl?
- someone else?
- a cat or a mouse?
- red or green?
- yes or no?
- a forest or a stream?
- rich or happy?
- a table or a chair?

Take three of the following and get the children in pairs or groups to choose between them:

- Would you rather live in the country or a town?
- Would you rather be a brick or a feather?
- Would you rather be a tree or a flower?
- Would you rather have £50 or five friends? Say why.
- Would you rather live in this country or in another country? Say why.
- Would you rather live at this time or at another time in history? Say why.
- Would you rather have one good friend or £1000? Say why.
- Would you rather go through a door to another world or have free sweets for the rest of your life? Why?
- Would you rather be a colour or a sound? Which colour or sound? Why?
- Which would you rather be: a door, a window or a hole in the roof? Why?
- Would you rather live in a house surrounded by the sea, snow or the jungle? Why?

(adapted from Fisher 2006a)

6 How many questions?

This activity may be done individually, with a partner or with a small group.

Test your questioning power by choosing an everyday object or topic, such as a chair, and seeing, with your partner or group, how many questions you can create. Discuss with a partner all the things that you do not know about that object or topic of study.

- How many questions can you think of to ask about this object . . . (show an object), e.g. How many questions can you think of to ask about a chair? (show a chair).
- Write down all the questions you can think of which have the answer . . . (e.g. '24').
- How many questions can you think of where the answer is 'green'?
- How many maths questions can you ask to investigate this room (or a given garment)?

Share and analyse questions together. How many different questions were created? Discuss the kinds of questions that were asked. What were the most interesting questions? What made them interesting?

7 Twenty questions

'Twenty questions' is a popular game for practising asking closed factual questions (remember: closed questions are those where there is only one right answer). For this you need two or more players. About six players are best although it can be played with any number. One (or more) of the players chooses an object, person or place. The others may ask up to twenty questions to try to find the answer. Only 'yes' or 'no' answers are allowed. Only three direct guesses are allowed. Play in groups of six (e.g. two choose, four ask). After each game discuss with children whether good questions were asked, whether better questions could be asked and how many questions might be needed to find the hidden answer.

8 Question what you read

This activity is about practising posing questions when reading a newspaper or a magazine. Ask children to create not as many questions as they can, but to pose questions that are as interesting and varied as possible. Reading news stories or articles is a wonderful opportunity to pose questions because most articles and stories do not have definite conclusions or all the possible facts.

1 Choose an interesting story or article for children to read in pairs or groups.

2 Try, in pairs, to pose ten questions about what they have read.

3 Ask them to make these questions as varied and interesting as possible by creating questions that other people might ask – such as the people referred to in the story or article.

9 Interview questions

Choose one person from the past or present that you would most like to question. It could be someone famous, someone you know, someone from literature, history or current affairs. It could be anyone living or dead. Imagine you are in a position to interview that person. Devise a list of questions you would like to ask them. These should include as many open questions as possible to encourage them to say as much about themselves that you want to know. When you have completed your interview questions, decide:

■ Which are your best and most interesting questions?

■ What order would you ask them?

■ Write down ten questions to ask this person . . . (name a person they all know) if you were to interview them.

Hotseating

A child then chooses to be the character and the others pose the questions to frame a dialogue with the child-in-role.

10 I wonder why . . .?

'I wonder why . . .?' Discuss with your partner ways to end this sentence. Choose, for example, three of the most interesting ways to end the sentence (Why have leopards got spots? or zebras stripes?).

11 Question an answer

Children devise questions to fit a given answer (e.g. a person, place, thing or number; or for older students a quote from a poem or play).

- Think of ten questions for which the answer is 'my house'.
- Why do we use cutlery? Design and draw your own cutlery.

12 Problem box

Collect any interesting or puzzling questions that arise in the classroom. Create a place to write, store or display your questions, such as in a box, on a board or in a book in which children can post their problems or questions about their learning or their lives. The teacher, being part of the community in the classroom, may add their own problems or questions too. Once a week share out the questions and problems for pairs or small groups to discuss. Here are some ideas for problems to discuss.

- What is a problem? Give examples. What is your recipe for solving problems?
- What causes fights between people? What can help prevent fights?
- How could life in school be improved?
- What is your recipe for keeping healthy?

13 Question the world

Using a globe, children in pairs brainstorm questions to ask about the planet. Share the questions out to pairs or small groups to discuss. Pairs share questions and answers with the whole group. Here are some sample questions to discuss:

- What are the most important problems we have to solve in the world?
- Many people are dying of hunger in the world. How could we help them?

- Many people are homeless. How should they be helped?
- How could the richer countries help people in the poorer countries? Should they? Why?
- How might the problems of too much traffic on the roads be solved?

14 What kind of question is this?

Ask students to think about what is strange, interesting or puzzling about a particular text, to generate and share questions. List their questions and then ask them to analyse the questions (e.g. using the Question Quadrant). Could they turn any of the closed questions into more interesting open enquiry questions?

15 Talk about questions

Some questions to ask to stimulate thinking and dialogue about the role of questions include:

- What is a question?
- Why ask questions?
- What is the value of asking questions?
- What is the difference between 'open' and 'closed' questions?
- What is the difference between 'factual' and 'reasoning' questions?
- Are some questions better than others? Why? What is your definition of a good question?
- Are there questions for which there are no answers?
- Do you sometimes get an answer, then ask the same question again? Why?
- Do you sometimes get different answers to the same question? When, and why?
- Do you ask yourself a lot of questions? What questions do you ask? Who answers?
- Do you ever ask yourself a question that you don't know the answer to? Is there a point in doing this?
- Do you ever ask questions when you know you are not going to like the answer?
- Do you sometimes ask questions when you already know the answer?
- Do you sometimes think of questions and don't ask them? Why is this?
- Would you rather ask questions or give answers? Which is more important? Why?

See also: Fisher (1996, p.86; 1997b, p.74; 2000, p.70).

3

Creative Talk for Thinking

Creativity is the way of thinking out loud original ideas and thoughts.

(Larry, aged 10)

Good talk is characterised by creative energy. This energy comes naturally from the meeting of diverse minds and is sustained by the interplay of different perspectives. When the energy is not there it needs to be stimulated. This chapter explores ways of stimulating creative talk.

Many attempts have been made to define what 'creative' and 'creativity' means. The following are three typical definitions:

- The ability to solve problems and fashion products and to raise new questions (Gardner 1993).

- Imaginative processes with outcomes that are original and of value (Robinson 2001).

- The capacity to make, do or become something fresh and valuable with respect to others as well as ourselves (Pope 2005).

Part of the reason for the diversity of definitions is that creativity may be seen as an act, skill or process (what we do), a property or quality of people (who we are), a product or outcome (what we make) or a concept or idea (what we think). It may also be thought of as an ideologic strategy or goal (how people should behave). Whether it is one, several or all of these things, it exists on a continuum. People can be more or less creative. It is a common human attribute, and is not limited to creative geniuses and it is not just expressed through the arts. As Georgie, aged 10, put it: 'Creativity is not just art. It is thinking deeply and having original thoughts about something.' Human activity of all kinds, whether at work or play, at home or school, present problems that people regularly solve with some degree of creativity.

A better question than 'What is creativity?' is 'Where is creativity?' Identifying the creative aspects of a work is never simple because creative thinking can be exercised on various levels, in various ways and in various locations. These dimensions include:

- self – the individual person or talent

- task – the domain or discipline in which the individual is working

- environment – the context or community which judges the quality of outcomes.

It is the interaction of these elements that allows us to identify creativity. What we call 'creativity' is not the product of individuals in isolation but of social systems and communities that make judgements about individual products or outcomes. In one nursery class the teacher asks each child to point to something creative they have done. Each child is able to identify some piece of creative work of their own on display, including questions they have asked that have been written up in their 'Questions Book'. When the teacher asks the children what makes their work creative a child responds: 'Because I have done it myself.'

A question that can always be asked about any dialogue is 'Where were the creative ideas?' Evidence for creativity might be found in individual responses, in the questions asked and ideas put forward, or in the solutions proposed to the task or problem, or in the way the group judged the process or outcomes of the dialogue. We will look later at some particular community settings in which creative dialogue flourishes (see Chapter 8).

Einstein believed that the key to improvement in learning was creative thinking. He said: 'To raise new questions, new problems, to regard old problems from a new angle requires creative imagination, and makes real advances.' According to Piaget, 'To understand is to invent'. We make knowledge our own, he thought, 'by reconstructing it through some creative operation of the mind'. Leaving children to think and learn on their own does not guarantee that they will engage in creative thinking. What they need to stimulate, challenge and stretch their thinking is dialogue. What any mind needs to retain its flexibility, in both young and old people, is the combination of creative thinking *and* dialogue.

Evidence that creative thinking is happening in a dialogue might include examples of individuals or groups engaging in one or more of the following elements explored in this chapter:

1 Questioning and challenging.
2 Making connections and seeing relationships.
3 Imagining what might be.
4 Exploring and extending ideas.
5 Reflecting critically on ideas, actions and outcomes.
6 Creative talk in practice.

These are some of the creative behaviours, or habits of intelligent behaviour, that need to be practised through dialogue with children at home or in the classroom. This chapter explores these features and suggests what needs to be done to develop them. As Johanna, aged 10, said: 'Creativity is not about knowing things, it's about doing things and knowing you have done them.'

Questioning and challenging

What promotes creativity is a questioning classroom, where teachers and pupils value diversity, and ask unusual and challenging questions; for example:

■ Asking 'Why?', 'How?', 'What if?'
■ Responding to ideas, questions, tasks or problems in an unusual way.

- Posing unusual questions or problems.
- Challenging conventions and assumptions.
- Thinking from other viewpoints.

Here is an example of the questions raised after reading a 'poem for thinking' ('The Magic Box' by Kit Wright) by a mixed group of 7- to 10-year-olds at Burunda State School in Brisbane:[1]

- Can your imagination change who you are?
- If a picture paints a thousand words can a word paint a thousand pictures?
- Does imagination only affect your mind?
- Can a poem affect your imagination?
- Can our imagination influence the way we live?
- Is our imagination a door into another world?
- Are there any limits to our imagination?
- Can a poem change your life/the world/ the universe?
- Can a poem lead to another poem?
- What gives us the will to live?

The following are some questions raised by a group of able 13- to 14-year-olds about Franz Kafka's story 'Metamorphosis'[2] about a boy who wakes one morning to find he is a beetle. The students choose to discuss 'What's the point of the story?' and play spontaneously with their own ideas, and with what the image of the boy metamorphosing into a bug might represent.

- How did he know it wasn't really a dream?
- How did it happen? Why did it happen?
- Why is it only his body that has changed and not his thoughts and feelings?
- Why was he not bothered that he was a bug?
- How does he still have a human voice when his features were like a bug?
- Why is he a bug and not something else?
- How do we know he is a bug?
- If it was a dream how do we know if he is awake now?
- What is the point of the story?
- If he is a bug, why is he such a big bug?

> *Child*: I don't think the point of the story is to ask questions about the story but to ask questions about yourself. How can you relate to this? Does he really turn into a bug? Or does he feel mostly that he's ugly or something?
>
> *Child*: Maybe he's like worried or something. Maybe he is feeling like everything is difficult, like his voice is changing, and he's just feeling really scary, about growing up and all that lot . . .

Child: Suddenly you just feel that your legs are so long, and your arms so much longer than you thought they'd be. And these are things you wouldn't normally think about so maybe its just how he feels. He's just realised it and that's it.

Child: Maybe he's just buried up so he thinks he's a bug.

Child: Or it could represent something else.

Child: Yes, but if you are buried you don't think you are a bug!

Child: It might have represented a change in your life or something, like he's changed into a bug and that represents a change in his life.

Child: But what does a bug represent?

Child: I don't know. It's just a comparison. Maybe he just chose that because that happened in a dream. Just that.

Child: Yes, but you can't choose your dreams can you?

Child: How do you know it was a dream? How do we know we are not dreaming now?

Child: Maybe it's just the writer's way of telling us how the boy is feeling.

Child: Maybe there's no point to the story. Perhaps it's just the writer's way to keep people confused. [Laughter from the group]

Child: Well I think he succeeded.

Child: I think the more questions you ask the more confused you get.

Child: Yes, maybe . . . or do I mean definitely?

[More laughter and clapping in agreement from the group]

This short dialogue shows how the students are playing with ideas and possibilities in a creative way; interrogating the meaning behind the story and starting to use their own experience as a reference point. Towards the end of the extract the concept of dream or reality gets thrown into the mix, opening opportunities for a more philosophical dialogue. The use of metaphor shows the playfulness characteristic of a creative dialogue as does the use of humour. Creative dialogue is about creative conflict, considering different points of view and the practice of solving problems together. It is about seeking to disturb the existing pattern of children's thoughts so as to expand their consciousness.

One way to broaden one's perception of self and others is to try to see things from another person's point of view. For the learner, and perhaps for us all, this is a difficult challenge. It requires an ability to listen to the views expressed by other people, and to make an imaginative leap to understand their feelings and ideas. This leap of imagination is fundamental to moral development, and to an understanding of others (part of social and emotional intelligence).

Role play can be an excellent way to challenge children to think and talk as another person. Another way into thinking about other points of view is to consider different views (peer reviews) of a piece of work, or to consider both sides of an existing argument or conflict. It can be fruitful to encourage different views when assessing a piece of work. Stories and drama, history and geography settings, art, design and IT also provide good opportunities to look at different viewpoints:

■ Does everyone think the same thing?

■ What do you think? What does s/he think?

- What do the others think?
- What are they feeling? Why?
- What do you think is going through his/her/their mind?

> *A man sold a well to a farmer, but when the farmer went to draw water from it the man stopped him. He said: 'I sold you the well but not the water. You will have to pay separately for the water.' The farmer of course refused and both came to Nasruddin to make a judgement on the issue. After hearing both points of view Nasruddin said to the man who had sold the well: 'Since you sold only the well, you have no right to keep your water in it. Pay a rent to this farmer for using his well or take your water out at once!' The man realised that he had been outwitted, and bowing to Nasruddin quietly left the court.*

For an activity which aims to encourage seeing other viewpoints see p. 67.

Think the opposite: try reverse thinking

A creative person is willing to consider alternative ideas or plans before, during and after an activity. Being open-minded means being willing to consider the opposite of what has been thought, said or done before. Some of our ideas will be wrong and sometimes the reverse of what we think might be true.

Creative dialogue may involve thinking about opposite points of view. Sometimes an idea can benefit from considering opposite points of view. We may gain new insights by turning an idea or problem around and thinking the reverse.

The reversal method for examining a problem or generating new ideas takes a situation as it is and turns it around, inside out, backwards, or upside-down. Any given situation can be 'reversed' in several ways. When discussing problems try 'turning' the problem around and considering it from another angle. For example, you might ask: 'What can I do to make my relationship with my family better?' Reverse this and ask: 'What can I do to make it worse?' Suggestions might be to have temper tantrums, use insults, pretend not to hear and so on. Try reversing these negatives – perhaps to control temper, use compliments or be thoughtful about your family's needs and requests.

The value of reverse thinking during a dialogue is that the rearrangement of information can provoke new ideas. Instead of asking 'Why?', it asks 'Why not?' Creative dialogue involving looking at a familiar problem or situation in a fresh way can suggest new solutions or approaches. It doesn't matter whether a reverse situation seems to makes sense, it may provoke new thinking. See the task 'Try reverse thinking' (p. 70) for another example of a dialogic activity that promotes creative disturbance.

Making connections and seeing relationships

Nasruddin was sitting among the branches of a tree, sniffing the blossoms and sunning himself. A traveller passed by and asked him what he was doing there. 'Climbing the Great Pyramid.' He replied. 'You are nowhere near a pyramid. There are four ways up a pyramid; one by each face. That is a tree!' 'Yes,' said the Mulla, 'But it's much more fun like this don't you think? Birds, blossoms, wind, sunshine. I don't think I could have done better.'

Creativity involves expanding existing knowledge. This is done through connecting ideas, building on them or thinking of new ideas. Creative dialogue should help children build on what is given through making new connections. They will be helped to think for themselves and benefit from the ideas of others through discussion.

Piaget argued that concepts are organised into 'schemas' or 'models' which are mental representations of things or ideas, and it is through these that we process information. For Piaget cognitive development was very much to do with conceptual development, and this was often best achieved through cognitive conflict when our existing concepts or 'schemas' are challenged, and our existing ideas disturbed. It is through dialogue with others, as Vygotsky said, that existing patterns of ideas are disturbed and new connections made; to learn is to have changes and new connections made in the mind. Cognitive development must entail some change, some rearrangement or enlargement of the conceptual structure. It is these conceptual structures that underlie skills and understanding, and it is primarily through dialogue that these changes occur.

Making connections, seeing relationships might involve:

- making unusual connections
- searching for relationships
- creating analogies and metaphor
- applying ideas to new contexts
- communicating ideas in novel ways.

Analogical thinking: create an analogy, make a connection

An important strategy in creative thinking and problem-solving is being able to see an issue or problem in new ways, making new connections and discovering new possibilities. One way of creating a connection is to talk about how two separate things may be linked with a connecting idea. When we think about one thing being also true of another we are reasoning by analogy. The American poet Carl Sandburg once said: 'Poetry is the synthesis of hyacinths and biscuits.' Here he was taking two unrelated words or images and putting them together to make the familiar strange. An analogy is created when one takes two seemingly unrelated words or ideas and sees a connecting idea. For example, when a class were asked to think of reasons why a teacher was like a ham sandwich, one child responded: 'because they both have a sell-by date.' Another said: 'You'll find there's goodness in the middle – if you look hard enough.'

The following are examples of students creating analogies about themselves:

- I am undiscovered gold lying in the hills, waiting to be discovered.
- I am like a grape, just one of a bunch, but I am full of juicy goodness.
- I am like a pawn in a game of chess, but without me the game would not work.

Many solutions to problems can be found by spotting a similarity or analogy with the solution of an earlier problem. So a question to ask about anything is: 'What is this like?'

Leonardo da Vinci was good at seeing analogies. One day he noticed that 'birds which ride on the wind in circles hold their wings very high, so the wind may serve as a wedge to hold them up.' He realised that birds fly not just by flapping their wings but by riding ramps of air. So he thought that if man could make a machine that did the same, with a propeller on top, it too would fly. He drew it but could not successfully make one. Children will also imagine, draw and talk about things that they cannot make.

Another use of analogy is through story. The great spiritual leaders of the past used stories as teaching aids to help people find solutions to their problems. These teaching stories, like those quoted in this book, are not about our problems but are analogies that enable us to see connections between what is told in the stories and the problems we face. Analogies are also used as a form of reasoning (see p. 68 for more on analogical thinking tasks).

'Creative thinking helps me to make connections between things and develop my deepness in thinking' (Matthew, aged 10). For activities that encourage children to make new connections see the 'What connections can you make?' tasks on p. 69.

Imagining what might be

> Imagination is more important than knowledge. For knowledge is limited while imagination embraces the whole world.
>
> (Albert Einstein)

To be creative is to activate one's imagination. As Miercoles, aged 10, put it, 'Creativity is like imagination because when you create something you need to imagine it first.' What imagination does is to enable the mind to represent images and ideas of what is not actually present to the senses. It can refer to the capacity to predict, plan and foresee possible future consequences. In short imagination is the capacity to conceive possible (or impossible) worlds that lie beyond this time and place. These possible worlds may derive from actual worlds or be re-created from our store of memory knowledge. As William Blake said, 'What is now proved was once imagined.'

Imagination can be exercised through dialogue and might involve:

- envisaging and seeing things in the mind's eye
- asking: 'What if?' and 'What if not?'

- visualising alternatives
- seeing possibilities, problems and challenges
- thinking about other possibilities.

Guided imagery can be a powerful stimulus to imagination as a form of meditation using 'the inner eye' to create and explore special places in the mind through guided images (for more on guided visualisation see p. 66). A focus such as a picture or word stimulus may be used to practise focusing the mind and stimulate visual thinking and imagination. Such experiences can help still the mind and focus it on positive images and emotions.

Every good lesson or learning conversation is in a sense a story. The story is a universal means of generating creative dialogue. We begin by telling our children stories, enriching their minds with narrative models, imaginative ideas and expanding their experience through inviting them into imaginary worlds and possibility thinking. A rich store of story experience enables children themselves to be story-creators and story-tellers. Any story that they hear or create for themselves can have more than one ending. For example, choose a short story or TV film, stop half-way through and ask the children how it might end. How many endings can they devise? Which is best? Why? How in fact did the story end?

Whenever we make up a story of what might happen we are using our imagination. See p. 70 for a story-making activity that encourages children to exercise their imagination through creating a story from a few given elements.

Possibility thinking: think of alternatives, possibilities and choices

When his friends asked him what he liked best about his new house in the city, Nasruddin replied that it was the garden. When his friends came to visit him he took them out into the garden. They were surprised to see that it was small and narrow, hemmed in by buildings on three sides. 'You're always praising your garden, Nasruddin', said one of the men, 'but it is so . . . so . . . small!'

'That is true', said Nasruddin, looking up at an eagle soaring in the sky. 'But see how high it is!'

The world is full of alternatives, possibilities and choices, but we don't always see them. This is especially true of children who often come to believe that there is only one answer, only one right way to do things. We need to alert them to alternatives, to possible new directions, and to encourage them sometimes to choose 'the road less travelled by'. We talk of being 'blinkered', and of 'tunnel vision'. As learners we talk of 'getting stuck', and of not knowing what to do, where to turn, which way to go. If children value the practice of seeking alternatives they will be better placed to think of alternative solutions when they need them.

There are many sorts of alternatives, including:

- viewpoints
- actions

- solutions

- ways of working

- explanations

- plans

- designs.

Encourage children to talk about alternatives, to be alert to multiple possibilities. As one child commented, 'There is always a different way, even if you can't find it.'

The most difficult thing to do is to look for alternatives when you don't have to. Like us, children prefer to do things out of habit, and often work mindlessly. What helps them to be more flexible in their thinking, and more alert to possibilities? Questions to ask as starters for dialogue include:

- Is there another way?

- Can we come up with an alternative suggestion?

- Is there a possibility we have not thought of?

- What other choices have we got?

- Have we considered all the options?

When we begin to look for alternatives we should be clear about the purpose of the alternative. So a key question becomes: 'Why are we looking for alternatives?' Here are some responses to that question from a group of 9-year-olds:

Teacher: Why is it good to look for alternative ideas?
Child: So we can find better ideas.
Child: Just in case our first thought was not our best thought.
Child: You never know what you might think . . . you might have a good idea.
Child: A better idea.
Child: Sometimes your first ideas are best.
Child: Yes, but you don't know that until you've had some other ideas.
Child: Sometimes I don't have other ideas.
Child: Sometimes I don't have a first idea!

See 'Possibility thinking' (p. 66) for a sample way to encourage looking for alternatives.

Sometimes creative dialogue needs provocation. We need a short, sharp shock to be jolted out of habitual thought patterns and provoked to look at things in a new way. De Bono has coined the word 'po' to describe this kind of 'provocative operation'. One technique is 'provocation in role', which entails the teacher or other 'agent provocateur' playing devil's advocate in discussion with children by challenging all or any received moral and scientific assumptions with a view to building up a child's confidence and resilience in argument. A provocative statement is any that will stimulate creative thought, response or discussion.

Examples of provocative statements that teachers, in role, can use to provoke discussion include:

- There is no point in going to school.

- Nothing is true.

- I can do whatever I want.

- I am going to call this four-sided shape a triangle.

- Adults know more than children so what they say is never wrong.

Provocation is about disturbing children's thinking so as to extend their ideas.

Exploring and extending ideas

'Reasonable people always see things in the same way,' said the Khan of Samarkand to Nasruddin one day. 'That's the trouble with "reasonable people",' said Nasruddin, 'some can only see one of two possibilities.' The Khan called his wise men to explain this, but they thought Nasruddin was talking nonsense. The next day Nasruddin rode to see the Khan and his wise men, sitting on a donkey, his face towards its tail. 'What have you just seen?' asked Nasruddin. They said: 'A man riding back to front on a donkey.'

'That is my point,' said Nasruddin. 'The trouble with them is that they did not think that perhaps it was me who was right and the donkey who was the wrong way round.'

Any learning that is not routine that takes account of new knowledge, develops new ideas, or design solutions to new problems requires creative thinking. Because learners do not have complete knowledge of an area of learning, creativity will be needed to help develop, adapt and apply understanding that is at present partial or incomplete. Creative or divergent thinking opens up possibilities, the chance to try alternative and fresh approaches in any situation.

'Creativity is stretching further on knowledge, inventing ideas to help your thinking' (Christopher, aged 10). Brainstorming is a traditional idea-generating strategy whose main goal is to break us out of our habit-bound thinking and produce a collection of ideas from which we can choose. Brainstorming can take place either individually or in groups of two to ten, with four to seven generally being the best group size for generating a range of ideas through dialogue. Everyone in the group should contribute any idea they wish in response to a problem, issue or idea.

The following guidelines aim to help bring the best results in terms of range of ideas.

- *Think freely.* All ideas are valid, accepted and recorded. Odd thoughts are fine. Impossible and unthinkable ideas are fine. In fact, in every session, there should be several ideas so strange that they make others laugh. Remember that practical ideas can often come from silly, impractical, impossible ones. By permitting yourself to think outside the boundaries of ordinary, normal thought, brilliant new solutions can arise. Some 'wild' ideas may turn out to be practical, too.

- *Suspend judgement.* When ideas are generated no critical comments are allowed. This is the most important rule. All ideas are written down. The judging of ideas comes later. We have been trained in school to be so instantly analytic, practical and critical in our thinking that this step is very difficult to observe, but it is crucial. To create and criticise at the same time is like watering and pouring weedkiller on to seedlings at the same time.

■ *Build on ideas*. Improve, modify, build on the ideas of others. What is good about the idea just suggested? How can it be made to work? What changes would make it better or even wilder? This is sometimes called piggybacking, hitchhiking, or batting ideas backwards and forwards adding something each time. Use another's idea to stimulate your own improvement or variation. Changing just one aspect of an unworkable solution can sometimes make it a great solution.

■ *The more ideas the better*. Concentrate on generating a large stock of ideas so that they can be sifted through later on. There are two reasons for desiring a large quantity. First, the obvious, usual and well-known ideas seem to come to mind first, so that the first, say, ten or more ideas may not be new and creative. Second, the larger your list of possibilities, the more you will have to choose from, adapt or combine. Some people aim for a fixed number, like ten, twenty or fifty ideas, before ending the session. Someone should be put in charge of writing down all the ideas. No attempt should be made to put the list in any particular order. Preferably, the ideas should be written on a board or large piece of paper so that the whole brainstorming group can see them. Some people say that using a large piece of paper increases their creativity, even when working on their own (See the task on 'Brainstorming', p. 65).

Being creative is about being able to overcome the mental blocks of routine thinking. Some of these blocks include the tendency to think that:

■ there is only one right way to do things

■ we know all there is to know

■ it is wrong to experiment with new ideas.

If we get stuck the best way is to alter our approach to a problem. To do this we need to be flexible, not rigid in our thinking. Being flexible is about being aware that there is always another way, a new approach or different idea to try. It is about doing things well but differently. Dialogue is important, since we think differently by listening to ideas that others think we would not have thought of. As Elaine, aged 10, said: 'You never know what others are thinking unless you ask them.'

Dialogue helps children to explore and extending ideas through:

■ playing with ideas and experimenting

■ responding to feelings and with intuition

■ keeping an open mind, ready to adapt and modify ideas

■ trying alternatives and fresh approaches

■ overcoming problems and thinking of improvements.

See p. 69 ('Improve it' for examples of ways to challenge children to think of ways to improve or add value to objects, places and ideas.

Reflecting critically on ideas, actions and outcomes

Nasruddin was once seen throwing handfuls of bread all around his house. 'What are you doing?' he was asked. 'It's a new idea I've had for keeping the tigers away,' said Nasruddin. 'But there are no tigers around here,' came the reply. 'Exactly,' said Nasruddin. 'It seems to be effective doesn't it?'

Creativity is the way you use your imagination to produce something that is original. This may be done individually or more powerfully as part of a creative dialogue. You can 'be original' in two senses – in a personal sense and a universal sense. If an idea you have thought of is new or novel to you, it is original in a personal sense. Many others may have had this thought or idea before, but if it is new to you and originates from you it is in this sense original. Another sense of original means that *no one* has ever thought of it before. This is a much harder kind of originality, for it is very difficult to create something that has never been seen or heard before – but you can do it, as the exercises below will show. You can create ideas you have never thought of before and you can create ideas that no one has ever thought of before. All you need is the confidence, stimulus and opportunity to be creative and to do it.

Many children do not consider themselves to be creative because they compare their efforts with those of their teacher or parents or talented friends and feel they are not much good. However, they should be comparing themselves only with their own past efforts. As Charlie, aged 11, said: 'When I compare myself with myself, I come out pretty good.'

To think of something that is original does not of course mean that it is of value. The true end of creativity is to use imagination to create things that are original *and of value*. There is no virtue in simply doing things differently for the sake of being different. There is virtue in doing things differently if it results in doing them better. So a crucial follow-up question to the generation of ideas is to ask: 'It may be original, but is it good?' (for more on the discussion of criteria see p. 188).

Reflecting critically on ideas, actions and outcomes might involve:

- reviewing creative progress
- asking: 'Have we had any good ideas?' 'Are these the ideas we need?'
- inviting and responding to feedback
- reflecting critically about the process of dialogue and ways of doing things
- making constructive comments about creative outcomes.

Exercise judgement

As Nasruddin walked down the street one day a gang of youths began to throw stones at him. 'Stop that and I will tell you something sure to interest you,' said Nasrudin. 'All right, what is it?' challenged a youth. 'The king is giving a free banquet for everyone,' said Nasruddin, going on to describe all the kinds of food, drinks and entertainment on offer. The youths ran off towards the palace. Suddenly Nasruddin started to run after them. 'I'd better go and see too,' he panted, 'in case it is true!'

Creative dialogue requires the exercise of judgement. The philosopher Plato distrusted poetic talk because it strayed from truth and reality. As Jamie, aged 6, put it: 'A story may be true or may not be true or may be partly true and partly fake.'

'Creative thinking is like thinking of all different objects or things in your own way' (Natasha). Any lesson can develop creative thinking if it involves pupils generating and extending ideas, suggesting hypotheses, applying imagination and finding new or innovative outcomes. Try to include opportunities for creativity in the lessons you teach. Look for evidence of pupils':

Creative thinking	**Questions to ask**
■ Apply imagination	*What might be . . .?*
■ Generate hypotheses, ideas and outcomes	*What is a possible (idea/way/solution) . . .?*
■ Develop creative skills or techniques	*What methods could you use for . . .?*
■ Assess own or others' creative work	*How well did you/they succeed in . . .?*

Teaching for creative dialogue should not be confused with creative teaching. In creative teaching the focus is on what the teacher does. Teaching for creative dialogue makes the focus the learner, not the teacher. Active teaching methods are necessary but not sufficient for creative learning. Teaching for creative dialogue helps students not only to learn, but to learn from their learning – to learn and practise the habits of creative behaviour. The best way to teach these habits is to model these behaviours ourselves.

In reviewing the process of creative thinking and dialogue we need to discuss with students what their concept of creativity is, as well as the criteria they would use to judge the quality of particular creative activities (see p. 71 for ways to engage children in discussing creativity).

Creative talk in practice

The creative dialogue tasks presented include ways to stimulate creativity and solve problems using the following strategies:

1 Solve a challenge together

2 Invent a word

3 Brainstorm ideas

4 Picture it

5 Find a use

6 Possibilities thinking

7 See other viewpoints

8 Thought experiment

9 Analogical thinking: create a metaphor

10 Make a creative connection

11 Improve it

12 Create a story

13 Reverse thinking

14 Consider what's best

15 Discuss creativity.

In stimulating creative dialogue with children try to make creative thinking visible by discussing the strategy and the reasons for it. The strategies presented may be adapted and developed in different ways. They are not recipes but suggestions for stimulating creative talk with children. The chapter ends with some questions for engaging children's thoughts about creativity – again expressing the central message of this book that if it's worth knowing about, it is worth talking about.

1 Solve a challenge together

Ask students in pairs or small groups to discuss possible methods to solve particular problems. They should try to think of different ways of solving the problem and decide what they think is their best solution. Groups then present and describe their different solutions.

Here are examples of some creative challenges:

- an improvement to the human body
- a new way to cut hair
- a way to pick fruit from a tall tree
- a better purse or wallet
- a chair that helps you to learn
- a way of watering house plants when you are away
- something to keep your desk tidy
- something to scare birds away from growing crops
- a litter bin
- a machine to help around the house.

Can you think of one or more unique solutions to each problem? Remember: it is a unique solution for you if it is one you have never thought of before.

Here is an activity to encourage you and your children to generate some novel ideas and to think of words that no one has ever thought of before. Words are the tools we use for thinking. We know thousands of words in our own language. We know there are many more in the dictionary. We know that new words are slowly but continually being added to languages. Creative minds create new words to express new ideas and inventions. This activity invites you to be creative in inventing new words.

2 Invent a word

The objective of this activity is to create new words. Words have many purposes. Think of the purpose for which this new word is needed. What job has it to do? For example, it could name something, describe something, identify a particular action. Here are some purposes your word could serve.

Try to create a word (or many words) to describe:

- a new kind of dinosaur
- a machine
- a strange plant
- a custom
- a new game or sport
- a new dish
- a new drink.

Ask children to play with the order of letters in their new words and to think how it sounds.

Invent two definitions for your word, one being the 'true' meaning of the word you have invented, the other a 'false' meaning. See if others can guess the 'correct' definition that you have given it.

3 Brainstorm ideas

Ask children to choose one of the following problems for a brainstorming session and to try, through discussion with a partner, to generate at least ten ideas for solving the problem:

- a new snack food
- how to entertain children at a party
- how to get more tourists to visit your country
- how to meet new friends
- how to keep a school free of litter
- how to reduce airport congestion and delays

- a name for a new laundry detergent
- how to keep your keys safe while at the beach
- a new toy
- a new electronic consumer product.

Once you have a list of ideas evaluate and distil your list into at least three practical, effective ideas. These ideas need not only to be expressed in words, they can also be expressed visually through drawing.

4 Picture it

Can you visualise it?

- Describe a picture without showing it to your partner. Can they visualise it? Can they draw it from your description?
- Shut your eyes and listen to a new piece of music. What pictures/words come into your mind? What does it make you feel or think? Discuss this with a partner.
- Discuss a geometric shape(s). Ask students to visualise the shape(s) in their mind's eye. Ask them to try to add to or turn the shapes in their mind to see different angles and combinations.

5 Find a use

Think of as many uses as you can for this design to make or improve a product. Ask yourself: How else could it be used? What are the most interesting and unusual uses you can think of? Can you think of a strange or surprising use? Write down or draw your ideas. Think of adapting it, changing colour, shape, position, combining it, moving it, making it in different materials, to appeal to sight, touch, taste and smell, using the design for different purposes (see also 'CREATE questions' on p. 37).

- Think up as many different uses as you can for a familiar object such as a blanket, barrel, brick, sock, paper clip, shoebox, elastic band, human hair, toothbrush, compact disc, milk bottle, sock.
- Discuss how a pattern or design might be used. For example, see the cobweb design in Figure 3.1.

Discuss how else it might be used in designing and making things.

6 Possibilities thinking

Make a list of options, alternatives and possibilities to help in making a decision about the following problems or situations:

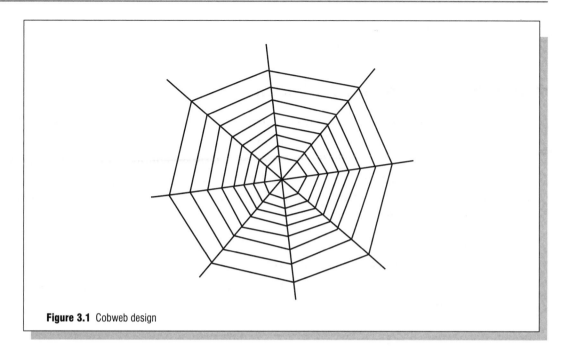

Figure 3.1 Cobweb design

- You discover your best friend is a thief. What alternatives do you have?

- As you are walking along the street you see a woman collapse to the ground. How could this have happened? What can you do?

- A car is found crashed in a ditch. There is no driver. What happened?

- Some places are dirty because people drop litter and cans everywhere. What could you do to solve this problem?

- You and your friends decide to raise money for charity. Which charity? What could you do?

7 Seeing other viewpoints

List what you think the views are of different people in these examples:

- A father and mother forbid their son and daughter to stay up after 10 p.m. to watch a TV programme they want to see. What are the different views of the parents, and of the children?

- Someone wants to sell you a second-hand bicycle. What are their views, and your views?

- You lend a friend some money to buy a lottery ticket. Your friend wins a prize with the ticket. Who does the prize belong to? What might be the different points of view of you and your friend?

- A burglar breaks into your house and steals everything of value that can be found. Your parents call the police, who say they will try their best to catch the thief. What are the views of your parents, the burglar and the police?

- Choose a book, picture or video programme and list the different thoughts, feelings and points of view of the characters.

8 Try a thought experiment: ask 'What if . . .?'

What if animals could speak? What if we could live forever? What if the Earth stopped revolving and the Sun did not rise? 'What ifs' provide a wishful thinking kind of provocation by adding some impossible feature or picking out some characteristic of an item and imagining it was missing. This kind of playful imagination is a kind of conceptual exploration. By examining what can or cannot be imagined or conceived, students are exploring the possibilities and limits of their thinking. For example:

- What essential features of the following could you imagine leaving out of a house: school, bicycle, library, birthday (e.g. 'What if your house had no . . .')?
- What features could you imagine adding to school, parents, clothes, sleep, sports (e.g. 'Wouldn't it be nice if . . .')?

Can you or your children create ten 'What if . . .' impossibilities? Choose, draw and discuss your most interesting idea (see also p. 165).

9 Analogical thinking: create a metaphor

Discuss these with a partner and find answers to these questions. There are no right or wrong answers, but find as many reasons as you can for your answers:

Riddles. What answers can you find for these riddles:

- Why is summer like a bridge?
- Which animal is like a rubber band?
- Which colour is quickest?

Create more metaphorical riddles of your own by linking two seemingly unrelated ideas.

Metaphors. Make up some metaphors (or analogies) about yourself:

- What kind of food are you?
- What kind of furniture are you?
- What kind of animal are you?
- How are you like a candle?

Think of some more categories, and make up some more metaphors.

Analogy. Think of a good, original analogy or metaphor for one of the following and then trace at least four similarities. Describe the similarities in complete sentences, for example:

'Studying is like walking down a long and winding road . . .'.

■ Your brain	'My brain is like . . .'
■ Driving a car	'Driving a car is like . . .'
■ Using a computer	'Using a computer is like . . .'
■ Learning	'Learning is like . . .'
■ Love	'Love is like . . .'
■ Your life	'My life is like . . .'.

10 Make a creative connection

■ Choose any word – a simple concept like 'tree' or 'wet', or something more complex like 'anger' or 'democracy'. Ask students to think about it, discuss and choose words they associate with it. Individually or in pairs they continue to add words, building up a sequence of associations. A more challenging version is to try to reach in a chain of association a very different word from the first word.

■ Make connections with key concepts in a unit of study by giving students a number of concept words from a unit of study; ask them to think of and try to pair up any two or more words with a connecting idea or ideas. Discuss or display these in visual form.

■ Write down lines or fragments from different poems on slips of paper. Students select at random some of these fragments of poetry and try to compose a poem (or prose) inspired by the fragments, making connections between them in their own words.

11 Improve it

Choose something, for example, one item from the following list, and try to think of as many ways to improve it as you can. Discuss possible improvements to:

■ a pencil

■ lighting in a room

■ a bus

■ a desk

■ a telephone

■ a bicycle

■ a spoon

■ your home

■ your life

■ your country.

After your discussion can you list up to ten ways to improve each of these items?

Refer to the 'CREATE' list of questions on p. 37 for ways to get you thinking about how to improve or add value to something.

12 Create a story

Choose six very different words or concepts (words that stand for things or ideas), or invite individuals to suggest these words. In pairs or groups children are asked to make these words significant elements in a story. Specify a story length (e.g. 500 or 100 words).

- Can you create the story?
- Can you complete other, very different stories using these words (e.g. a comedy, a tragedy, a fairy-tale, a creation story, a news story)?
- Discuss these alternative stories and decide which of the stories you prefer and why.
- Discuss ways of condensing a chosen story into fifty and then ten words.

13 Reverse thinking

In 'reverse thinking' children are asked to consider and discuss the reverse of a given situation. Supposing the opposite were to happen? For example, consider and discuss: *How might a teacher improve teaching in a classroom?* Ask children in pairs or small groups to discuss the reverse of the situation; for example, 'a teacher teaching students' could be reversed as:

- children teaching the teacher
- the teacher not teaching the children
- children teaching themselves
- children teaching each other
- the teacher teaching him/herself
- children unteaching (correcting?) the teacher.

Ask children to consider what value there might be in discussing these 'reverse' situations.

14 Consider what is best

Consider the possible views of the main characters in a chosen story. Ask the children to discuss:

- What are they thinking?
- What should they be thinking?
- What are they feeling?
- What should they be feeling?

- What could they do?
- What is best for them to do?

Real-life situations sometimes present us with one and often many alternative options. Thinking 'What else could be done' encourages us to think more widely, that there may be more than one or two options or obvious answers. Being creative means broadening our thinking by using our imagination to think about alternatives.

15 Discuss creativity

Here are some questions about creativity to think about and discuss:

- What is creativity? What does 'being creative' mean?
- Is creativity important? Why?
- Can everybody be creative? How?
- What helps people to be creative?
- What questions can help stimulate creative ideas?
- What is the evidence that you (or we) are creative?
- What stops people being creative?
- What would help me (you or/us) be more creative?
- Is too much creativity a bad thing?
- How creative a person are you?
- What can be improved in life? Can you give an example?
- What do you want to improve? How could you set about it?
- What would you most like to create?

4

Critical Talk

Developing verbal reasoning

Nasruddin once went on a journey with his son and a donkey. He let his son ride on the donkey. On the way they met some people who said, 'Look at that healthy young boy! That is today's youth for you. They have no respect for elders. His poor father should ride on the donkey!' Hearing these words the boy felt ashamed and insisted that he walk and his father ride the donkey. So Nasruddin mounted the donkey and the boy walked at his side. A little later they met some other people who said, 'Well, look at that! That poor little boy has to walk while his father rides on the donkey.' Hearing this Nasruddin told his son, 'The best thing to do is for both of us to walk. Then no one can complain.' So they continued on their journey, both of them walking. A little way down the road they met some others who said, 'Just take a look at those fools. Both of them are walking under this hot sun and neither of them are riding on the donkey!' Nasruddin turned to his son and said, 'That just goes to show how hard it is to escape the opinions of others.'

Children often absorb the attitudes and opinions of the significant adults in their lives and can become dependent on the thinking of others. They need to learn to question their own ideas and the ideas of others, to value and exercise their own reasoning capacities. If children are to become open-minded and critical, their thinking cannot be left to chance. They should be taught how to think critically. This chapter on critical dialogue is about helping children develop verbal reasoning through learning how to:

1 Give reasons.

2 Evaluate the reasons.

3 Assess the evidence.

4 Argue well.

5 Distinguish fact from opinion.

6 Exercise your judgement.

7 Develop critical talk in practice.

Children need to learn about reasoning to help them understand some of the differences between good and bad reasoning. They need to develop critical thinking to gain a more grounded knowledge and understanding of the world.

In this chapter the focus for dialogue is on helping children to learn to reason and how to use arguments to support what they believe. Reasoning well – the giving of reasons for one's beliefs and actions, and evaluating the reasons which others give – is an important skill for all of us. Like other aspects of living and learning it is a skill that can be improved through dialogue.

The word 'reason' is derived from the word 'ratio' which means balance. A child can only think critically or reasonably to the extent that he or she is able carefully to examine experience, assess knowledge and ideas, and to weigh arguments before reaching a balanced judgement. Being a critical thinker also consists in developing certain attitudes, such as a desire to reason, a willingness to challenge, a passion for truth and for what is right. The critical thinker should be willing to submit his or her ideas to scrutiny, to the challenge of reason, and should also be open to self-correction.

Critical thinking helps young people develop insight into the problematical nature of learning, and the need to be willing to subject what they read, see and hear to critical enquiry (Table 4.1).

TABLE 4.1 Challenging children to think critically

CRITICAL THINKING	QUESTIONS TO ASK
Make reasoned evaluations	*What reasons are there for . . .?*
Make choices informed by evidence	*What kinds of evidence support . . .?*
Ask critical questions	*What questions could be asked?*
To argue a case	*How would you justify thinking?*

To be an effective thinker and learner one needs both creative and critical thinking. Table 4.2 lists different ways in which these two kinds of thinking have been described.

Children are surrounded by people telling them what to think and do. These people may be parents, teachers, friends, people they know or complete strangers. Most of what they are told may be true and helpful. Some may be false information or wrong advice. Some may deliberately try to deceive them into feeling, thinking or doing things that are wrong. For all these reasons they need to learn how to be critical, to use their powers of reasoning in thinking for themselves and with others.

Being critical means having a critical or questioning approach to all that we see, hear, think and do. It means developing children's ability to judge whether something should be believed, or some action taken. The sorts of questions they need to ask about what they see, hear or read include:

- Is this true?
- How do I know it is true?

TABLE 4.2 Different forms of two kinds of thinking

CRITICAL THINKING	CREATIVE THINKING
analytic	generative
convergent	divergent
vertical	lateral
probability	possibility
judgement	suspended judgement
hypothesis testing	hypothesis forming
objective	subjective
the answer	an answer
left brain	right brain
closed	open-ended
linear	associative
reasoning	speculating
logic	intuition
yes but	yes and

- ■ What are the reasons for believing this?
- ■ What is the evidence that supports or justifies this?
- ■ What else do I need to know?

If children learn to simply accept what everyone tells them, then, like Nasruddin in the story, they are going to be led into error and false belief. Humans only have a partial grasp of truth, and know only part of all there is to know and only partial understanding of all that might constitute right action. We, and our students, can develop our judgement so that we have fewer false beliefs, have fuller knowledge and make fewer mistakes. To do this we need to use our powers of reason and judgement.

Reasoning is a special kind of thinking in which we draw conclusions about what to believe or do. If the reasoning is good then the conclusions are likely to be correct; if the reasoning is faulty then the conclusions may be wrong. One way to introduce children to reasoning is to give them a claim to truth such as the following sentence to consider: 'Omar loves Paula, therefore Paula loves Omar.' Is this sentence true? Why? (Paula may love Omar, but of course the reasoning in this sentence is faulty – just because Omar loves Paula does not mean that Paula loves Omar. Nor is Omar's love of Paula a good reason, in itself, for believing that Paula loves Omar. We would need other reasons or evidence to believe that Paula loves Omar.)

Much trouble in the world arises from false belief; that is, beliefs which are not true, or which have no good reasons or evidence to support them. Consider the following Nasruddin story:

> One day someone enquired of Nasruddin how old he was. 'Three years older than my brother,' replied Nasruddin. 'How do you know that?' he was asked. 'By reasoning,' he said. 'Last year I heard my brother tell someone he was two years younger than me. A year has passed since then. So that means I am older by one year. Soon I shall be old enough to be his grandfather!'

Some questions for children to ponder about Nasruddin's use of reasoning this story include:

- Was Nasruddin using good reasoning?
- What was wrong with his reasoning?
- What do we know from this story about Nasruddin's true age?
- What is the reason given for knowing this? Do you think it is a good reason?

Children are often in situations where someone is trying to persuade them that something is true. They need to think about whether they should believe what other people tell them, just as they need to think about what they should do and why they should do it. Sometimes it will be easy for them to see the reasons for believing things or doing things, sometimes not. They are drawing conclusions about the world all the time but they do not always pay attention to the reasons why they think or do things. However, we might ask children to discuss questions such as the following:

- Is it a good idea to cross the road without looking? Why?
- Is it a good idea to believe everything we are told? Why?
- Should we believe every word we read? Why?

Reasons are the words we use to justify what we believe or do. Reasons give us the confidence to believe that some things are true and some actions are right. Reasons answer the question 'Why?' Not all things are believed because of reasons. Some of people's most important beliefs, such as belief in God, may be held not through reason but through faith. As one child explained: 'Believing in God depends on the heart.' Religious beliefs are usually different from beliefs about the world. In the material world we need reasons and evidence to justify what we believe and know, otherwise we are easily led into error or false thinking.

Question to discuss

What problems may be caused by people believing what is not true? Give an example.

Give the reasons

> There are reasons for everything, if only you can find them.

> (Child, aged 11)

We will only understand the world if we use our reason. There are reasons why the world is as it is if only we can work them out. We may not be able to understand all that there is to be found out about the world, but we can practise finding the reasons that underlie everyday situations. Being critical means using our powers of reasoning by asking questions such as:

- What reasons might there be for this?
- What reasons, if any, are given?
- Do the reasons make sense?

When reasons are given in support of a conclusion it is called an argument. Sometimes people argue without giving reasons; for example: 'I think it is wrong for people to smoke in public places.' This is an opinion but it is not an argument, since no reasons are given for this view. If, however, someone said: 'People should not be allowed to smoke in public because smoke pollutes the atmosphere and can cause lung disease even in non-smokers,' this is an argument because the speaker has given reasons for his view. This argument consists of two reasons and a conclusion:

Reason 1:   People who smoke in public pollute the atmosphere.
Reason 2:   Smoke can cause lung disease even in non-smokers.
Conclusion: People should not be allowed to smoke in public.

Arguments are not just about saying what you think but are about giving reasons for what you think. If you accept the reasons you are persuaded to believe the conclusion of the argument or reasons given. So we have seen that:

- Arguments have reasons.
- Arguments are meant to persuade you that what is said should be believed.
- Arguments have conclusions.

An argument must have one reason, but it can have many. If the reasons are poor then the argument is a poor one. Not all efforts to persuade are arguments; sometimes they are just statements or claims. Advertisers are doing this all the time (e.g. 'Buy brand x', 'Brand x is best', 'Brand x will make you happy'). Sometimes words are clues as to whether what is said is an argument. Such words include 'therefore', 'so', 'then', 'thus', and 'because'. Sometimes it is difficult to see what the reasons or conclusions are. Therefore it will be useful to practise your skill in identifying reasons and conclusions.

Ask children to discuss and list the reasons for and against a contentious subject such as whether it is right to allow people to smoke in the street. Can they think of reasons or arguments for and against smoking in public? Which of these reasons convinces you most? What conclusion do you come to?

Inferences and deductions

Reasoning is the mental process of looking for reasons to support beliefs, conclusions, actions or feelings. Different forms of reasoning may be used to support or justify conclusions. The main division between forms of reasoning or inference is between informal or inductive reasoning and deductive or logical reasoning (Figure 4.1).

The process of using reasons to support belief in the truth of conclusions is also called inference. In inductive reasoning, the truth of the premises does not guarantee the truth of the conclusion; the conclusion only follows with some degree of probability. In deductive reasoning the conclusion is contained in the premises and so is certain, as in the following example:

Premise: Socrates is a man.

Premise: All men are mortal.

Conclusion: Therefore Socrates is mortal.

The conclusion of an inductive argument offers more information than is already contained in the premises. Thus this method of reasoning is explanatory. Because our understanding can change in the light of new evidence, the meanings of words we use to describe the world can change, and so our conclusions and knowledge are always in a sense incomplete and therefore provisional. Rahim put it another way when he said during a discussion: 'You don't know for certain you are not God.'

It is important to distinguish the two sorts of reasoning since we can easily fall into the trap of thinking that past regularities make conclusions about the future certain. Only in a closed system of fixed meanings, such as maths or formal logic, can our reasoning be certain. In an open system like the living world our conclusions can only be probabilities. As the philosopher

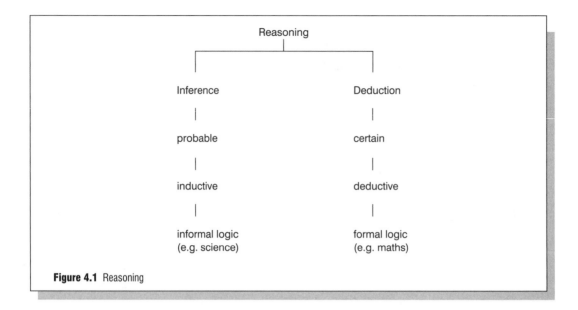

Figure 4.1 Reasoning

Bertrand Russell put it, 'The hand that feeds the chicken one day wrings its neck.' Conclusions are only probable because the world is changeable. If something has always happened so far, we cannot be certain it will always happen. In the real world any term is open to redefinition in the light of changing evidence. Where terms are fixed and unchangeable, fixed conclusions must follow. As Russell put it: 'In maths, no surprises.'

When you use reasons to support a conclusion it is called an argument. Critical thinking is about students giving reasons to support any claim to belief or knowledge. Teaching for critical thinking means never accepting a claim from a child in a dialogue without asking for the reasons for their belief. The keyword for young children to use in dialogue is 'because'. We turn a mere conversation into critical talk when we prompt them with: 'Because . . .'.

Questions to discuss

What are 'reasons'?
What is an argument?
What is the difference between an opinion and an argument?
What makes maths different from science?

Evaluate the reasons

In the last section we found that an argument offers one or more reasons in support of a conclusion. Sometimes the words used, such as 'so' or 'therefore', are clues that an argument is being used. Children need to learn the vocabulary of critical talk (see p. 189 for a list of thinking words).

Reasons lead to conclusions but conclusions do not have to be at the end of arguments. Sometimes people say the conclusion first, or in the middle of an argument. Sometimes reasons are not stated in an argument, they are simply assumed to be true. The reasoning may be implicit. One of the purposes of critical talk with children is to help them to make their thinking and the reasons behind their thinking explicit. So, 'What do you mean by that?' and, 'What are your reasons for thinking that?' sustain the dialogue and the critical thinking.

For example, we might ask what assumption is implicit (not stated) in this argument:

Women's brains are on average smaller than men's brains, so women are less intelligent.

(What is not stated of course is that the physical size of a brain is related to intelligence.)

Once we understand the reasons given explicitly in words or implicitly as assumptions we can then judge whether the reasoning is good. There are two ways of judging whether the reasoning is good:

■ Are the reasons or assumptions (unstated reasons) true or supported by good evidence?

■ Does the conclusion follow from the reasons given?

If the answer to these questions is 'yes' then the argument is good (that is, sound but not necessarily true).

Questions to discuss

Ask children to consider the following. Is it a good argument?

All London buses are blue, so if you see a bus that is not blue it is not a London bus.

If the reason given, that all London buses are blue, was true it would be a good argument since the reasons support the conclusion. But we need to know whether all London buses are blue to establish whether the argument is true. As London buses are currently red, not blue, the reasoning and conclusion are not true. Arguments like this one can make sense even if they are not true. The danger for human thinking is that if it sounds right as an argument we may tend to believe it. That is why advertising is so effective. Even if what we are told sounds right we still need to ask the question: 'Is it true?'

Questions to discuss

Ask children to consider the following. Is it a good argument?

All London buses are red, so if you saw a red bus it would be a London bus.

Here the reason given is true, but it is not a good argument, since the conclusion is not established by the reason given. The fact that all London buses are red does not rule out the possibility that other buses might be red (since if some buses are red we cannot assume that all buses are red). We must always check whether the conclusion follows from the reasons given. We need to check whether the facts given are true, and what other relevant information might be missing. For an example of this see the activity on 'Judging the reasons' (p. 98).

Analogical reasoning is a special type of inductive reasoning by inference. An analogy infers that if two or more things are similar in some respects they are probably also similar in some further respect. We use such comparisons to explain, illustrate or argue what we mean (see p. 98 for more on the use of analogies). We need to help children to critically assess the evidence that supports their conclusions. Factors to consider include: number of instances, variety and relevance of reasons.

Questions to discuss

Why is reasoning important?

Assess the evidence

Children should learn how to question what they hear, think carefully about what others claim and have the courage to ask when they need to find out more. To be critical of and ready to assess evidence can only be learned through dialogue. Children should only be confident that their beliefs are true if they are founded on reasons and evidence. The trouble with information and evidence is that there is a lot of it and not all of it is accurate or true. As Shakespeare's 'Othello' shows, false belief based on false evidence can lead to tragedy. Many a person has been falsely accused because of false evidence. Have you ever been falsely accused? Have you ever falsely accused another because you thought you had evidence that they had done wrong?

When we are presented with evidence we need to check that it is correct and relevant. We need to be critical in our thinking and not accept everything we are told at face value. Like sales people and politicians there will be many who seek to persuade us with 'evidence' that they are right and should be believed.

In assessing the information and evidence they are given, children need to practise keeping an open mind. Important questions for them to remember include:

- Who is telling me this?
- What are they saying? What is the point?
- Why are they telling me this?
- So what? What does this mean?
- What else do I need to know?

The following section is about developing children's ability to assess whatever evidence is presented to them by focusing on:

1 Finding the point.

2 Identifying what is significant.

3 Thinking about what else they need to know.

In any learning conversation or dialogue we need to try to find the main idea; otherwise we can easily get lost in a mass of detail and words. It is sometimes difficult to see the wood for the trees or to see the whole because there are so many parts. Whatever the topic, the first question we might ask is: 'What is the main idea or point of this?'

What is the evidence?

Anything worth reading or hearing will always have a main idea that is the topic or focus of what is being said. In newspapers this main idea is often summed up in a headline. In an argument it will be the conclusion. Sometimes, as in a newspaper headline, the main idea will be presented first (the 'headline'), sometimes in the middle of what is being said, and sometimes at the end. The best way to get your main idea across in a teaching situation is to say what the main point is first, repeat it during the account and again at the end as a summary or conclusion (see also p. 116).

Get children to practise by trying to summarise the main point of a dialogue. If they are not sure, ask: 'What were the main points of what you were saying?' Try to summarise in your own mind, or in notes, the main points of the dialogues you have with children. Putting the main points down on paper can be helpful. Find out at the end of a dialogue what you and they can remember of the pattern of talk they have had. See ' What is the evidence?' (p. 99) as an example of how to practise looking for the main point and the evidence given to support an argument.

What is significant?

When people make a claim about the world they should offer evidence to support their main points and be prepared to say where their claim comes from. Children need to learn to be cautious with what you claim. To say 'All boys are lazy' *might* be true, but do you have the evidence? (It would need only one boy shown not to be lazy to prove the claim is wrong.) 'Some boys are lazy' would be easier to illustrate with examples. Ask them: 'Whose evidence is this? What is the source, and is it reliable?' We know that memory can be very unreliable from the evidence of witnesses at the scenes of crimes who remember very different details.

Try this test. Ask children to try to remember everything that happened this morning from the moment they got out of bed. Children should come to see that their personal experience may not be enough to 'prove' that something is the case. Can they prove the exact time they got up this morning? To prove they are right you would need not to rely on memory but to draw their evidence from elsewhere (e.g. alarm clock). To convince others, their evidence needs to be significant.

Is there a difference between evidence and illustrating a point with an example? Giving an example can be very helpful in supporting a point, but to say, 'All girls are selfish because Sarah is very selfish' is not significant evidence. It is one small example and there may be many oppo-site examples. The purpose of illustrating a point is to help explain it with an example. We need to be wary of the truth of such examples from life, as the report may not be reliable. It is only a partial view. It does not prove a case, but other more significant evidence might.

Children need to be able to identify many possible sources of evidence including:

- research from different sources
- information from reliable sources
- testimony from different people
- pictorial records
- real objects
- facts and figures.

For more on sources of evidence see p. 98.

What else do we need to know?

After looking at the evidence that has been collected or presented and the conclusions that have been drawn from it we can always ask: 'What further evidence do we need?' This is an important question for children to ask since there is always something more to be found out, more facts to know. Further evidence might suggest a different or a better conclusion. Further evidence might also confirm that we were right in the first place. Much research in the world merely confirms what we already know. It helps to make our knowledge more certain. Further evi-dence may change our views completely. We need to get as many examples as we can, check on the reliability of our information and be aware of what further information is needed.

Ask older children to consider the news that car thefts in your area have increased over the past year by 100 per cent. What does this tell them? What does this not tell them? What else do they need to know? Invite them to be critical, to withhold judgement until they have more facts. If it means that two cars have been stolen rather than one, then not much has changed (in fact thefts may have gone down if in the year previous to these three cars had been stolen).

We often need more background information than we are given to form a sound judgement. In the following activity try to assess what else you need to know. Adverts provide good examples of claims that may need more evidence, as in the example 'What else do you need to know?' on p. 100.

Questions to discuss

1 What questions should you ask when assessing evidence?
2 Why is it useful to summarise the main point of what you say, read or hear?
3 What different sources of evidence are there?
4 Why might getting further evidence be important?
5 In what ways is assessing evidence like being a detective?

Argue well

All arguments aim to establish some sort of truth. In some kinds of arguments we can know for certain that the conclusion is true – deductive arguments. Other arguments, where the conclusion is only probably true, are inductive. Ask children to consider the following example of a deductive argument:

If all queens are women and Cleopatra is a queen, Cleopatra must be a woman.

If you accept the reasoning the conclusion must be true. It is true by definition. It would not be logical to disagree with the conclusion if you accept the reasoning. All mathematics is based on the logic of deductive reasoning, for example $1 + 1 = 2$, and there cannot be any other answer. With inductive arguments the conclusions are only *probable*. Because inductive conclusions are not certain, two people could accept the same reasoning but come to different conclusions.

Questions to discuss

Ask children to consider the following argument:

Some of the ice-caps in Antarctica are melting, therefore the whole world must be getting warmer.

Some of the ice-caps are melting but there is much disagreement among scientists about whether this is proof of global warming. Without further evidence we cannot say for sure it is true, but we can argue that it is more or less probable.

Even if we cannot claim to be *certain* about many things in the world we can use good arguments to persuade others that what we believe is true. The most important aspect of a good argument is that the conclusion is supported by reasons. Muhammad Ali said, 'I am the greatest.' He was heavyweight champion of the world in boxing at the time so he had a good reason for his boast. If you or I said it, it would not be believed unless we could find a good reason to support it. It is a better argument if we can find many good reasons to support our conclusions. To strengthen any argument you need to provide more reasons or evidence. Another way to strengthen your argument is to limit your conclusion. If I did not say I was the greatest but that I was 'quite good' it would be much easier to support, more probably true and more people would believe me.

When many reasons are given we call this a chain of argument. Encourage children to assess chains of argument. For an example of this see 'Assessing the argument' (p. 99).

Children may think that arguing is simply about 'winning' an argument by persuading others you are right. If an argument means people saying, 'I'm right and you are wrong', or if they keep restating the same idea all the time it can become unpleasant and pointless. This sense of argument means to 'have' an argument or dispute. These sorts of arguments, or quarrels, often happen in life. But this is not what an argument should be about.

Children need to learn that to 'give' an argument means to offer reasons or evidence in support of a conclusion. It is not just a restatement of certain views or a dispute or a quarrel. Arguments are attempts to support points of view with reasons. They are essential because they are a way of trying to find out which views are more believable or true. Some conclusions are supported by good reasons, others may have little evidence or few reasons to support them. It is often not easy to judge how strong the arguments really are or if we should believe them. An argument then is a means of investigating what views we should hold in light of the reasons and evidence.

Argument is vital for another reason. Once we have a view that is well supported by reasons, argument is how we explain and defend it. A good argument does not just say what we think, it gives reasons and evidence to help others make up their own minds. If you believe meat-eating or vegetarianism is right it is not enough to say it is right; you need arguments to show others how you arrived at your conclusions. It is not wrong to have strong views, but to have strong views with no arguments to support them is simply to be prejudiced.

A good argument is a means of enquiry that explores the reasons for and against a point of view in order to find the strongest or most convincing argument. A good argument is also a means of justifying your conclusions to yourself and to others. A weak argument may have few or poor reasons to support it, or may contain mistakes in reasoning or misleading information. Weak arguments lead people into error. They do not persuade and may confuse.

To argue well we need to be clear about:

- what is assumed
- what is meant
- what is being claimed.

The following sections look at each of these aspects and present some general rules for arguing well.

What is assumed?

Very often in life we do not say everything there is to say because we assume that people know a lot already about what we are going to say. An assumption is a belief that is not said but is taken for granted. For example, if someone were to say: 'It must be true because it says so in the newspaper,' what is that person assuming? He or she is assuming that what the newspaper says is true, although they have not said it.

Children who have not been taught about giving reasons often make assumptions because assumptions act as unstated reasons. We should not let children just assume that what others say is true. They need to develop what one teacher called 'built-in bullshit detectors'. When they are told things they need practice in asking themselves: 'Who is telling me this?'; 'What are they assuming without saying why?'; 'What are they trying to prove?' Before they can do it for themselves they need a dialogic teacher to do it for them and with them. Children can be taught to look out for assumptions being made and then to challenge them. Here is an example of it happening in the classroom:

Child 1: Everyone knows that killing animals to eat them is wrong.

Child 2: How do you know that?

Teacher: That's a good question. What have you spotted?

Child 3: I know . . . an assumption.

Child 1: Yes but it's true. You ask anyone.

Teacher: But that's not a reason, it's still an assumption even if lots of people think it.

Child 1: Well, would you want an animal to kill and eat you?

Child 2: A lot of animals would like to. . . .

Most assumptions may not be obvious until they are pointed out. Stories are a good way to practise spotting assumptions by asking questions like: 'What is the assumption here . . .?'; 'What is x assuming?' A famous example occurs in Arthur Conan Doyle's story 'The Adventure of Silver Blaze' when Sherlock Holmes says that an important clue was the fact that a dog did not bark. When asked to explain the reasoning behind this assumption, he says: 'A dog was kept in the stalls, and yet, though someone had been in and fetched out a horse, the dog had not barked. Obviously the visitor was someone whom the dog knew well.' We might then ask children: 'What was Sherlock Holmes assuming by saying that? Was Holmes right to assume that?'

Assumptions can lead to misunderstandings when there is not a common understanding or explanation of the words or concepts being used. So a key question in any dialogue is: 'What do you mean by that?'

What is meant?

One day the doctors of law called Nasruddin to court to face a trial. Nasruddin had been accused of saying that the wise men of the country did not know what they were talking about. This was a serious charge which the King himself had come to judge. 'You may speak first,' said the King to Nasruddin.

'I would like each of these seven wise men to write their own answer to one question,' said Nasruddin. Pens and paper were brought. Nasruddin asked, 'What is bread?'

The wise men's answers were handed to the King who read them out. The first said: 'Bread is a food.' The second: ' 'Bread is flour and water.' The third: 'Bread is a gift of God.' The fourth said: 'Bread is baked dough.' The fifth: 'Bread is a nutritious substance.' The sixth: 'The answer depends on what you mean by "bread".' The seventh said: 'Nobody really knows.'

Nasruddin said: 'When they have decided what bread is it will be possible for them to decide other things; for example, whether I am right or wrong. How can you trust the judgement of people who cannot agree about something that they eat every day?'

Sometimes it is not easy to define what words mean, but in reasoning we need to be as clear and consistent as we can about what our words mean. To be critical, and to be skilful in our thinking we need first to understand what we are talking about. If we are nor sure what others mean we should ask. If we are not sure that others understand what we mean we should tell them, explain our terms, clarify our meaning. If the words we use are unclear, imprecise or vague, then our meaning becomes unclear and we have to rely on others interpreting what we mean. When we do not understand what words mean we cannot fully understand the message. When the meaning of what is said is vague it is easy to jump to the wrong conclusions. So it is not surprising that philosophers and wise people often respond to a difficult problem or question by asking, like Nasruddin, 'What do you mean by . . .?'

Encourage children to be clear and precise in what they say. Try to get a clear idea of what they mean. Ask them what can they can do when there is a word or expression they do not understand. The context may help you to guess but, when stuck, look up a dictionary definition. A dictionary definition reports how most people in society at the time interpret the word. It can be interesting to look up the definition of a word in more than one dictionary. It is probable that the two dictionary definitions will vary slightly because people differ in their interpretation of words. A dictionary gives a common definition but not the only definition. The meanings of words may change gradually over time and dictionaries of different periods will reflect some of these changes.

Another way to find out the meaning of a word is to ask someone with special knowledge, for example, a teacher if it is a word used in education, a lawyer if it is a word used in law or a scientist if it is a scientific term. Many important words that stand for ideas (or concepts) have no fixed meaning but are endlessly debated. For example, how would you define the word 'democracy' to someone who did not know what it meant? (Compare your definition with one you find in a dictionary or textbook.)

We must try to be precise but we cannot be more precise than words allow. Words are not the things they describe, they are only what people use to describe things. They are abstract symbols on a page but they come to life when we can give an example of what we mean and what we do not mean. For example, if I was trying to explain what I thought a 'good teacher' was it would help if I gave an example of what a good teacher does, such as 'is patient in explaining things', and does not do, such as 'does not ignore questions from students'. How would you describe what a good teacher is? What examples would you give of what a good teacher does and does not do?

Exploring children's understanding of concepts is a powerful stimulus for dialogue (see p. 163 for more on conceptual/philosophical discussion). For an example of an activity when children are challenged to clarify a concept that is important in everyone's life see '*What does this mean?*' (p. 100).

What is being claimed?

> One morning Nasruddin sat down for breakfast and saw that there was no cheese on the table. 'Get me some cheese,' he said to his wife. 'Cheese is good for your health.'
>   'There is no cheese in the house,' said his wife.
>   'No cheese? Oh, all right,' said Nasruddin. 'It's not good for the stomach anyway.'
>   His wife was confused. 'One moment you say cheese is good for you, and the next you say it is bad,' she said. 'Now which of your statements is true?'
>   'The first one if cheese is available,' said Nasruddin, 'and the second one if it is not.'

Not everything that we say is an argument. Often we just make a statement, like 'It's raining today', or give an opinion, as does Nasruddin when he says, 'Cheese is good for your health'. Sometimes what we say contradicts something else we say; for example, when Nasruddin says, 'Cheese is good for your health,' and, 'It's not good for the stomach.' This breaks the rule of logic which says that something cannot be true and false at the same time. No wonder his wife was confused.

Children are also in a confusing world of competing claims. These claims are of different sorts, including:

■   factual claims

■   causal explanations

■   value judgements.

These different kinds of claims need to be evaluated in different ways. Some claims present facts, evidence or data. A newspaper, for example, might report that, 'A survey shows that 10 per cent of the population cannot read.' This would be a factual claim. Should we accept this as true? Whether we should accept it as true might depend on two things:

1   *Is it from a reliable authority?* – should we believe everything we read in this paper?

2   *What is the strength of the evidence?* – was it a valid, representative survey?

A factual claim may be used as a basis for a causal explanation – certain things happen (factual claim) and these *cause* certain other things to happen (*causal* explanation). If the report above went on to explain the cause – for example, by saying that some people never learn to read because they do not attend school or because their reading difficulties are not diagnosed – these would be causal explanations. Whether we agree with the argument about causes might depend on:

1   *What evidence makes this a likely cause?* – do we know that those who cannot read had no schooling?

2   *Is it the only cause?* – might there be other causes?

Sometimes factual or causal claims are linked to value judgements – certain things happen and are caused which we judge to be right or wrong, good or bad. If the report above went on to claim that, 'It is shameful that in a modern society 10 per cent of the people cannot read,' this would be a value judgement. It assumes that the fact is true and says that it is not a right or a good state of affairs. Whether we agree or not might depend on the following;

1 *Are the terms clearly defined?* – are we sure what exactly is meant by saying that people 'cannot read'?

2 *Are good reasons given?* – why should it be regarded as 'shameful'?

Whenever a claim is made, whether it is a factual claim, causal explanation or a value judgement, we should take a critical view of it. This means that we should not just uncritically accept it at face value. Nor does it mean that we should not believe what is said. It means withholding judgement until we are clear about what it means and are convinced by the arguments given. Being critical means asking questions to understand more clearly what is being claimed, and considering the reasons or evidence that support the claim rather than just assuming it to be true.

Invite children to be critical of claims, including factual, causal and value judgements, as in 'Assessing the claims' (p. 100).

Questions to discuss

1 What is the difference between an argument and a quarrel?
2 What should we do to argue well?
3 What are some of the faults of bad arguments?
4 What is an assumption?
5 Why should we try to argue well?

Distinguish fact and opinion

Nasruddin said, 'One day a magnificent horse was brought to court. No one could ride this noble beast because it was wild and high spirited. Suddenly in the heat of my pride I cried out, "None of you dare to ride this splendid horse. None of you can stay on its back. None of you – except me!" And I sprang forward.'

'What happened?' they asked.

'I could not ride it either.'

All arguments make some sort of claim. Some arguments are factual; they claim that certain facts or statements are true, like 'it was a rainy day' or 'the horse was wild'. Other arguments express opinions such as value judgements about how good or bad something is thought to be, for example, 'it was a magnificent horse'. Sometimes it is difficult to tell whether an argument expresses a fact or an opinion. People disagree whether moral principles are facts or opinions. Is the moral principle 'you should not steal' a fact or an opinion?

The way we describe the world is through words which express facts (we claim or know to be true) and opinions (we believe to be true). Facts are how we put into words the way we describe the world, the way we think it *is*. Opinions are how we put into words what we think *ought* to be, the way we judge the way the world is and what actions we think should be taken. We can analyse any argument in terms of whether it expresses facts or opinions or both. Confusion can occur when people mix up facts and opinions. So of any argument we can ask:

■ What are the facts of the matter?

■ What opinion is being expressed?

Try to analyse the different claims in the Nasruddin story into facts and opinions. Which of the following statements is a factual claim, and which is opinion?

1 'One day a magnificent horse was brought to court.'

2 'None of you can stay on its back.'

3 'None of you except me.'[2]

Different sorts of claims need to be judged and evaluated in different sorts of ways, by asking questions such as:

■ Is it fact and an opinion?

■ Is it relevant?

■ Is it valid?

Is it fact or opinion?

It is essential that children distinguish and can talk about the difference between fact and opinion. Ask children what the difference is between a fact and an opinion. We use the word 'fact' as a way of saying something that is true, and by true we mean that it is a justified true belief. A fact is what we claim to know, an opinion is what we believe but do not know for sure. An opinion is a belief which may or may not be justified or true. The trouble comes when people mistake facts for opinions. They may do this deliberately or without knowing. Just because someone thinks something is right or true does not make it right or true. Even if there are reasons and evidence to justify it, an opinion may still not be a right or true belief. The same reasons and evidence can be used to support very different opinions.

Ask children to discuss the following argument in pairs or trios, and to identify whether the claims being made in each argument are fact or opinion.

> Tobacco companies have known since the report of the Royal College of Physicians in 1962 that smoking tobacco is harmful because it causes lung cancer. They know that smoking is addictive and once people start to smoke they find it very difficult to stop. Manufacturers of any product should try to minimise risks to customers. Tobacco companies have not done this and so should pay compensation to smokers who have become ill as a result of smoking.

The first two sentences present factual claims. This does not mean they are correct because we might have to check on the accuracy and reliability of the facts quoted; just that if we accept them as facts they cannot be disputed. We check whether facts are true or reliable by trying to find a good source of information to confirm them, such as an encyclopaedia, dictionary or the opinion of an expert.

The last two sentences represent opinion. Sometimes different sorts of evidence may be used to support different conclusions. Sometimes the same evidence may be used to support different conclusions. In the following argument the same factual evidence is used to support a different conclusion. Can you see how this argument differs from the one above?

> Tobacco companies have known since the report of the Royal College of Physicians in 1962 that smoking tobacco is harmful because it causes lung cancer. They know that smoking is addictive and once people start to smoke they find it very difficult to stop. Tobacco companies have produced low tar cigarettes to cut the risk of disease. People have a choice. Nobody is forced to smoke so people who smoke and become ill should receive no compensation.

Can the children think of further reasons or evidence that are relevant to this argument?

Give children another argument to assess, such as task 'Assessing the argument' (p. 101). What claims are being made and what kinds of evidence would help persuade you whether the claim is true or false?

Is it relevant?

A good argument makes sense. The points it makes are connected to one another. They are linked in a chain of reasoning. Each part is relevant. It has no irrelevant parts, no 'red herrings'. Red herrings are characteristic of conversations with children. Once, when discussing whether what someone in a story had done is right or wrong, James, aged 6, said he thought the character was a bad man. When asked why, he replied: 'Because he is wearing red.' Other children have said that you can tell whether someone is good or bad from where they were born or what they liked to eat. These observations seemed to have nothing to do with what we were talking about, although of course they may indicate assumptions which the children in question believed to be very relevant. Hence the need for extended dialogue.

Another way of introducing something that is not relevant is to be personal, by attacking the arguer rather than the argument. Examples of this are when people dismiss an argument by dismissing the arguer because of their sex, position, nationality, religion or other personal reason ('You can't believe him [or her] because he's [she's] a . . .'). This kind of illogical argument (or fallacy) is called *ad hominem* (against the man) in Latin. Children should learn to criticise the argument rather than trying to discredit the person.

Another irrelevant form of argument is the 'two wrongs don't make a right' kind. Here is an example: 'It's not fair to punish me for doing wrong. There are plenty of others who do wrong things too.' It is a common form of false argument and one that children pick up on quickly. It is a way of deflecting an accusation or argument by blaming others. However, the conclusion has nothing to do with what is claimed. What others have done is not directly relevant to the person being accused. In Latin this false argument or fallacy is called *tu quoque*, which means 'the same thing'. You may accuse me of the same thing but it is not relevant to this argument – two wrongs don't make a right.

There are many arguments where the arguer brings in something not relevant to the argument, for example:

■ *Appeal to authority* – for example, 'Everyone knows it is bad luck to walk under a ladder'. Even if everyone believes it, or some special person believes it, this does not make it true.

■ *Appeal to pity* – for example, 'It is wrong for people to starve. I am starving. So you should take pity on me and give me money to buy food.'

■ *Appeal to ignorance* (ad ignoratium) – for example, 'You should try this as there is no proof that it does not work'. Just because we are ignorant of the causes or consequences of an action does not justify accepting the argument. Similarly, just because there is no proof, that is no reason to believe it could not be true. If there is no proof it may or may not be true, but we cannot say for sure that it is true.

Discuss arguments with children and encourage them to decide whether the reasons given are relevant to the conclusion. An example is given in the task 'Asking are the reasons relevant?' (p. 101).

Is it valid?

To be valid an argument must be soundly based. Ask children to consider the following argument. Is this a valid (or sound) argument?

> Plato, Galileo and Darwin were wise men. They all had beards. So to be a wise man you must have a beard.

There are two major weaknesses (or fallacies) in this argument that are common to most bad (invalid) arguments. First, the conclusion that all wise men must have beards from just three examples is not justified. This is the fallacy of *incomplete evidence*. You cannot draw a general conclusion from just a few cases. More evidence is often needed to prove a point. For it to be a strong argument a lot more evidence would be needed. To make it more than half probable, over half the wise men who ever lived would have to have had beards. Some does not imply all. From the statement that some wise men may have beards we cannot say that all wise people must have beards. When some things are true we cannot say all things are true. To make it certain, you would have to check that every wise man who ever lived had a beard.

The second major weakness is that it *overlooks alternatives*. Even if all wise men had beards there may be other, more important features or alternative factors that were just as important or more important. Just because A (wise men) and B (beards) sometimes appear together it does not mean that they are in any way linked or related. It may be pure chance or the fashion of the times or other factors that might account for this fact. A connection is not a cause. Because two things occur together (i.e. wise men and beards) it does not mean that there is any necessary connection or cause that links them. There may be other reasons to explain why they were wise.

We should never accept the first explanation that occurs; there may be other, better explanations. We should keep our minds open to alternatives. We overlook possible alternatives if we are rushed into making a decision (for more on decision-making see p. 133). Try always to increase the number of possible options you consider. Being critical means keeping your mind open to alternatives.

To be valid, an argument must pass the test of adequacy and relevance:

- Are the reasons or evidence *adequate* to justify the conclusion?
- Have we considered all *relevant* alternative arguments?

In seeking to strengthen our arguments we try to add to the reasons and evidence given and we consider the alternative arguments. Children need to understand that you do not have to agree with an argument to see that it is soundly argued.

Is it logical?

A deductive inference uses logic or reasoning by deduction. Pure logic is based on a mathematical approach to knowledge; it relies on lines of reasoning that can be set in symbolic form. Deductive arguments aim to be valid. An argument is valid if the conclusion must be true when the premises (the reasons given to support that conclusion) are true. One traditional form of logical reasoning is the syllogism, which takes the form of two statements (assumed to be true), followed by a conclusion which is drawn from them. For example,

> All children love sweets.
> Mary is a child.
> Therefore Mary loves sweets.

Give children practice in making similar deductions by supplying conclusions to given premises, for example,

> All fish can swim.
> The trout is a fish.
> Therefore. . . .

Discuss instances of faulty reasoning, for example:

> All children love sweets.
> Peter loves sweets.
> Therefore Peter is a child.

The drawing of circles or sets can help to show whether the relationship of one part to another is clear or whether it is ambiguous (and might be contained in another set; for example, Peter may be an adult or a horse). Ask whether the evidence or information given is sufficient to reach definite conclusions. What else do we need to know?

Ask students to write, analyse (draw in sets) and discuss their own experiences, for example:

> All teachers are . . .
> David is . . .
> Therefore David is. . . .

Encourage children to distinguish 'some' from 'all' in analysing arguments; for example, if most road accidents are caused by fast cars, what can we say about fast cars or any particular fast car?

Exercises in deductive logic do not easily transfer to talk about the real world unless there is a process which links the two, such as the scientific methods to establish 'proof'. Everyday reasoning depends on the ways we use language to create meaning. But even when meanings are clear, everyday reasoning is prone to error (to being invalid). That is why we need the tools of deductive reasoning. Help children to practise thinking logically by exercises such as 'Think logically' (p. 101).

Questions to discuss

1   What is the difference between fact and opinion?
2   What is a 'red herring'?
3   What is a fallacy in argument?
4   What does it mean to be 'logical'?

Exercise your judgement

Once Birbal's 5-year-old daughter accompanied him to Emperor Akbar's court. The emperor wanted to see if she had inherited a little of her father's wit and so he began talking to her.

'Can you speak Persian?' he asked her.

'Just a little lesser and a little more,' replied the little girl.

Birbal smiled at his daughter's reply, but the emperor was puzzled and asked her what she meant by a little lesser and a little more.

'I know Persian a little lesser than those who know it well, and a little more than those who don't,' replied the girl.

The emperor was convinced that Birbal's daughter had inherited her father's good judgement and wit.

Have your children ever made a wrong decision in life? Has anyone ever said to them: 'How could you be so stupid!' Have you ever said to yourself: 'I wish I had never done that!' We all make mistakes. Some decisions we make turn out badly. How do we avoid making mistakes? How do we avoid repeating our mistakes? How do we make the best decisions? There are two answers to these questions.

Children make the best decisions when:

■   They develop their own powers of judgement; that is, their ability to think well and with wisdom.

■   They benefit from the judgement of others who think well and are knowledgeable.

Ask children to think of a poor decision they made in life, something they did or failed to do, and then to try to think of why they made that wrong decision. It is often hard to put one's finger on why something went wrong or a wrong decision was made. Often mistakes are made because not enough thought was given, with people doing the first thing they thought of and not thinking of other possible options or alternatives. Sometimes mistakes are made when we do not consider the risks or consequences of actions. We are too hasty. According to Reuven Feuerstein, impulsivity is the major weakness of human thinking.

We can learn to tackle these weaknesses in judgement if we practise taking time to consider:

- all options
- risks and consequences
- our moral values.

Consider all options

It is not enough that you have a good argument. You must try to show that your argument is better than others. Why should people believe you if they think they have another, better argument or solution?

Ask children to consider the following argument:

> The roads are becoming so overcrowded with cars. Therefore there is only one solution. Build more roads.

Is there anything wrong with this argument? As an argument for building more roads it is weak in several ways. The word 'overcrowded' is vague. What precisely does it mean? Is every road overcrowded? Overcrowded for whom? Overcrowded when? Even if we define fully what is meant by overcrowded, the fact that roads are overcrowded does not in itself justify the conclusion. There may be other ways of easing congestion than building more roads. What other options might there be? Maybe existing roads could be improved; for example, widened? Maybe motorists could be persuaded to use other forms of transport; for example, buses, taxis or trains? Maybe there are ways to make the traffic move more smoothly on existing roads; for example, by introducing tolls to make the use of some roads more expensive? Maybe there are ways of cutting down the number of motorists using the roads; for example, by only allowing cars with odd or even registration numbers to use the roads at particular times?

Children must learn to beware of thinking there is only one option. Ask them to consider the following claims that some people might have made throughout history:

- 'We have always done it this way, so this is the only way to do it.'
- 'We have always done it this way, so this is the way you must do it.'
- 'We have always done it this way, so it must be the best way.'

All of these statements commit the 'fallacy of the single function'; that is, the mistaken belief that there must or can be only one explanation, one way of doing things, one use to which things can be put or one purpose for things. To be critical means being able to think of more than one thing at a time, realising there may be other options or factors to consider. Every situation in life contains more than one variable, more than one option. Only in a closed system, like mathematics, are there no other options to the correct answer. Life is about judging what is the best, right or true answer from other possible answers.

When children are interpreting a text or event in life they need to consider alternative interpretations. No matter how true something seems, how fully explained, how cleverly argued, there may be another explanation. Science is also about finding the most likely explanations and causes of things. That is why judging what is right and what to believe is not easy. It is not easy because there is more than one thing to think about, more than one possible cause, more than one possible solution. Ask children to exercise their judgement by discussing common dilemmas such the exercise 'Considering the options' (p. 102).

Consider the risks and consequences

Nasruddin was cutting a branch off a tree in his garden one day. While he was sawing, a man passed by in the street and said, 'Excuse me, but if you continue to saw that branch like that, you will fall down with it.' He said this because Nasruddin was sitting on the branch that he was sawing. Nasruddin said nothing. He thought, 'This is some foolish person who has nothing better to do than go around telling other people what they should do and what they should not do.' So Nasruddin ignored the man and continued sawing. The man shrugged and went on his way. Of course, after a few minutes, the branch cracked and fell, and Nasruddin fell with it. Nasruudin lay on the ground, feeling battered and bruised. Then he remembered the man's warning. 'My God!' he cried. 'That man knows the future!' Nasruddin got up and ran after him. He wanted to ask how long he was going to live. But the man had already gone.

After the story ask the children:

Why did Nasruddin fall from the tree?
Has an accident ever happened to you that could have been avoided?

Sometimes mistakes happen that are unavoidable; sometimes they happen when we have not been mindful of the situation and considered possible risks and consequences. How often, when things go wrong, have you said, 'I just did not think what might happen.' Sometimes things go wrong when we do not realise the dangers. We cannot always depend on others to warn us of possible risks and consequences. We need to think for ourselves about what might be the results of our actions or decisions. If we do not think things through we may realise too late that the branch we are sawing is also the branch we are sitting on.

When you are faced with a decision you should pause and ask yourself what the alternatives are. This sounds easy enough but it is often hard to put into practice. We get used to doing things quickly without much thought. We often jump to conclusions (the human mind, including yours and mine, would rather not work hard if it does not have to) and later think of the justification. Most of us find it hard to stop and think of the alternatives. We would rather do things and think later.

If the decision is between two simple alternatives, for example, whether to go down one road or another, it may only be necessary to think of two alternatives. But if the decision is a complicated one like where to go on holiday or who to invite to a party, there may be many factors to consider. The more important the decision the more time you should give to thinking through the alternatives and to making sure you have enough information to make the right choice.

There is no way of avoiding risk in life. In every situation there may be some foreseeable consequences and some unpredictable consequences. Risks also provide opportunities. Great travellers like Marco Polo and Ibn Battutah would never have discovered new lands if they had been too afraid to take risks. What successful explorers take are *calculated* risks; they think about how likely or unlikely and how valuable or undesirable the possible consequences are. They think carefully about how the opportunities for new knowledge might or might not outweigh the possible risks and dangers. Thinking carefully and critically about the possible opportunities, risks and consequences helps them to be best prepared and contributes to their ultimate success.

Ask children to discuss a given situation critically and to consider possible opportunities, risks and consequences as, for example, in 'Considering the consequences' (p. 102).

Consider what is right

Nasruddin was sometimes asked to be a Qazi or Judge, and to make judgements about the rights and wrongs of local disputes. One day he was sitting in judgement when a neighbour ran in and said, 'If one man's cow kills another's, is the owner of the first cow responsible?'

'It depends,' answered Nasruddin.

'Well,' said the man, 'your cow has killed mine.'

'Oh,' answered Nasruddin. 'Everyone knows that a cow cannot think like a human, so a cow is not responsible, and that means that its owner is not responsible either.'

'I'm sorry, Judge,' said the man. 'I made a mistake. I meant that my cow killed yours.'

Judge Nasruddin thought for a few seconds and then said, 'When I think about it more carefully, this case is not as easy as I thought at first.' And then he turned to his clerk and said, 'Please bring me that big black book from the shelf behind you. This case is more complicated than I first thought. . . .'

In life, children are surrounded by complex social situations that challenge their thinking. What should they believe? What should they do? Which side of an argument should we take? Arguments are made complicated by moral values that may be involved. Moral values are those beliefs you have about what is right and wrong, or good and bad behaviour. As Nasruddin found, cases are often more complicated than we at first thought. One risk in any decision is that what we decide may not be morally right. Ask the children, for example, if they found something valuable lying in the street, what should they do?

If doing what is right is important then children should practise, through dialogue, thinking about what is right (the moral values or principles) in any decision. Moral values are based on general principles of what is right or wrong, good or bad. There are many kinds of principle; for example, legal rules, moral guidelines, school rules. These principles may function as reasons in arguments, or as unstated assumptions as in, 'You should not do this because it is wrong . . .' (to turn this from an assumption to a reason we would have to say *why* it was wrong).

Ask children to consider the following argument against capital punishment (the right of the state to punish certain criminals with death):

> *Killing people is wrong. Capital punishment means killing people. Therefore capital punishment is wrong.*

'Killing people is wrong' is a moral principle. However, it is a moral principle with a very wide applicability. If we are to accept it as a principle that guides our decisions and actions, then killing people in wartime or in self-defence is wrong. If we believe that some killing is justified we have to modify our original principle. To modify a principle is not to invalidate it or to say it was wrong, it is to be more accurate and specific about the cases to which it applies. We should always be prepared to modify or change our views for a better, truer or more accurate belief. We must be prepared to change our mind if we are to seek better judgements. Simply to have a moral value or principle does not, of itself, justify a conclusion. Moral principles must be backed by reasons (for someone who believes in God this must be true, since God is the origin of all knowledge and reason). To be critical means asking why this should be so and what the consequences might be, and because humans are and should be moral creatures, it means asking what the moral issues and consequences might be.

The trouble with moral principles is that sometimes they are in conflict with each other. For example, many people have strong moral views about whether abortion (the termination of pregnancy) should be allowed. Some people argue that an unborn child has a 'right to life' and therefore abortion should not be allowed. Others argue that women have a 'right to choose' whether they have a baby or not. What you think is right in this argument will depend not only on how you interpret these two principles, but which you think is more important.

Children should be asked to consider the moral values in deciding what is the right or best course of action, as, for example, in the task 'Asking what is right?' (p. 103).

Questions to discuss

1   Why is good judgement important?
2   Why should we try to consider different options when making a decision?
3   Why and when should we be prepared to change our minds?

For more questions to discuss see 'Discussing critical thinking and reasoning' (p. 103).

Develop critical talk in practice

The following are examples of dialogic tasks to stimulate critical thinking and verbal reasoning with children using the following strategies:

1 Reasoning from evidence: making inferences.

2 Judging the reasons.

3 Assessing the argument.

4 What is the evidence?

5 How do you know?

6 What else do you need to know?

7 What does it mean?

8 Assessing the claims.

9 Assessing the argument.

10 Asking are the reasons relevant?

11 Thinking logically: are the arguments sound (valid)?

12 Considering the options.

13 Considering the consequences.

14 Asking what is right.

15 Thinking about critical thinking.

In stimulating critical dialogue with children try to make critical thinking visible by discussing the strategy and the reasons for it. The strategies presented can be adapted and developed in different ways. They are not recipes but suggestions for stimulating creative talk with children. The chapter ends with some questions for engaging children's thoughts about verbal reasoning – again expressing the central message of this book that if it's worth thinking about it is worth talking about.

1 Reasoning from evidence: making inferences

Give the students a picture, text or object and a sheet of paper with three headings: Questions, Knowledge, Inferences.

Ask them to discuss together what they can see and to record under 'Questions' what they do not know and want to find out; under 'Knowledge' what they know for certain about it; and under 'Inferences' what they do not know for certain but can infer through reasons or evidence. These inferences are of course hypotheses.

2 Judging the reasons

Think about, be critical and judge the reasons given in the following argument. Do the reasons given justify the conclusion?

Most parents would prefer to have sons, so if people can choose the sex of their child it is likely there would be many more boys than girls and this would lead to serious social problems; therefore we should not allow parents to choose the sex of their children.

Questions to consider in judging the argument are:

1 Are the reasons given true?

2 Do the reasons support the conclusion?

3 Are there other reasons, arguments or evidence we should consider?

What is your evaluation of this argument? What are your views about this question?[3]

3 Assessing the argument

Assess the following chain of argument.[4] Discuss and try to answer the questions below:

> *Courts of law should be televised because justice should not only be done but be seen to be done so we are sure justice is done. Evidence shows that when trials in court are televised a lot of people are keen to see it on TV. There is also evidence that criminals commit fewer crimes if they have the prospect of being tried on television. Many lawyers and judges are in favour of allowing TV cameras to film in court. Most people have not seen a case being heard in court, so if it was televised it would help to educate them. Therefore we should try an experiment in which trials in court are televised.*

1 How many reasons for televising courts of law are given in this chain of argument?

2 What are the reasons given? Which are good reasons? Why?

3 What evidence does the writer say supports the argument?

4 What is the conclusion?

5 Is it a good chain of argument? Why?

6 Do you agree with the argument? Why? (It may be a good argument but you do not have to agree with it.)

4 What is the evidence?

Consider the following extract about the Pueblo people:

> *Once the Pueblos had a surplus of food they could turn their attention to other things besides finding and growing food. They developed a high degree of artistry in one particular activity – pottery making. Potters became artists and developed new styles of painting and decoration. Pueblo pottery has been found decorated with geometric designs and different life forms. The paints they used were improved and pots came to be decorated in three or four different colours.*

1 What is the main point that the author is trying to make?

2 What evidence does he use to support his argument?

5 How do you know?

In the following story Nasruddin faces an unexpected problem. Can you help him?

One day Nasruddin suddenly realised he did not know who he was. So he rushed into the street to try to find someone who might recognise him. He ran into a shop and said to the shopkeeper, 'Did you see me come into your shop?' 'Yes, I did,' replied the shopkeeper. 'Good. Now, have you ever seen me in your life before?' asked Nasruddin. 'Never in my life,' said the shopkeeper. 'Then,' said Nasruddin, 'how do you know it is me?'

What sorts of evidence might Nasrudddin need to be sure of knowing who he was? What would be the most significant piece of evidence? Think this through for yourself or discuss it with friends.

6 What else do you need to know?

Someone posts an advert through your door. It is an advert from a local builder and decorator. It reads:

> Use Bodgers the Builders for all your building and home decorating – we already have dozens of completely satisfied customers in your area! We are the best. Hurry, don't delay, call today!

What reasons do Bodgers the Builders give for using them? What evidence supports their claim? What else do you need to know before deciding whether Bodgers the Builders' claims are true?

7 What does it mean?

What do you think it means when someone says they *love* someone? Ask children to discuss a concept that is important in life, but has a variety of possible definitions such as love, hate, fear, jealousy, anger, happiness, and to explain the concept with examples drawn from their experience.

8 Assessing the claims: is watching television harmful?

Consider the following argument:

> Over the past twenty years children have watched more and more television. Over the same period children have spent less time reading books. If children watch a lot of television their reading will suffer. It is not right that children's reading should suffer. So children should be made to watch less television.

Identify in the argument the:

- factual claims
- reasons given
- the judgements being made.

What questions would you want answered before accepting or rejecting this argument?

9 Assessing the argument: does watching violence on TV make people more violent?

Consider the following argument. Be critical and try to judge whether the argument is good. Consider the significance of the evidence. Is it a strong argument? What further evidence or reasons would make it stronger?

> Many people claim that watching violence on TV makes people more violent. This is not true since I watch violence on TV and this has not made me more violent. You should be free to watch whatever you want.[5]

10 Asking: are the reasons relevant? Do ghosts exist?

Consider the relevance of these arguments. Which are facts and which opinion? Which might support the view that ghosts exist?

> Most people believe in ghosts so there must be some truth in it. After all there is no proof that ghosts do not exist. I know someone who has seen a ghost so at least one ghost must exist. Some things exist even if we cannot see them so ghosts could exist. There are many stories and films about ghosts. People who say ghosts don't exist just haven't yet seen a ghost.

What other arguments might support belief in the existence of ghosts? What might be good arguments against the existence of ghosts?

11 Thinking logically: are the arguments sound (valid)?

Consider the following arguments. Are they sound (valid) arguments? If so, why? If not, why not?

1 It is my turn to have the ball. After all, it is my ball.

2 If you eat an apple a day you will keep the doctor away. You do not eat an apple a day. You will not keep the doctor away.

3 If there is a red sky tonight tomorrow will be shepherd's delight. There is a red sky tonight. Tomorrow will be shepherd's delight.

4 If people were meant to fly they would be born with wings. People were not born with wings. They were not meant to fly.

5   When Red Riding Hood became ill she went to her home in the woods rather than follow the doctor's advice and go to hospital. Although it was very cold she left all the windows open. She got well again and attributed her cure to fresh air. She said this proved that air from the pine woods had cured her.

Answers in Notes.[6] *Think logically.*

Now ask children to make up some of their own examples of logically valid and invalid arguments. Remember, a good argument does not have to be true!

12 Considering the options: why get married?

Consider the following argument:

Statistics show that 40 per cent of marriages end in divorce. Many people who stay together are unhappy in their marriage. Therefore it is likely that young people who marry will divorce or be unhappy in their marriages. So young people should not get married.

■   What are the alternatives to getting married?

■   What are the factors that might account for unhappy marriages?

■   What are the factors one should consider in deciding whether to get married or not?

13 Considering the consequences

We should consider the possible risks, opportunities and consequences of any important decision. Risks are the potential problems or dangers you might face. Opportunities are the potential benefits that might arise. Opportunities are positive factors. Risks are negative factors. The consequences of any decision may include both positive or negative outcomes.

Analyse the following in terms of risks, opportunities and consequences:

You have been invited to visit a relative in a far-off country that you have never been to before. The relative has written to you to say they will meet you at the airport on your arrival. What do you need to consider before deciding whether to go?

List the things you need to think about when considering such a visit. Think of the consequences of each factor. List them under two headings:

Opportunities (benefits)   **Risks** (problems or dangers)

_____   _____

_____   _____

_____   _____

_____   _____

_____   _____

14 Asking what is right. What should Shun have done?

Mencius (372–289 BCE) was a famous Chinese philosopher. His writings have been preserved because they discuss human problems that are still with us. He argued that in any argument we should consider what is right for the people in that particular situation, and that a way of doing this is to think what the wisest people in the past would have done. For Mencius, one of the wisest men whom he knew of was the legendary King Shun. One day Mencius was presented with the following problem:

> What would King Shun have done if he had discovered that his father had murdered someone? Should he arrest his own father?

Now consider or discuss the following questions:

- What could Shun do (what are his possible courses of action)?
- What should Shun do?
- What moral principle(s) should be considered?
- What would you do if you were Shun?
- Compare your answer to the last question with the answer Mencius gave.[7]

15 Discussing critical thinking and reasoning

The following are some questions to reflect on and discuss.

- What is critical thinking?
- Is giving reasons important? Why?
- Should one be willing to change one's mind? Give an example.
- Is having evidence important? Why?
- What is the difference between good evidence and poor evidence?
- What does 'being logical' mean? Is it important?
- Is there a difference between making an argument and having a quarrel?
- Can words mean different things to different people? Give an example.
- Is it important to think about consequences? Why?
- Is it imortant to think about what is right? Why?

5

Talking to Learn Across the Curriculum

You have to work on what you know to fully understand it.

(Child, aged 10)

This chapter explores ways to help children process information and to learn about learning. Opportunities for dialogue should be built into any lesson to help learners to:

1 Focus on concepts and understanding.

2 Become a dialogic model.

3 Use technology as a dialogic tool.

4 Develop dialogic research.

5 Define learning objectives and goals.

6 Know and use a range of learning strategies.

7 Develop talking to learn in practice.

The first part of this chapter discusses some key principles of dialogic teaching and strategies to help children to learn through talk in any subject area. The second half presents twenty practical activities to stimulate talk for learning across the curriculum.

Children's learning is always about something, some form of knowledge or information. At a literal level knowledge is about 'knowing that' something is the case. Learning at its most basic is about gaining knowledge and processing that information so that it connects with what is already known and stored in the memory. We may know things that we cannot remember. As Jamie, aged 9, pointed out in a discussion about knowing: 'I know something I can't remember. I know I was born but I can't remember it.'

Information-processing is also about 'knowing how'; that is, knowing what skills and strategies to use to find out about or to do things. Knowledge is fully understood only when expressed in words or concepts. We need to make thinking explicit not only by pointing things out but by saying what they are. Concepts are the organising ideas we use to express what we think, know or believe. All subjects include key ideas or concepts that students may or may not fully understand. We need to check their knowledge of facts and also their understanding of

TABLE 5.1 Dialogue

INFORMATION PROCESSING	QUESTIONS TO ASK
The literal level – 'knowing that'	*What do you know about?*
The strategic level – 'knowing how'	*What strategy do you use to?*
The conceptual level – organising ideas	*What does (the key idea) mean?*

concepts. There is not much point telling children we live in a 'democracy' without checking they understand what 'democracy' means.

If knowledge is important, children also need to be helped to remember it. Studies on memory have shown that rehearsal is important in memorising and storing verbal information. Dialogue helps children to rehearse, rethink and relate what they think and are learning (Table 5.1).

Fields of knowledge and research are classified as subjects within a curriculum. Whatever the subject, children should be encouraged to interpret information in their own words and to process it through critical and creative thinking. Critical thinking involves analysing and understanding relationships that exist between beliefs, strategies or concepts. Creative thinking is concerned with the ability to make new connections and generate new ideas. Creative and critical thinking are essential to teaching for understanding.

Information-processing is taking place when young people engaged in:

- accessing knowledge
- understanding key ideas and concepts
- knowing what rules and strategies to use to solve problems
- researching to create new knowledge (see 'Students as researchers' below).

But not all knowledge is of equal value:

> *One day, as Nasruddin was ferrying a scholar across a piece of rough water, he said something that was ungrammatical. 'Have you never studied grammar?' asked the scholar.*
> *'No,' replied Nasruddin.*
> *'Then half your life is wasted,' replied the scholar.*
> *A few minutes later Nasruddin turned to the passenger. 'Have you ever learned how to swim?'*
> *'No. Why?' asked the scholar.*
> *'Then all your life is wasted,' said Nasruddin, 'for the boat is sinking!'*

Two key questions in any learning situation are, 'What do you need to know?' and, 'What do you need to do?' The following are some important principles of dialogic teaching and possible activities to help children to learn through talk in any subject.

Dialogue in any subject can help teachers and learners to:

- develop concepts and understanding
- create a dialogic model
- use technology as a dialogic tool
- train students to be researchers
- define learning objectives and success criteria
- know and use a range of learning strategies.

The information that children need to process is not just the odd fact picked up here and there, but the organising of ideas which link items of knowledge into meaningful wholes that have relevance to what they learn and to the real world. These organising ideas are called concepts and a prime purpose of creative dialogue in any discipline is to develop conceptual understanding.

Focus on concepts and understanding

We know from research that students may have hazy or confused notions about the nature of different subjects. Helping them to discuss subject knowledge and explore key concepts within that subject will help develop deeper understanding of subject matter. The following are some questions children might discuss related to any subject:

- *Reflection on the nature of the subject* through discussing such questions as:
  - What is . . .? (e.g. history, geography, science) Who studies . . .? Why do they study . . .?
  - Who is better at . . ., girls or boys?
  - Do you need a special talent to be good at . . .? Is . . . useful? Why study . . .?
- *Reflection on personal experience* in a subject through, for example:
  - keeping a learning diary or notebook to record ideas, feelings and problems;
  - discussing experiences in learning, such being stuck, explaining, problem-solving, being tested;
  - having a help or question box where students can post any problems they have for later discussion.
- *Reflection on concepts* in a subject through, for example, discussing within a field of study:
  - problematical concepts;
  - stories or relevant news items;
  - knowledge and concepts.
- *Reflection on processes of investigation* in a field of study; for example, by discussion of:
  - ways of investigating and solving problems;
  - ways of gathering and interpreting data;
  - particular skills and strategies needed.

Every subject has its puzzles. For example, in mathematics: are mathematical entities, as Plato believed, real, independent objects of study about which discoveries (and mistakes) can be made? Or, as constructivists believe, is it we who construct what we talk about in maths? See p. 119 for discussion plan about the nature of mathematics.

Another mystery is music: what is it and why does it have such power? As Amy, aged 10, said: 'Music is a kind of language that you can't quite understand. Sometimes talking about it helps you understand.' See p. 120 for some starters for thinking and talking after listening to music. See p. 124 for an activity about the nature of art.

Become a dialogic model

Nasruddin used to stand in the street on market-days. People thought he was an idiot. No matter how often people offered him a large and a small coin, he would always choose the least valuable coin. One day a kindly man said to him, 'Nasruddin, you should take the bigger coin. Then you will have more money and people will no longer laugh at you.'

'That may be true,' said Nasruddin, 'but if I always take the larger coin, people will stop offering me money to prove that I am more idiotic than they are. Then I would have no money at all!'

When teaching *through* dialogue teachers are also teaching *about* dialogue by modelling the habits of dialogue that children may learn to copy. Teachers create dialogic models. Such modelling can have a powerful influence on children – through repeated demonstration they learn what active listening is, how to use questions to prompt and probe, how to share ideas and seek alternative viewpoints. Through modelling these behaviours, teachers help children to develop the habits of successful learners. Developing good dialogic habits enables children to express themselves and to engage in cooperative talk in any field of study.

Dialogue is modelled when:

- the teacher talks to individual children;
- two or more children talk together;
- when the whole class is involved in discussion.

One powerful dialogic strategy is 'Think–pair–share', because it provides opportunities for all three of the above – individual thought, talking in pairs and sharing with the class. All lessons need to include 'thinking time' for individuals to give them time to process information and translate their thoughts into words. Talk with partners extends opportunities for thinking and is particularly supportive of children with learning difficulties or those learning English as an additional language. Talk in trios is a good alternative to pairs, as in groups of three roles can be assigned for speaker, questioner and note-taker or reporter who can observe how well they fulfil their roles and report back both on what was said and the quality of the dialogue. These roles can then be rotated, so that each has a turn. Talk in trios also adds a level of challenge by introducing a third alternative point of view, with more potential for cognitive conflict and argument.

Group children in pairs or in trios to talk to each other at particular points in a lesson; for example, to:

- discuss the learning objectives at the start of the lesson;
- share and reflect on learning experiences during the lesson;
- review what they have learnt or remembered after the lesson.

Retain pairs or trios for a period of time (e.g. for up to half a term), so they can become confident with each other, establish routines and develop more extended turns. For examples of activities see 'Talk partners and trios' (p. 119).

Every lesson can become a dialogic lesson by ensuring that one or more of these elements is included. If including opportunities for dialogic learning is important, then lesson plans should include a space where dialogic teaching is made explicit.

Use technology as a dialogic tool

Despite the dangers of relying too heavily on technology (ICT) for learning (noted on p. 194), computers have many features that can help facilitate dialogic learning (see Table 5.2):

TABLE 5.2 Features of computers to facilitate dialogic learning

Speed	Computers can access information from around the world in a few minutes using search engines. They can do complex calculations and change information into different formats in moments.
Capacity	Computers can store and make accessible huge amounts of information.
Automation	Automatic features include use of templates for recording data.
Communicability	Computers can communicate in a variety of ways from a range of sources.
Provisionality	Computers can constantly change, be amended and added to.
Interactivity	Computers can respond to the learner.
Non-linearity	Computers can navigate in many ways, in many formats.
Multi-modality	Computers can express data in text, image, sound and movement.

These features support dialogic learning if children are actively engaged in discussing the process and outcomes of their experience with ICT. For example, the provisional nature of ICT can encourage creativity. Through working in pairs learners can discuss, experiment with, add and delete ideas and 'play around' with ideas and possibilities. ICT can present the viewpoints and lives of others with reality and immediacy. It can allow people to connect directly with materials and thoughts from others.

ICT interfaces can be effective in supporting talk, for example in:

■ showing evidence or multiple choices on the screen for discussion;

■ presenting choices embedded in a motivating narrative;

■ making problems sufficiently complex to benefit from being analysed through discussion;

■ using simulations to discuss, predict, analyse and reach agreement.

Teachers can ask children to discuss in pairs or small groups many of the features and facilities of ICT; for example, when involved in:

■ demonstrating

■ modelling

■ accessing, presenting and communicating

■ representing and analysing

■ investigating, testing and confirming.

Demonstrating

Using ICT the teacher or child can more easily demonstrate methods, illustrate procedures and set out instructions and creative processes. These can be modified in the light of dialogue with children; for example, in maths, interactive teaching programmes allow teachers or children to demonstrate the four number operations in a range of interactive ways.

Modelling

ICT may be used to model the concept, process or idea being presented. For example, in literacy, story structure can be discussed and represented by children as a table or graph, and this is then translated into a writing frame. In mathematics, concepts relating to number or shape can be discussed and modelled in ways not previously possible using traditional methods. In history, electronic timelines can be created to model the passage of time and evolution at key points in history. In science, physical and chemical reactions can be modelled and controlled by children to show a dynamic and visual representation of changes of state. Similarly, in geography, physical processes such as beach erosion or the rain cycle can be shown and discussed by children in dynamic and interactive ways.

Accessing, presenting and communicating

ICT can present data and information in forms that can be manipulated and presented to accommodate different learning styles and engage children in learning approaches other than their preferred learning style. These include still and moving images, audio files and materials which involve learners in interactive responses. For example, this can include the discussion and presentation of reading texts in interactive, multi-media format. Texts can also be created in electronic and multi-media formats and communicated through e-presentations, e-mail and on the Internet as a spur to further dialogue.

Re-presenting and analysing

The use of ICT to quickly change and reconfigure data or information provides children with opportunities to engage in dialogue that offers cognitive challenge and develops higher order thinking; for example, in geography, discussing changing data into a variety of graphs and charts, analysing and agreeing on how to present the same information in different ways.

Investigating, testing and confirming

ICT allows speedy access to information and instant modification of data. This can be a powerful tool to enhance the development, through dialogue, of children's skills in analysis and hypothesis. Children can be encouraged to deepen their level of shared enquiry and generate, in pairs or in groups, their own questions and hypotheses, which they can then test and confirm.

See p. 125 for some questions to help review the use of ICT in dialogic learning.

Develop dialogic research

> If you know how to find out, you can find the answer to everything.
>
> (Child, aged 10)

A common complaint about many national curricula is that there is too much content. The problem with too much content is that it encourages a surface approach to learning. Many countries, however, are trying to 'declutter' the curriculum to help teachers to focus more on deep learning and understanding. One of the best ways to deepen children's learning is to train them in the skills of dialogic research.

Engaging children in challenging contexts for research, 'rich tasks' with 'rich talk', can help them practise the skills needed for independent research. Research begins as a social process where learners create and reconstruct knowledge through dialogue, questioning, collaborative working, debate and argument. The teacher needs to set up opportunities for such activities to take place but also needs to enable learners to acquire the skills to participate fully in collaborative research. This may involve teachers working with colleagues from across subjects and sectors to present projects to pupils that are motivating and challenging. For an example of dialogic research activity see 'Jigsaw' (p. 119).

Helping children to take control of their own learning means helping them to learn how to make plans. 'Planfulness' is a characteristic of good researchers that can be developed in any area of the curriculum. A lesson plan is a model of planfulness. Children can also be taught to plan, or to discuss plans for learning or for problem-solving. 'I like to plan with others,' said Chantelle, aged 10, 'because they always think of something different to you and even if they are wrong it's worth talking about.'

The easiest way for children to create a plan that is original is to take a plan that is given and to alter it in some way. Creativity, like evolution, works through variation. For example, ask them to think of any everyday activity, like their routine when getting up in the morning, to discuss what they do and the order in which they do it. Could they vary this plan in some way to make it more interesting or different? Think of your journey to school or work. Could they vary this or add something interesting or change something that is boring about it? Share and discuss ideas. You could also involve children in discussing a plan for the next lesson as part of their lesson evaluation.

The activity 'Create a new game' (p. 124) encourages children to plan a new game with agreed rules.

Personal learning planning may involve students identifying what research strategy they need to employ. At other times it will mean identifying a range of processes needed to tackle a specific research task. Students should be encouraged to plan their research tasks using a step-by-step approach, breaking down complex tasks into manageable stages. The planning process might involve:

- Defining the problem (What do we want to achieve?)

- Gathering information (What do we need to know to tackle the problem?)

- Forming a strategy (How can we tackle the problem?)

- Implementing the strategy (How are we tackling the problem?)

- Monitoring outcomes (have we achieved our aim?)

A research plan does not need to be a set order of steps; plans often need to be flexible to allow for the use of a range of possible strategies that may help in achieving an objective. As we move to a solution they may need to try out new ideas, to take account of new obstacles and opportunities. Planning for children in its simplest form means they have thought about and made explicit what they are going to do. In teaching children to plan we are teaching them to be thoughtful about what they are doing, to focus and share their thinking, as in the activity 'Plan a research topic' (p. 121).

Teachers can model dialogic prompts to planning such as: 'What do you need to think about first . . .?', 'What are we trying to achieve . . .?', 'What strategy could we use . . .?' When a teacher asks questions that probe children's assumptions about their learning, it can help develop metacognitive awareness of:

- Self (What must I remember?)

- Group task (What must we do?)

- Strategy (What plans do we have? Is this the best plan?)

For more on developing metacognition through dialogue see p. 122.

Discussing and formulating plans can take place before, during or after a task is completed.

The following are some possible personal learning activities for children to discuss and plan:

- *Daily plan*: record/discuss their planned learning for the day.
- *Weekly plan*: record/discuss the planned learning objectives for the week.
- *Long-term* plan: record/discuss the major learning objectives of the term or year.
- *Research plan*: record a study plan for a project.
- *Life plan*: record and discuss their possible future life plans.

Encourage children to take ownership of the research agenda. What would they like to find out about? The Community of Enquiry is a useful strategy for encouraging students to take control of an agenda for enquiry (see p. 121). Encourage children to suggest questions for the rest of the class to discuss. Make a 'Wonder Wall' of all the things they want to question and wonder about. Ask children to research answers for homework and discuss current research.

The following are some stages of research to discuss:

- *Designing a research plan* to show stages and possible timetable for your research.
- *Identifying the key question(s)* that your research will try to answer.
- *Deciding on research methods* for collecting information (data) (e.g. reading, Internet, observation, interview, recording).
- *Systematically collecting data* about your research topic.
- *Analysing, summarising and presenting* your data.
- *Critically discussing* your conclusions/answers to research questions.
- *Discussing what further research is needed.*

Consider how you could make part of your teaching a joint research project with your students. One important step in any research is identifying the goal of the research – what are we trying to learn or find out?

Define learning objectives and goals

Why are you doing this? is a question we can ask of ourselves or others. When children are asked this question in school they often find it difficult to give a clear answer. A common response is, 'Because my teacher told me'. Children may do things without knowing why, not knowing the reasons for or purpose of an activity. Help your students define the purposes of their learning activities; for example, by discussing: Why are you doing this? What do you hope to achieve? How will it help (to fulfil your needs/ambitions, or the needs of others)?

Helping students define the learning objectives is to get them to think about the purposes of their learning. Trying to distinguish between 'aims', 'goals', 'intentions' and 'objectives' may not be time well spent. What is important is helping children understand why they are engaged on a learning activity. Questions to ask might include:

- What are we trying to do?
- Why are we doing this?

- What is the purpose?

- What objective are we trying to achieve?

- How will we know we are successful?

- What will it look like? What criteria should we use to judge success?

The activities on p. 121 focus on defining aims or objectives.

Know and use a range of learning strategies

Children need strategies that help them overcome the natural weaknesses in human thinking. One of these weaknesses is that human thinking tends to be narrow. Another is that it tends to be impetuous, wanting its first efforts to be its only efforts and to jump to the solution. This is partly because the brain wants to use the least energy possible to complete any given task. Hence the common experience of children saying, 'Finished!' when more effort and longer discussion might produce a better outcome. They need to be encouraged to sustain their attention and to extend the possibilities of learning. The following are examples of ways to help them to sustain attention on a learning task:

- consider all factors

- discuss priorities

- map what you know

- analyse

- summarise

- discuss memory strategies.

Consider all factors

'Have I considered all factors?' (HICAF) is important. It is not simply for brainstorming ideas, but is an attention-directing tool that encourages thinking time. As with all strategies, skill, practice and familiarisation are needed (for example, by having the acronym written on a chart or bookmark). The more a strategy is used in a deliberate manner the more useful it becomes by being internalised through practice.

Here is a story about Nasruddin that illustrates this point:

> *Nasruddin used to take his donkey across a frontier every day, with bags loaded full of straw. As he trudged back home every night the customs men at the border asked him whether he was a smuggler. Nasruddin admitted to being a smuggler and so the guards searched him again and again to find out what he could be smuggling. They searched his person, sifted the straw, steeped it in water, even burned it from time to time, but they could find nothing but straw and there was no customs tax to pay on straw. Meanwhile Nasruddin*

> *grew prosperous from his smuggling activities. Then he retired and went to live in another country. There, many years later, he met by chance one of the customs officers again, 'Now you can tell me, Nasruddin,' said the customs man. 'What was it that you were smuggling with the straw, all those years ago, when we could never catch you out?'*

What do you think Nasruddin replied?[1]

HICAF, like other habits of thinking, will be quickly forgotten if used only once. But if repeated in a variety of learning situations over a period of time it becomes a 'thinking frame' that is remembered and used. HICAF is a useful strategy to remind children of when asking them to discuss or choose or make a decision. The following tasks provide practice in the use of the HICAF technique. 'See List the characteristics and consider all factors' on p. 121.

Discuss priorities

What are your priorities (in this piece of work or research)?

Some things are more important than others, some values are more important than others. Priorities should be taken into account in planning and reviewing what has or should be done. Priorities provide a focus for effort and assessment of learning. A lot of things may be important but which are most important? For example, discuss:

- 'Can you agree on the priorities?'
- 'What are (or were) your priorities?'
- 'Are your priorities the same or different from other people's?'

In reviewing a list of factors – for example, in planning a piece of writing – we may think that all the factors are priorities – spelling, presentation, ideas, word length, topic – and a case can be made for the importance or value of all of these things. The role of 'Decide priorities' (or any prioritising strategy) is that it forces us to make choices and to decide what the really important things to consider should be.

In doing a prioritising exercise (see p. 122 for an example), it is useful to set a limit on the number of priorities; for example, three, four or five.

Map what you know

Researchers need to locate, extract and record relevant information. Mapping keywords or ideas is one way to make visible a conceptual structure out of information, to record, process and build on it in any area of the school curriculum. The aims or purposes of information mapping (also called cognitive mapping, think mapping, mind mapping, concept mapping) include to:

- explore what we know
- help planning
- aid evaluation.

Visually, a map consists of an arrangement of shapes, such as boxes, circles, rectangles and triangles, connected by lines and/or arrows drawn between and among the figures. The map should contain verbal information within and among the shapes to create a pattern or relationships of ideas. The whiteboard or computer is ideal for displaying networks of visual information. Software enables children to create their own visual diagrams, ready-made visual organisers that enable them to experiment with ways of presenting information and ideas.

Mapping encourages children to:

- actively engage in thinking about, interpreting and building on information and ideas;

- communicate information to, from and among pupils and teachers;

- organise information, to show understanding of relationships between ideas;

- develop a visual strategy to aid memory;

- understand the structure of any text or body of knowledge.

Mapping the information about a topic is only useful if it helps children to think more clearly and to discuss it. Individual maps, paired maps or maps drawn up by different groups can be shared and discussed. Mapping may be useful as an evaluative tool, for example, by getting pairs or groups to map what they know before their learning experience, then after their research is over. Compare and discuss the before-and-after knowledge maps, carefully noting any developments (see also p. 122 for a mapping activity).

Analyse

There are various strategies for analysing concepts and categorising information. These include analysing what is similar and different and which in any set might be the odd one(s) out and why (see p. 124 for other tools of analysis).

Similar and different

'What is the difference between 100 real and 100 imaginary dollars?' (Immanuel Kant). Comparing and contrasting are the basic building blocks of thinking. Noting sameness and difference are the foundations of human cognition and all reasoning depends on these skills. Psychologists who wish to assess a child's level of reasoning use tests that require a child to look for similarities and differences between two objects. Acts of comparing and contrasting enable children to relate one experience to another, to classify concepts and build a coherent and interconnected picture of the world. Help them to notice details, to look from different angles to compare features, to look at similarities and differences, and to see what changes are wrought over time.

Children can be asked to analyse what is similar and different in two objects, pictures, places, times, events, texts and so on. What is similar does not have to be identical but should have one or more shared variables. Force them to think by getting them to choose and say why. Encourage them to try to reach a consensus or to identify differences of opinion, choosing which they prefer and why. All such judgements should be based on analysis of evidence and the giving of reasons (see the 'Similar and different' activity on p. 124).

Odd one out

> We are all odd in some way or other.
>
> (Janie, aged 11)

'Odd one out' is a good strategy for developing reasoning, critical and creative thinking skills. The strategy is to present children with three objects and ask them which is the odd one out. Here there are no right or wrong answers, but a number of possibilities to think about and analyse. The process of reasoning and justification is the point of this activity. In pairs, the children must discuss and answer the question: 'Why is this the odd one out?' They must give reasons to justify their choices. They must also be open-minded to other possibilities. They should be asked to consider, 'Could it be a different one?' The answer to this is always 'yes', since there are many ways we can analyse the factors and variables that make up the potential similarities and differences between objects.

'Odd one out' may be used to identify pupils' understanding of key concepts in different subjects. A teacher in a numeracy lesson may write down three numbers on the board, such as 9, 5 and 10; or in science, three materials; or in English, three characters to compare and contrast – then ask the children to choose the 'odd one out' and to give a reason.

In any subject area, can you think of three or more items, words, objects or people, and challenge children to discuss and give reasons why one, two or each of them might be the odd one out? Teachers who use this strategy claim it can reveal gaps in the knowledge that has been taught and the knowledge and vocabulary that the children are then able to use. The children think of it as a game and are used to thinking up examples and ideas which show their thinking in different curriculum subjects. This approach encourages creative thinking and reasoning (See 'Odd one out', p. 125).

Summarise

Summarising means to check understanding of the whole of the topic, for example, by asking: What was said? Can you say it in a few/your own words? Can you say what you think now? This also involves helping students to discuss and clarify what they mean, for example, by asking What does that word/point/detail mean? Can you explain it? Are you saying that . . .?

'Reciprocal teaching' incorporates the key dialogic thinking tools of summarising, questioning, clarifying and predicting. It follows the principle that the best way to learn a process is to teach it, and uses the four strategies of successful learners:

- summarising
- questioning
- clarifying
- predicting.

The teacher first models the process by summarising, asking a question, clarifying a point and predicting what will come next. Next time around the learner takes on one or more of these activities with a partner, and gradually expands this role. The aim is to encourage the learner to take more responsibility in the learning situation and in helping others to learn.

Summarising is useful as a means of synthesising the meaning of any complex message, in the process of assessing learning. The ability to provide a good summary is an advanced, higher order skill. It involves a number of important cognitive processes including:

- judging which ideas are important;
- applying rules for condensing information;
- practising the communication of key ideas.

Summarising can be spoken or written, and older children should gain experience of both. The practice of taking notes and concept mapping can help in this process. As these are advanced skills plenty of guided practice is needed. Students will need to be shown what to do and told the strategies that will help them, such as:

- deleting unnecessary material;
- grouping key ideas and information into larger concepts;
- picking out key terms, phrases or sentences;
- creating new sentences which summarise the important points.

Children should be encouraged to 'look for the big ideas' and to discuss them with each other in all that they learn. A good way to begin is for the teacher to model the process, and for the teacher to think aloud while searching for the main ideas (see p. 123 for an activity to help in develop the skills of summarising).

Discuss memory strategies

Do you help students to try to improve their power to memorise information? Do you practise memory games with them? Remember that it is the discussion of strategies that stimulates thinking about learning. Just doing it is not enough.

Think about the ways in which the mind can try to process information into the memory. The mind tends to remember more when it can link units of meaning into patterns. A famous psychological study showed that the human mind can recall about seven (plus or minus two) unrelated items of knowledge. Memory can of course be trained, for example, by making patterns out of the information given, and repeating these patterns until they become internalised as long-term memories. These patterns can be created in visual ways, for example, through remembering how things looked, verbally through how things sound or physically through activities such as writing things down to remember them. These patterns can be processed in different ways.

Ask children to discuss how they prefer to process information:

■ *verbally*: through listening and saying or repeating the information;

■ *visually*: through seeing visual patterns, or pictures 'in the mind's eye';

■ *logically*: through seeing a pattern of logical or mathematical relations;

■ *physically*: through physical representation or bodily gestures;

■ *musically*: through melody, rhythm or musical association;

■ *personally*: through linking information to personal experiences or memories;

■ *socially*: through learning with and from others, sharing a task.

There is no one way of remembering or learning, but many ways. Some people call different ways of learning *styles* (for more on thinking about learning styles see p. 181), others say they reflect different types of intelligence. We know that staring at a textbook is one of the most inefficient ways of learning facts. It is when we are actively processing the facts, doing something with them, that they are likely to stay in the memory (for memory activities see p. 122).

Develop talking to learn in practice

The following are examples of activities that may be used to develop dialogic learning across the curriculum. They may be adapted and developed in different ways. The activities are about helping children to make thinking explicit and again expressing the central message of this book that if a topic is worth learning it is worth talking about.

The talking to learn tasks presented here offer ways to stimulate dialogue through using the following strategies:

1 Jigsaw: an approach to dialogic research

2 Talk partners and trios

3 What is mathematics?

4 What is music?

5 Plan a research topic

6 Defining objectives

7 List the characteristics

8 Consider all factors

9 Decide on priorities

10 Map the concepts

11 Memorise the information

12 Summarise what you have learned

13 Predicaments and problems

14 Use photos and pictures

15 Hold debates

16 Just a minute

17 Radio or TV report

18 Create a new game

19 Similar and different

20 Odd one out

21 Review your use of ICT

1 Jigsaw: an approach to dialogic research

When working on a theme, perhaps across several curriculum areas, divide the children into five or six 'research teams', and ask each team find out about one aspect of the theme. After they have been practising their research skills for a while, reorganise the class into 'jigsaw groups' that contain one delegate from each of the research teams. Get the children to explain to their 'new colleagues' what their research team has been doing, and what they have found out. Each jigsaw group should then consider the project as a whole, and be ready to contribute to a whole-class discussion about overall progress, and what needs to happen next.

2 Talk partners or trios

Put children in pairs or trios to talk to each other at particular points in a lesson, for example to:

■ Discuss the learning objectives at the start of the lesson; for instance, by asking them to put the learning objectives in their own words or identify the criteria for success.

■ Share and reflect on learning experiences during the lesson; for instance, by identifying what they need to remember or discussing progress with a partner.

■ Review what they have learned or remembered after the lesson; for instance, by asking them to summarise the key points or identify the plus, minus or interesting points in terms of their learning.

Retain pairs or trios for a period of time (e.g. for up to half a term), so that they can become confident with each other, establish routines and develop more extended turns.

3 What is mathematics?

Questions to encourage reflection about the nature of mathematics include:

■ Is mathematics useful?

■ What does 'useful' mean? How is maths useful?

■ Who uses mathematics?

■ What is a mathematician?

- Are you a mathematician?
- What do you do to become good at maths?
- Can everyone succeed in maths?
- What does 'succeed' mean?
- Is success in maths the same for everyone?
- What makes maths a challenge (hard)?
- What is a 'challenge'?
- Is a challenge in maths the same as other challenges, such as in sports?
- What is mathematics? Is maths invented or discovered?
- What does 'invent'/'discover' mean?
- What have you invented or discovered in maths?
- Does maths have a purpose?
- Does all maths have a purpose?
- What is the purpose (or usefulness) of what you have been doing in maths?
- How important is maths compared to other subjects?
- What questions do you have about maths?

(Fisher 2008a, p.211)

4 What is music?

The following are some questions to discuss about the concept and nature of music:

- Which sounds are musical and which are not musical?
- Make a list of all the places where you hear music. Which place do you like best?
- What would the world be like without music?
- [*Play some music*] Listen carefully to the music. What does the music make you think and feel? Write about your ideas.
- [*Play some orchestral music*] Listen carefully to the music. List all the instruments you can hear. What does the music make you think of?
- If you were making a CD of your favourite music with ten tracks, what would you choose to include?
- If you could play one musical instrument really well, which would you choose and why?
- Why do people like to listen to music or learn to play an instrument?
- What for you are the most beautiful sounds in the world?

For more discussion plans about the nature of subjects across the curriculum see Fisher 2008a, p. 202ff.

5 Plan a research topic

Using a chosen topic, write down or ask students to discuss and list under three headings:

- What do we know (about the topic)?
- What do we need to know?
- How can we find out? (Where? Who might help us?)

6 Defining objectives

List what you think the following may be trying to achieve:

- Your school.
- Your teacher in a lesson.
- Your teacher in assessing your work.
- Your aims in going to school.
- Your parents or carers at home.
- The students in your class.

7 List the characteristics

This is best begun as a group or class activity, and later as a paired or individual activity.

It presents that most basic of problem-solving strategies – consider all factors, list all characteristics, find out what you know/find out what others know, define the concept.

- Choose a concept.
- Write it down on a board, a large piece of paper or a digital whiteboard.
- Ask each group to give as many characteristics/definitions as possible of the concept word.
- List all suggestions.
- After listing, discuss similarities/differences. Could they be grouped into any order?

8 Consider all factors

Discuss with a partner and make a list of factors for each of the following:

- Your family have decided to move to a new home. What factors should they take into account in deciding on a new home?
- You are choosing a summer holiday. What factors should you keep in mind?
- What factors make for a good teacher?
- What makes for a good story? List all the factors that might be included in writing a good story.
- You are designing a chair. What factors should you take into account?

9 Deciding priorities

Make a list of factors and then prioritise three or four items in order of importance:

- In choosing a friend what are your first most important priorities?
- A sum of £1000 has been given to improve your school. What would be your priorities in spending the money?
- What do you think are the most important factors in choosing to buy a new bicycle?
- What rules should a school or class have? Which are the most important?
- What should parents consider in choosing a school for their child? Which are the most important points to consider?

10 Map the concepts

- After brainstorming/listing words connected to a concept write the concept word in the middle of the board or on a page.
- Link the connected words to the central concept word with lines.
- Write along the lines the relationship between the concept and connected words.

Mapping a text

- Give each pair of children a page from a reading, story or text book (a text of ten to thirty sentences). Ask them to list or mark every concept word they can find.
- How often does the same concept word appear? Which concept word appears most often? Which are the most important concept words (which words could you not leave out for the passage to still make sense)?
- List or mark words that are not concepts, that don't mean anything by themselves.
- Share and discuss.

11 Memorise the information

- Ask children to look at a line of numbers or words for about ten seconds, then cover them up and see how many they can remember by writing them down.
- See how successful they were at remembering (processing the information).
- Ask them to discuss with partners what helps them to remember.

What strategy did you use to try to remember the information? What helps us to remember and learn things by processing information?

12 Summarise what you have learned

Ask students to take turns to summarise a text, lesson or learning experience; for example, by noting the main points first in a hundred words, then in fifty words and then in one sentence.

13 Predicaments and problems

Use opportunities across the curriculum to solve a problem or a predicament; for example:

■ An historical figure at a critical turning point in history.

14 Use photos and pictures

Use photos and other kinds of pictures to encourage pairs or groups to construct a story or report; for example:

■ *Geography*: a photopack of a particular place or environment.

■ *History*: compare photos with illustrated impressions or artists' drawings of events and objects.

■ *Design and technology*: discuss from photos how buildings were designed and built.

15 Hold debates

Hold a debate on a disputed issue in your chosen topic or subject area, for example, in history:

■ What kind of king or queen was – ?

■ Was the British Empire a good thing?

Or in geography:

■ Should we fly less?

■ Are China's carbon emissions our concern or theirs?

16 Just a minute

Give children a topic to speak on without hesitation, deviation or repetition for up to one minute. Others can challenge them when rules are broken and if the challenger is successful they continue the topic (or nominate the next speaker) for up to a minute unless challenged.

17 Radio or TV report

In pairs, children prepare a short report for radio or TV, for example:

■ Informing them of what has been learned about a given topic.

■ Explaining an event.

■ Persuading the audience to a particular point of view.

18 Create a new game

In pairs or small groups, think of one of your favourite games. Whatever game it is it will have rules. The easiest way to create a new game is to take a game you know and change one or more of the rules of the game.

The game you choose might be a board game such as chess, where you might like to:

- change the way different pieces move, or the object of the game (for example, the object might be to lose rather than win);
- the nature of the pieces (for example, the pieces could be the characters in a book);
- the nature of the playing board (for example, landing on certain squares might incur certain penalties).

You might make up a new card game, adapt an existing game or invent an entirely new game (for example, a learning game which includes facts to be learned or remembered). You might invent a maze game, a word game, a quiz game, a game to play outdoors, a game for teaching something to younger children, a word game or party game.

When you have created or adapted your new game teach it to another group of children.

19 Similar and different

Choose two similar real objects (e.g. stones, feathers, seeds, fruits, vegetables, flowers, people). Discuss: How are these objects similar? How are they different? Which do you prefer? Why?

Choose two very different things and ask children to discuss and categorise similarities and difference; for example:

- tree and book
- boy and dog
- a poem and a story
- a photo and a painting
- two photos of the same scene, object, person, taken over time
- two pieces of music or a piece of music and sound of a bird singing
- two works of art (use these to discuss criteria for what makes a work of art)
- two characters in a book
- two stories or poems
- two events or places.

20 Odd one out

Which of these could be the odd one out? Discuss and give reasons for your answer (remember there are no right or wrong answers, only good or not-so-good reasons):

- fish, bird, frog
- bus, car, lorry
- wood, seeds, trees
- 9, 5,10 (or 36, 11, 25)
- sun, moon, stars
- violin, drum, flute
- silk, leather, fur
- true, good, beautiful
- police officer, fire officer, hospital worker
- Spain, France, Germany, England.

Create your own 'odd one out' puzzle and possible answers for it.

21 Review your use of ICT

Working in cross-pairs, ask children to reflect on and discuss their own and others' recent use of ICT for learning in a particular curriculum area or topic.

Possible questions for discussion include:

- What ICT did you use and how did you use it?
- Did it involve discussion or sharing with others?
- Was the discussion helpful?
- What did you learn from using the ICT?
- Were there any problems or limitations in what you could learn or do?
- What did you find interesting?
- How could you improve on what you did?
- How could the ICT have helped you more?
- What do you need to do next?
- How might you use ICT to help you learn in the future?

6

Talking Together

Talk to think in groups

> *A fruit seller with a basket of mangoes was walking down the road when he saw another man coming towards him. 'Please buy a mango for me, Nasruddin,' said the other man. The fruit seller was puzzled. 'Who is it you are you talking to?' he asked.*
>
> *'To Nasrudin,' said the man.*
>
> *'But there's nobody here except you and me,' said the fruit seller. 'Show me this Nasruddin you were talking to and I'll give you a mango free!'*
>
> *'Let's have it, then,' said the man, 'because I am Nasruddin.'*

This chapter explores children talking to think in groups. It discusses some key principles and strategies to help children to learn through talking together in groups and concludes with practical activities to stimulate children talking to think in groups. Talking together in pairs, trios or groups helps children understand what they need to think about and do when faced with a learning task.

This chapter on talking together is about helping learners to:

1 Talk in pairs, trios and groups

2 Achieve success in talk

3 Solve problems with others

4 Talk together in practice.

Children should experience talking together in groups of different sizes. Talking together in groups can help learners to:

■ ask questions and pose problems

■ investigate and solve problems with others

■ think more widely and deeply

■ learn collaboratively as part of a group

■ develop dialogic skills

■ practise social and cooperative skills.

This chapter discusses some key principles in talking in groups and ends with a range of practical activities to stimulate children talking to think in groups.

Talk in pairs, trios and groups

The trouble with children working on their own is that they may run out of ideas, repeat the same errors or get stuck, and therefore it is helpful to have someone with whom they can talk through any problems. Sometimes 'A problem shared is a problem halved', though not always; for if both become stuck it can be a problem doubled (see p. 137 for an activity based on this dilemma). However, a partner will often give the child a different way of looking at the problem, some new ideas to try, or help by simply listening as they talk through their ideas.

Talk partners

Find learning partners for your children so that they can then support each other through dialogue. Talk partners, or 'study buddies', offer opportunities for children to share ideas, express opinions, discuss different approaches or help to assess progress in learning.

Having a learning partner also helps them practise the skills of cooperation. The ability to work with others, share thinking and build on each other's ideas are key social as well as dialogic skills. One of the most important ways talk partners can help each other is through learning from each other's mistakes. Mistakes spring from ignorance or carelessness, but if spotted by a critical friend they can promote learning – unless they have both got it wrong! A potential problem is that one partner may come to rely on the other partner to find the answers. As Jason, aged 10, remarked: 'I don't like to rely on others, otherwise you end up with twice as many mistakes!'

The talk partner does not have to be the same person each time. Find different learning partners for the children to work with over time, including less able and more able partners. Sometimes 'the best way to learn is to teach', because the child is learning something again every time they teach it to others, and this can help them to understand it better as well as helping them develop useful metacognitive and social skills. The child's metacognitive skill lies in coming to understand the needs of a learner, and in helping others they can come to learn how to help themselves. Social skills develop from the practice of supportive talking and listening. The best way for them to practise what they have learned is to have someone to teach it to if they are more skilled or knowledgeable in that area of learning. They can be particularly supportive to children still learning the language. But make sure the mentor is someone who is encouraging, supportive and willing to be a source of information and support. It is not always easy, as this vignette shows:

Child [exasperated]: I have told her and told her and she still doesn't get it.

Teacher: Is that her fault or yours?

Child [grudgingly]: A bit of both I suppose.

Teacher: So what might help?

Child: Get someone else to try, or try again in a different way. . . .

A mentor should be someone who can offer positive advice. Discuss with children what they think is needed to be a good learning partner (for an activity involving 'talk partners' see p. 137. For an activity to encourage children to think carefully about what being a learning partner means see p. 137).

Talk trios

Children should also experience talk in trios. Three heads should have more ideas to offer than two. In a talk trio, or listening triangle, one of the problems as with any threesome is that one person may be left out of the dialogue. To overcome this and provide more of a shared focus, assign different roles in the dialogue, for example:

- *a speaker* who explains their thinking about a topic;
- *a questioner* who asks for further information or clarification;
- *an observer* who notes how well the other two fulfil their roles and reports back at the end.

These roles should be discussed before the dialogue and some criteria agreed for each role. The roles should be rotated so that each participant has a turn (see p. 137 for the activity 'talk tennis' for making a story in pairs or trios).

Talk groups

People working in groups or teams can achieve much more than people working alone. Help the children understand how best to work in a group and explain that working with others can help them achieve success in learning and in life.

Children may not find it easy working within a group, either because others are difficult to work with, do things in the wrong way, or ignore them. Many a child has echoed the complaint: 'It's not me! It's the others!' Working with others can be frustrating, and it takes time to learn how to handle others and oneself within any group.

There are a number of factors that affect working in groups. These include: group size, behaviour of others, the roles they take on, their relationships, their motivation and effort. The smaller the group the more chance children have, as individuals, to have their voice heard and to contribute to group effort. Working in fours can be ideal, since it gives members the chance to partner with three other people or for two sets of conversations to take place at the same time. Children can first talk in pairs, then two pairs can join in groups of four; for example, by sharing anecdotes of a time when they were in trouble in pairs, then sharing these anecdotes and working one up into a longer story in groups of four. They also need experience of talk within larger and more diverse groups.

All groups benefit from having goals to give them a purpose for being together. A learning group should begin by deciding what it wants to achieve. These goals may include working well together or achieving success in a common task. The behaviour and attitudes of people to each other will be important factors in ensuring successful working of the group. The following are some of the vital ingredients of good working groups:

- all relevant information and ideas shared among the group;
- no one person dominates;
- everyone is encouraged to contribute;
- everyone listens to whoever is talking;
- every contribution is valued;
- suggestions and opinions can be challenged and discussed;
- alternatives are considered before a decision is made;
- the group tries to reach agreement.

Learning how to work well and cooperate in a group requires the exercise of many skills. But the better children are able to work in groups the more they will benefit from the learning and effort of others.

Achieve success in talk

What makes talking together successful? Some groups work well, others do not. Talk with children about the many different groups in which they may participate (see p. 138 for dialogic questions to get children thinking about groups). Ask them to list the possible opportunities that they have for working and learning with others. Discuss how in any group there will be people who share ideas and information, help in planning what to do and who work well with others, as well as people who try to dominate, are aggressive or who block other people and their ideas. Discuss what people do in groups that are working well. Remind them that in a discussion listening is as important as talking. Discuss the old Chinese saying: 'Listen a hundred times, ponder a thousand times, speak once!'

Certain characteristics or logical conditions define dialogue or discussion. These are the conditions that have to be met for us to say that people are actually engaged in discussion. They include that people participating must:

- talk to one another;
- listen to one another;
- respond to what others say;
- put forward more than one point of view on the topic;
- try to develop their knowledge, understanding or judgement on the issue.

Get children to put their rules for good dialogue into their own words. The following are some suggestions for making discussions work well from a group of 10-year-olds:

- Each person in a group has time to say what they think.
- Try and keep to the point.
- Speak clearly so that other people can understand.
- Let people ask when they don't understand.

- Say whether you agree or disagree and why.

- Show respect to other people.

- Explain what you mean.

- Make sure everyone knows and agrees what to do.

Questions that can be used in assessing whether genuine discussion has taken place include:

- Have the group talked to one another?

- Have they listened to each other?

- Have they responded to what others have said?

- Have they considered different viewpoints?

- Have they developed some knowledge, understanding or judgement?

A checklist like this can act as success criteria which can be given to each group as an *aide-memoire* and used by them as a tool for self-valuation. Ask the groups to assess not only what they did but also how the members related to each other. The relationships between individuals in any successful working group are underpinned by moral values. These moral principles include:

- *Courtesy*: by observing the rules of discussion, such as not interrupting or shouting.

- *Reasonableness*: being willing to listen to the reasons, evidence and arguments of others, and being prepared to allow the arguments of others to influence their views.

- *Truthfulness*: speaking what they believe is true, not deliberately lying, deceiving others or pretending to believe what they do not believe.

- *Freedom of expression*: being free to express an opinion, not restrained by being ridiculed or made to feel embarrassed.

- *Equality of opportunity*: equal access for all to opportunities to speak and having the attention of others, not being dominated by the few.

- *Respect for others*: respect for the rights and opinions of others, paying attention and thinking about what they say, responding with care and respect for them as individuals.

- *Open-mindedness*: being open to the views of others, willing to change one's mind, being sensitive to the views of others, and willing to suspend judgement.

See p. 138 for a dialogic activity that asks for views on the uses of discussion.

Solve problems with others

Children will face problems throughout their lives. Some problems will be easy to solve, others difficult and some will seem insoluble. Discuss your children's experience of these different kinds of problem. There are questions that they may ask at different stages in solving a problem. These include:

- Understand the problem   *What is the problem?*
- Plan what to do   *How should we tackle it?*
- Make a decision   *How do we decide what to do?*
- Implement the plan   *What do we do to solve it?*
- Review the outcomes   *What have we learned?*

Understand the problem

One day some tourists became lost while driving. They stopped a local and asked him the way to the town they wanted to find. 'Oh, that's easy,' said the man, 'but if I were you I wouldn't start from here.'

One way to begin is to ask children: *What is the problem?* A possible answer might be that a problem usually has a starting point, a goal that is sought and some obstacle that is preventing one from achieving the goal. As one child put it: 'A problem is when there is something that is wrong with the world that you want to put right, but it's not easy.'

It is easier for children to solve a problem that they fully understand. Many fail exams because they have not understood the question correctly. If children understand fully what the problem is, they are more likely to find a solution. As the Indian sage Krishnamurti put it: 'If we can really understand the problem, the answer will come out of it, because the answer is not separate from the problem.'

Help children to understand their problem by getting them to express it in their own words. Do not assume they know what the problem is until they have said what it is. In a complex situation, identifying the problems involved and separating the central problem from other problems is challenging. Help them to understand the elements of a problem by asking them, for example, to define:

- The initial situation   *What is the problem?*
- The goal or objective   *What is the goal?*
- The obstacle(s)   *What is blocking them?*

Children face many real-life problems but they find it easier to discuss problems that do not relate directly to their own lives. Stories provide a useful source of problems to discuss – for example, what are the precise problems that a character faces? See p. 139 for an activity which asks children to identify the problems involved for each of the characters in a story.

Understanding a problem might include knowing what is the objective to be achieved and what obstacle(s) prevent them from achieving it. Have your children ever faced a problem that seemed overwhelming? Ask them whether they have ever said: 'I shall never be able to do that.' Discuss what they actually wanted (the objective) and what precisely prevented them (the obstacle). A problem once discussed may not seem so overwhelming. Whatever the challenge, remind them to try to tackle one obstacle, problem or step at a time.

Questions to ask to help children to understand a problem include:

- What do we/they want? What are we/they trying to achieve?

- What is preventing us/them from getting what we/they want?

- What exactly is the problem?

See p. 140 for an activity aimed at identifying obstacles in a problem situation.

Plan what to do

When facing a problem, children should plan what to do before they tackle it. Discuss the proverb: 'Look before you leap', and whether it is always good advice. Why or why not?

Planning means thinking ahead, and discussing one's plans with someone often helps. Illustrate this with your own examples or tell children the following story about a problem that Birbal faced, which he was able to solve once the had the chance to think and to talk about it:

Several courtiers were competing for the post of royal adviser. The Emperor Akbar told them he would put them to the test, and the one who passed the test would be appointed to the post. Akbar then unfastened his cloak and lay on the floor. He challenged the courtiers to cover him from head to toe with the cloak. Akbar lay there and one by one the courtiers took the cloak and tried, but their attempts proved useless. If his head was covered, Akbar's feet remained exposed. Some tried to pull and tug at the cloak to make it bigger, but in vain. The cloak was not long enough to cover the Emperor. The Emperor then asked Birbal if he could do it. Birbal took the cloak and then looked at the emperor lying on the floor. How could he cover a large man with a small cloak? He stopped to think and a plan formed slowly in his mind. What do you think it was?[1]

Once children have defined the problem the next stage is to solve it. There has been much research into the best ways to solve problems. A useful strategy for children to remember when confronted with any complex puzzle or problem is to use a step–by–step approach.

> The centipede was happy quite
> Until asked which leg came after which
> This threw him into in such a fright
> He fell into a ditch.

A step-by-step approach to planning makes it easier for children to see progress by taking one step at a time. As Wayne, aged 9, said: 'If I get something right I will try the next step.' Questions to ask children about their plans include:

- Have you thought of everything?

- What else do you need to think about?

- What do you need to remember?

See the 'Crossing the river' activities on p. 140 to encourage children to follow a step-by-step approach to finding solutions.

Make a decision

One day, Nasruddin was asked to judge a case in court. The prosecutor argued so persuasively that the defendant was guilty, that after he had finished arguing his case Nasruddin cried out: 'I believe you are right!'

The clerk of the court begged him to be patient, for the defendant had not yet spoken. When the accused person spoke in his defence he was so convincing that when he completed giving his evidence, Nasruddin cried out: 'I believe you are right!'

The clerk of the court could not allow this. 'Your Honour,' he said, 'they cannot both be right.'

'I believe you are right!' said Nasruddin.

Questions to ask children to think about before making any important decision are:

- What do I think?
- What do others think?

What do I think?

When faced with a problem, children need to think about all the facts they have (see 'Consider all factors, p. 113) but also the information they are not given but which may be relevant. Encourage them to discuss what they think with others and to take time to consider all factors (see the activity 'Youth or age?' on p. 141). In any dialogue children need to consider not only what they think but also what others think.

What do others think?

There are two main reasons for talking to others to find out what they think. The first is that they may have ideas and advice that we have not thought of. The second reason is that talking to others helps to clarify our own thinking. When children are confused about what to do, it is always a good idea to encourage them to talk more about it. Share and discuss stories about people whose decisions went wrong because they did not take time to think or to take advice from others. The following is one such story:

Nasruddin was about to throw a special party. He realised he did not have enough glasses or bowls for his guests. So he went to a shop selling glassware and bought a great number of fine glasses, dishes and bowls. The shop owner asked him if needed any help in carrying them. Without thinking, Nasruddin said, 'No. I can manage.' Nasruddin left the shop with his arms piled high with delicate glassware. On his way home he stumbled in the street, and with an almighty crash dropped all that he was carrying. Everything was smashed. A crowd soon gathered and stood staring at what had happened. 'What's the matter with you idiots?' cried Nasruddin. 'Have you never seen a fool before?'

Discuss with children: Was Nasruddin a fool? Why? What does this story teach us?

Ask children to try to remember one bad decision they made in their lives and discuss what they did, or failed to do, in the process of making that decision. The following is a list of ten common flaws in human thinking. Ask the children whether any of these apply to their thinking?

- Did it in too much haste (an Irish proverb says: 'Haste is of the devil').
- Did it without thinking.
- Did the first thing I thought of.
- Did not give the matter enough thought.
- Did not think of alternative courses of action.
- Did not consider the consequences.
- Did not ask for help, thought I could do it by myself.
- Did not have enough information.
- Did what others told me I should do.
- Did it while I was upset or feeling too emotional.

There is nothing wrong with making mistakes. We all make the wrong decisions from time to time. If we are going to learn from our mistakes and make wiser decisions we need to '*think ahead*,' which means thinking carefully about what we are going to do rather than rushing into decisions. These questions can help children think more deeply about any decision:

- What are the alternatives?
- What are the likely consequences?

What are the alternatives?

One day Nasruddin decided he wanted to learn to play the flute, so he went to visit a flute player.
'How much does it cost to learn to play the flute?' asked Nasruddin.
Thirty pounds for the first lesson,' said the flute player, 'and fifteen pounds for the next lessons.'
'That sounds fine,' replied Nasruddin. 'I'll start with the second lesson.'

The simplest kind of decision, though not necessarily the easiest, is to ask children to make one of two choices. They might, for example, be asked to discuss and make a choice between two texts, artworks or courses of action.

A decision is made more difficult when children know the alternatives but like none of them or neither of them. Discuss with children the saying: 'On the horns of a dilemma', and 'Being between the devil and the deep blue sea'. Share situations involving being forced to choose between equally unpleasant alternatives. See p. 142 for a story where children are asked to consider a decision in which people are faced with the dilemma of having to choose between two possible courses of action.

What are the possible consequences?

'Thinking ahead' means taking time to discuss the possible consequences of decisions, as in the story of a man who jumped from the top floor of a skyscraper. As he fell past a window about half-way down he said: 'All right so far.' A common human mistake is not thinking about the consequences of a decision – 'I just did not think about what might happen'. Practise thinking about possible consequences with children, both good and bad (the benefits and drawbacks or pros and cons) of a course of action by giving them tasks in which they have to discuss and list the pros and cons of any decision.

Thinking ahead and discussing alternatives and consequences will produce better decisions about learning and life, though it will not guarantee 'good' decisions. As Robert Burns said: 'The best laid schemes of mice and men gang aft a-gley.' However, they are less likely to go astray if they have been talked through first.

Implement the plan

> To do something that's difficult you've got to get your mind right first.
>
> (Ben, aged 11)

One of the characteristics of experts in any field of human effort is that they take time to prepare well. This was summed up by a group of children as: *Use your head to think ahead.* Part of good preparation is getting in the right frame of mind. In any difficult task, such as trying to get reluctant children engaged in dialogue, you need to be positive and persistant, and prepared to try different ways or to start again if necessary. A plan, like a lesson or dialogue plan, is always provisional, and open to change during implementation.

Success in any planned endeavour is more likely if one is:

- *prepared* – by thinking about what you will say before you begin;
- *positive* – by being in the right mind for the task;
- *persistent* – by taking the time you need to do it.

When children are stuck they need the resilience to try again, to try another way or seek further help. Discuss with them the attitudes that make for success, such as 'resilience' and 'resourcefulness', and ask them how to discuss and describe what they think the best frame of mind is for solving a problem.

Review the outcomes

We learn from thinking back or reviewing what has been done and trying to answer the key question: What have we learned? A review has two important aspects – time to think things through and time to discuss it with others. For more on helping children assess what they have learned see Chapter 8.

Remind children that not all outcomes will be successful. They must learn to fail, but to fail intelligently by learning from their experience. Problems have a habit of recurring in different forms and some human problems will have no final solution. There will always, for example, be evil in the world. As the old rhyme says:

> For every evil under the sun
> There is a remedy or there is none.
> If there is one, seek till you find it,
> If there is none, never mind it.

There are many evils in the world that return to haunt us as problems in one guise or another. Discuss with the children what they think are evils in the world; for example, the way some people attack others with verbal abuse or insults. Ask children if they have ever been on the receiving end of verbal abuse or insults from others for no apparent reason. It is a painful problem that any child may face and it can provide a useful focus for discussion. For an activity based on this problem see pp. 143–4.

Talk together in practice

The 'talking together' tasks presented here may be adapted and developed in different ways to stimulate dialogue through the following strategies:

1 Is a problem shared a problem halved?
2 The telephone game.
3 What is a good learning partner?
4 Talk tennis.
5 Working in a group.
6 Why use discussion?
7 Whose problem?
8 What is the objective?
9 What might the obstacle be?
10 Crossing the river.
11 Youth or age, which is better?
12 The king who foretold the future.
13 The lady or the tiger?

14 The world's oldest puzzle.

15 The Gift of Insults.

1 Is a problem shared a problem halved?

Proverbs can be a good focus for talk between children, particularly if they are asked to consider positive, negative and their own interesting examples of the proverb in use. For example, there is a proverbial saying, 'A problem shared is a problem halved.' It is usually thought that talking through a problem with someone else is a good idea. But is this always the case? Might sharing a problem make it worse? When might this be so?

Discuss with children the proverb, 'A problem shared is a problem halved.' Ask them to discuss:

- Is it always good to share a problem?
- When is it good to share a problem? Give examples.
- When might sharing a problem make it worse? Give examples.

2 The telephone game

The telephone game aims to develop your speaking and listening skills with a partner. You need a telephone and two or more people to play this game. Players take turns to speak to an imaginary person who has telephoned them, using a mobile (not switched on) or ordinary phone. They must speak for one minute on the phone to the imaginary caller, then hand the phone to the next player saying there is a call for them. Players must try to sustain the 'conversation' for one minute without undue hesitation or repetition. A theme, problem or scenario can be given, or roles assigned before the pretend telephone call is made. Afterwards ask the children to discuss how talking on the telephone differs from talking to people face to face.

3 What is a good learning partner?

Ask children in pairs or small groups to discuss the characteristics of someone who is a good learning partner and try to agree the five or more most important elements and rank them in order of importance.

A good learning partner is someone who:

1 ....

2 ....

3 ....

4 ....

5 ....

4 Talk tennis

This is a way of creating a story with a partner. It encourages an emphasis on partners listening for keywords, ideas and events, focusing on trying to create a narrative line and to make sense. Each person says one word, sentence or number of sentences (verbal paragraph) in turn so that the story is passed backwards and forwards. For example: Once there was a girl/who wanted to fly/so she looked on the Internet/ and found. . . .

This game can be played in pairs, trios or small groups.

5 Working in a group

Not all learning is to be found in books, the Internet and other printed sources. You can learn a lot through and with other people. Other people are human resources that can help you learn. Think who might help you to find out more, or who might help if you have a problem. The groups in which you participate might include friendship groups, family groups, sports groups, activity groups or learning groups.

Discuss these questions with your partner:

- What groups do you belong to?

- What are the similarities and differences between the groups?

- What do you like or dislike about each group?

- What makes a group successful?

- How could each group you know improve what it does?

- What rules do you think would help a group to work well?

6 Why use discussion?

What are your views on the value of discussion? Think about your answers to the following questions and discuss them with others:

- What is a discussion?

- Is every kind of talking together a discussion?

- Do discussions need rules? If so, what should they be?

- What good can come out of discussing things with others?

- What do you like/not like about discussions?

- Can you remember a good discussion? (What made it good?)

- What things are best for discussion?

- Are there some things you would not want to discuss?

- Do you prefer to talk or listen in a discussion?

- What would you like to discuss with others?

7 Whose problem?

Read the following story. Try to identify who has problems in this story and define what the problems are:

> *Nasruddin could not write very well. His ability to read was even worse. Usually this was not a problem for him, for he was good at asking others to help him. One day, while he was staying in a village where few could read or write, he agreed to help a villager write a letter. Nasruddin slowly wrote the words the villager dictated. 'Now read it back to me,' said the man, 'so I can see that nothing is left out.' Nasruddin began reading what he had written. He began, 'My dear Brother . . .' then got stuck. 'I am not quite sure what the next words are,' he said. 'But that's terrible,' said the man. 'Who is going to read it if you can't?'*
>
> *'My good man,' said Nasruddin. 'My problem is to write the letter not read it.'*

- What problems can you find in this story?
- Who has these problems?
- Why is it helpful to define what the problem is and identify whose problem it is?

8 What is the objective?

In the following example Omar has a problem. Look at the situation and decide what Omar and his sisters' objectives might be. Complete the problem plan by suggesting possible solutions which would allow both to achieve their objectives.

Problem

Omar wants to do his homework but he has a problem. He can only work well when it is quiet and his younger sister, Layla, is playing loud music on her stereo in the next room.

Objectives

Omar:

Layla:

Possible solutions

_____

_____

_____

_____

_____

9 What might the obstacle be?

Discuss the following Nasruddin story:

> One day Mullah Nasruddin lost his ring down in the basement of his house, where it was very dark. There being no chance of his finding it in that darkness, he went out on the street and started looking for it there. Somebody passing by stopped and enquired, 'What are you looking for, Nasruddin? Have you lost something?'
>
> 'Yes,' said Nasruddin. 'I've lost my ring down in the basement.'
>
> 'But why don't you look for it down in the basement where you lost it?' asked the man in surprise. 'Don't be silly!' said Nasruddin. 'How do you expect me to find anything in that darkness?'

- What is wrong with Nasruddin's interpretation of the problem?
- What is the real obstacle preventing Nasruddin from solving the problem?
- What lesson do you think this story may be teaching us?

10 Crossing the river

Ask children to discuss and demonstrate the best solution to the following problems about crossing a river. These are problems they could tackle in different ways. They could discuss how to get to the answer. They could write it down, for example, using mathematical symbols to represent the boys and the men. Short-term memory is limited. It is very hard to think more than three or four moves ahead, so we need to record the steps in words, symbols or pictures if we want to remember them. Recording what we do or think is also useful, as we can look back to see where and what exactly needs to be changed. So it is a good idea for the children to write down and record what the initial situation is and then what they might do about it. They could draw diagrams to show the solution, or use real objects to illustrate how it can be done.

Two men and two boys want to cross a river. Their boat is only big enough to take one man and two boys. How do they all get across?

Ask them to try to solve the problem. If they succeed, ask them which way of doing it suited them best. There are different possible solutions but only one way to solve the problem in the fewest moves. Can you solve the problem in the fewest moves?

Hobbits and Orcs is a another version of the crossing the river problem.

Three Hobbits and three Orcs are travelling in the same direction. They find their journey interrupted by a river. There is a ferry boat, but the boat is so small it will only hold two of them at a time. There is a danger. Orcs are hungry creatures and if they outnumber the Hobbits on either side of the river they will eat them. Can you devise a series of trips to transfer the six by ferry from one side of the river to the other without the Orcs outnumbering the Hobbits on either side of the river?

Clues to the solution: *As in the earlier problem not every trip needs two travellers, and sometimes travellers who have been across may need to return if the problem is to be solved.*[2]

Ask the children in pairs to discuss and create their own crossing the river problem.

11 Youth or age, which is better?

Read the following story about Nasruddin and the merits of youth and age:

At a gathering where Nasruddin was present, people were discussing whether it was better being young or old. They had all agreed that it was better being young because a person's strength decreases as years go by. However, Nasruddin disagreed.

'I don't agree with you,' said Nasruddin, 'for in my old age I have the same strength as I had in the prime of my youth.'

'How do you mean, Nasruddin?' asked one of the gathering. 'How can you prove that?'

'Easily,' replied Nasruddin. 'In my garden there is a massive stone. In my youth I used to try and lift it, and I never succeeded in lifting it when I was young. And now I am old I still cannot lift it!'

Discuss the following questions about the story:

- What is strange, interesting or puzzling about this story?
- Is Nasruddin's test of strength a valid test?
- In discussing the merits of youth and age what else should be thought about apart from strength?
- What do you think are the benefits of being young and of being old?
- Youth or age, which is better? What do you think?
- Do you think young or old people are better at solving problems? Why?
- What remains important in life whether you are young or old?

12 The king who foretold the future

The following activity presents a teaching story. Discuss what this story means. Are there any analogies between this story and other problems which people face? What does this story remind you of?

> *A king who was proud of his ability to read the future one day read in the stars that on a particular day a disaster would happen to him. He therefore built a house of solid rock and posted many guards outside. When the day came he stayed safe within, but realised there was still a small gap by the door where the sun came in. He blocked the gap with rocks which could not be moved. Later he realised that he was a prisoner within his own house. Because of this the king died.*
>
> Attar of Nishanpur

- In what way is this story like other problems people face? (How is it an analogy?)
- What lessons does this story teach? (What does this analogy suggest?)
- How might these lessons be applied to other situations? (How might this analogy be applied?)

13 The lady or the tiger?

The following story presents a dilemma. In it you are asked to consider a decision in which people are 'on the horns of a dilemma', trying to choose between two possible courses of action. This is a version of a famous dilemma story published in 1884 by American writer Frank Stockton.

> *A long time ago, in an ancient land, there lived a king who built a big stadium, like a Roman amphitheatre, in which not only shows would be put on but also in which justice would be done. When a man was accused of a serious crime he was taken to the arena in which there were two doors. The accused man could open either door. Behind one would be a hungry tiger who would tear him to pieces; behind the other there would be a lady whom he would marry. The trial would either end in death or in the celebration of a marriage. The king thought this a fair system, for did not the accused have the choice in his own hands?*
>
> *The king had a daughter who fell in love with one of his subjects; not a prince but a common man. When the king found out he flew into a rage. The man who loved the princess was arrested and sent for trial in the arena. A big crowd gathered to see which of the two doors the man would open. The king and the princess were there too. Both knew which door hid the hungry tiger and which hid the lady. The princess hated the idea that*

her lover would be eaten by a tiger, but hated as much the idea that her lover would be married to another woman. The man stared up at the princess looking for some sign to help him decide which door to choose. She raised her hand and made a slight quick movement to the right. He then turned and walked with a firm tread towards the door on the right and opened it.

The point of the story is this: Who came out of the door – the lady or the tiger?

- What choice do you think the princess made (who came out of the opened door)? Why?
- The king thought this a fair system. Was he right? Why, or why not?
- Sometimes one must choose between equally unpleasant options. Have you ever been in this situation? What did you do? Would you do it again? Why?

14 The world's oldest puzzle

Try with a partner to solve what is the world's oldest mathematical puzzle. It comes from the Rhind papyrus written about 1650 BCE by an ancient Egyptian scribe called Ahmes. He states that he copied it from a work written two centuries earlier. Here is the puzzle:

There are seven houses each containing seven cats. Each cat kills seven mice and each mouse would have eaten seven ears of corn. Each ear of corn would have produced seven hekats of grain. What is the total?

Can you work out the right method to find the right answer?[3]

Many years later, the Italian mathematician Fibonacci posed this problem in his *Liber Abaci* (1202 CE). Is this a similar problem to the one above, with the same method and answer?

Seven old women travel to Rome, and each has seven mules. On each mule there are seven sacks, in each sack there are seven loaves of bread, with each loaf there are seven knives and each knife has seven sheaths. The problem is to find the total of all of them.

Can you work out the right method to find the right answer?[4]

15 The Gift of Insults

The following activity asks children to discuss the possible messages of a teaching story from Zen Buddhism. It aims to provide a model of one way to solve a real-life problem: How do you respond to insults?

There once lived a great warrior. Though quite old, he was still able to defeat any challenger. His reputation extended far and wide throughout the land and many students gathered to study under him.

One day an infamous young warrior arrived at the village. He was determined to be the first man to defeat the great master in a sword fight. Along with his strength, the young warrior had an uncanny ability to spot and exploit any weakness in an opponent. He would wait for his opponent to make the first move, thus revealing a weakness, and then would strike with merciless force and lightning speed. No one had ever lasted with him in a match beyond the first move. The only man he had not beaten was the old warrior.

Much against the advice of his concerned students, the old master gladly accepted the young warrior's challenge. As the two squared off for battle, the young warrior began to hurl insults at the old master. He threw dirt and spat in his face . . . For hours he verbally assaulted him with every curse and insult known to mankind. But the old warrior merely stood there, motionless and calm. Finally, the young warrior exhausted himself. He knew he was defeated, and left without saying another word.

Somewhat disappointed that he did not fight the insolent youth, the students gathered around the old master and questioned him. 'How could you endure such an indignity? How did you drive him away?'

The master replied, 'If someone comes to give you a gift and you do not receive it, to whom does the gift belong?'

'The Gift of Insults', from *Values for Thinking* by Robert Fisher (2001)

- What did the master mean by saying: 'If someone comes to give you a gift and you do not receive it, to whom does the gift belong?'
- What is the message of this teaching story?
- Have you ever faced a problem involving someone who insulted you?
- What would be your advice to someone who faced similar problems?

7

Extending Talk for Thinking

What you want is to be given something to think about that you have never thought before and to say things you have never said before.

(Rahim, aged 13)

This chapter explores how to extend children's talking and thinking in large groups or classes. It explores ways to extend talk with a group or class or through a special form of dialogue called 'community of enquiry' which draws upon the long tradition of philosophy for children.

This chapter is about enabling learners to:

1 Engage in philosophical discussion

2 Create a community of enquiry

3 Extend dialogue by digging for depth

4 Extend talk for thinking in practice.

It discusses the nature and practice of philosophical discussion and how to create communities of enquiry in the classroom, and ends with practical activities to promote creative dialogue in the classroom.

The philosopher John Stuart Mill said that the only way to knowing the whole of a subject is by hearing what can be said about it by persons of every variety of opinion, and studying all modes it can be looked at by every character of mind (*On Liberty*). The advantage of dialogue and discussion in large groups is that dialogue benefits from the thinking of many 'characters of mind'. Philosophical discussion with many 'characters of mind' in a community of enquiry enables learners to:

- engage in philosophical dialogue in large groups
- identify philosophical problems, questions and issues
- create their own agenda for dialogue
- practise critical and creative thinking
- develop social and emotional skills
- extend the range and depth of their thinking
- internalise the habits of intelligent behaviour.

The ability to speak and listen comes naturally to children (unless their abilities have been impaired) but not necessarily the skills they need to engage in productive dialogue in large groups. These need to be learned. For this children need to be exposed to models and frameworks of good dialogue to help them learn the skills of effective talk in large groups. The 'community of enquiry' described below provides just such a model where children can develop the skills of creative dialogue in a safe community setting.

The skills of constructive discussion in large groups help children to develop habits of intelligent behaviour. These habits and how they are developed in a community of enquiry through philosophical discussion are the focus of this chapter.

Engage in philosophical discussion

The main teaching method for engaging children in philosophical discussion is an approach called 'Philosophy for Children' which is practised in more than forty countries around the world. The aim of Philosophy for Children is to help children develop dialogic and thinking skills as well as the capacity to engage in democratic and productive discussion.

There are two factors unique to Philosophy for Children (PforC) that make it especially effective in developing children's intelligence and dialogic skills. These are that children's capacity for thinking and dialogue is extended through their:

■ taking responsibility for creating the agenda and rules of the discussion

■ engaging in the practice of philosophical enquiry.

What makes PforC special is that the children set the agenda for enquiry and the teacher or leader facilitates discussion that involves philosophical thinking. What 'philosophical thinking' means is explored below (for more on the history, research and development of PforC see p. 168).

What makes a dialogue philosophical?

> Philosophy is the way you sort out problems in life when nobody knows the answer.
>
> (Simon, aged 11)

Philosophical thinking arises from the human need to question experience and to understand the meaning of puzzling ideas and concepts. The ability of humans to express their sensory experiences in words and concepts (organising ideas) enables philosophical thinking to take place. This happens not by asking, 'Who is that?' or, 'What is that?', but, 'Why is that?' and, 'Why do you think so?', and is activated by the search for answers to the problems posed by the human mind. It is the way we sort out problems using words as the tools for thinking.

Philosophy is not just an intellectual exercise, it also involves attitudes, habits or dispositions towards being in the world characterised by curiosity and questioning, by reasoning and by speculation. The knowledge that comes from philosophy is conceptual and arises from making meaning and creating ideas. Here is an example of a new idea or concept created by a child during classroom dialogue:

Child: I am iffing.

RF: What do you mean by 'iffing'?

Child: Its when you say 'suppose if . . . trees could talk or birds ruled the world.' So if someone says, 'That's crazy!' you can say, 'I am only 'iffing'.

Philosophy is necessary because human knowledge is incomplete, and life, as Richard, aged 6, said, 'is full of puzzlings'. Human knowledge is never complete owing to the ambiguity of experience, the unreliability of our perceptions and the fallibility of reports from others. In using words to describe the world we are inevitably faced with ambiguity, uncertainty and vagueness of meaning. The following is an example from classroom discussion illustrating a struggle to explain the relationship between the world and mental experience.

RF: What is a horizon?

Child: A horizon is as far as you can see with your eyes.

RF: So you can't see beyond the horizon?

Child: You can sort of see beyond the horizon, but you have to use your imagination.

RF: So is your imagination like an eye?

Child: Yes, you have a kind of eye in your mind.

RF: Like a camera?

Child: Yes . . . no, not like a camera, because a camera can't see what's not there, but your mind can.

'Philosophy', said the philosopher Wittgenstein, 'is a battle against the bewitchment of our intelligence by means of language' (*Philosophical Investigations*, p. 109). The meanings of words are not consistent and transparent; people use words in vague and inconsistent ways. Words used by different people or in different contexts can alter in meaning. Some people, advertisers for example, may knowingly use words to mislead or 'bewitch' our intelligence. Adverts can therefore be a stimulus to philosophical enquiry (see p. 163 for an activity that encourages children to explore the philosophical meanings of words used in adverts).

'Real concepts are impossible without words,' said Vygotsky (1978/1991), 'and thinking in concepts does not exist beyond verbal thinking.' Daniel, aged 7, put it this way: 'You can only speak with words because you can't speak with clicking; you can only speak with words!' The 'mark' of a concept being philosophical, in any field of enquiry, is that it is common, central and contestable. For example, what is love, death, truth, goodness, beauty, fairness or God? With some of these questions, such as 'Why are people cruel to each other?', 'Does God exist?', 'What is love?' the right answer may not be known, or there may be several possible answers. These questions arise out of a child's natural curiosity, but they are not scientific or open to empirical investigation. There is no one right answer; they are questions open to many possible answers and viewpoints. They are philosophical because they are about using words to make sense of life. Or as one child put it: 'Philosophy is trying to find out whether something is true when you say something is so and not everyone agrees.'

Asking and answering philosophical questions is where philosophy begins. For an activity that helps children practise asking questions see pp. 161ff.

Questions at the heart of philosophy include:

- What does this mean?

- Is it true?

- How do we know?'

Children bring with them into the world a mind capable of being stretched in many directions and an ability to ask not only everyday questions like 'Where's my food?' but also deep and challenging questions like the following questions from 4-year-olds: 'Why do people die?', 'Why do chickens lay eggs?' and 'How does an oak tree fit into an acorn?' This curiosity is evidence of the philosophical intelligence that we all have, that can be developed through creative dialogue (see p. 162 for some questions to stimulate children's philosophical thinking and dialogue).

Leading a philosophical dialogue

Philosophy helps you solve problems you didn't know you had!

(Joel, aged 10)

Socrates was famous for his pose of 'scholarly ignorance', saying he was the wisest of men because he knew his knowledge was limited. Philosophic dialogue seeks understanding through sharing and challenging different opinions and ideas. It is not like concealed forms of teacher talk where questions lead only to a closed conclusion. This kind of dialogue is typified by questions like, 'Who can tell me the answer to this?' rather than, 'Who can give me an (or another) answer?' Philosophical dialogue is a creative process because it is open and invites the free expression of ideas, and is not confined to a 'right answer'. The dialogic teacher is a questioner and encourages the child's voice to assert itself in unpredicted and challenging ways. As Terri, aged 10, describes: 'Its like an adventure – you never know where a discussion is going . . . and it always seems to end up with another question!'

Philosophical dialogue requires a community approach to enquiry in the classroom, with many voices creating multiple viewpoints. The aim is to enable the child's mind to become a moving prism catching light from many different angles. An enquiry is sustained by open-ended questions from the teacher as well as from children. For example, a teacher using a story that includes the theme of truth, such as Aesop's fable, 'Mercury and the Axe' (Fisher 1999, p.44) might prepare a number of open-ended prompt questions to encourage children to discuss the nature of truth (see p. 150 for some philosophical questions about God raised by children to stimulate philosophical thinking and discussion).

Here is an excerpt from one such classroom discussion with 6-year-olds, prompted by a teacher who used questions like those about 'truth' on p. 167:

Teacher: What do we mean when we say something is true?
Child: It means it really happened, it's not pretend . . . it's real, that's true.
Teacher: Can you think something is true when it is not true?
Child: Sometimes you say something you think is true. It's not a lie if you think it is true.

Child: I disagree with that because you could think something was true and say it was true when it was not true.

Teacher: Can you give an example?

Child: Well, if you could say it is raining because you thought it was raining and it was only birds on the roof. You can say something you think is true although in fact it is not true.

Child: You can only tell if something is true if you or somebody sees it with their own eyes and ears. That is why there are many people who think things are true, like ghosts or witches, that sort of thing. But you might be wrong so you have to check it first before you say it's true.

Child: It's not true because you say it is, but it might be.

This philosophical dialogue is beginning to explore the concept of truth. Key ideas are starting to emerge. These key ideas might be recorded by the teacher and reflected on further, either at the end of the dialogue or at a future session, for example:

True

- really happened
- think it's true
- you have to check it.

Create a community of enquiry

It helps you ask questions. It shows you there can be many answers to one question [and] it makes you think that everything must have a reason.

(John, aged 10)

Discussion in a community of enquiry is an opportunity to do more than just speaking and listening to others. As Gavin, aged 13, put it: 'Its more than just a talking shop. It's more like a workshop where ideas can be created and shared.' Such a 'workshop' provides opportunities to think deeply, raise questions and investigate ideas and issues of importance. The community of enquiry provides a model, or framework, for dialogue that is:

- serious
- sustained
- systematic

in order to investigate matters of importance.

A community of enquiry is a form of dialogic teaching with a whole class or large group that emphasises critical and creative thinking through questioning and dialogue among children and teachers and among children and children. Researchers have reported striking cognitive gains through this approach in the classroom, including enhancing cognitive and communicative skills (Topping and Trickey 2007; Trickey and Topping 2006). The practice of being in a community of enquiry also helps develop habits of intelligent behaviour, including being:

- *Curious* – through asking open and interesting questions.
- *Collaborative* – through engaging in thoughtful dialogue.
- *Critical* – through giving reasons and evidence.
- *Creative* – through generating and building on ideas.
- *Caring* – through developing awareness of the needs of self and others.

Being curious: getting children to question

A community of enquiry begins by getting children to question a given topic or stimulus. They will find it difficult to ask questions if there is little that is interesting or puzzling about the story or stimulus being used. Children need to be encouraged to question; for example, by being asked:

- What was strange about (what you have heard, read, seen)?
- What was puzzling?
- What was interesting?

Some children feel inhibited in asking questions in front of their peers. As Jude, aged 15, put it: 'Sometimes I want to ask something but I don't feel comfortable to ask because I know that they will all look at me. But if there are others asking it is easier. It starts to get usual and people won't look at me, because I am just doing what everyone does.' One teacher tries to overcome the inhibitions of her young children by telling them they are going to practise being 'brave talkers' and saying that 'brave talkers' ask questions. With practice in an atmosphere of trust the children will tend to ask more questions, better questions and to express themselves in more interesting and experimental ways.

The following are some of the questions raised by a group of 7- to 8-year-olds who had asked if they could discuss God at their next philosophy session in the community of enquiry. The questions reflect the breadth of their vision and imagination:

- Who made God?
- Who is God?
- How was God made? How old is God?
- How did God make the world?
- Why was God made?
- Is God real?
- How did He make us?
- What does Heaven look like?
- Why is God so special?
- Why does God make thunder?
- Why did God make us?

■ Why did God make the devil?

■ Why does God kill us?

■ Why did God make swear words?

(Quoted in Fisher 2006, p. 37)

The questions that children raise can be connected, extended and refined through further discussion. For example, when one class chose as the question for discussion, *What does it mean to be beautiful?*, the teacher asked them what kind of question this was, and received the response, 'an open-ended question' and, 'a philosophical question'. She then asked: 'What is a philosophical question?' 'A question that has no one right answer but many possible answers that might be right or wrong or partially right and partially wrong.' She delved deeper by asking probing questions such as: 'What do *you* mean by beautiful?'; 'Can you be beautiful and ugly?'; 'Is beauty on the inside and outside?'

The unique value of PforC is that it is the only well-researched approach to teaching thinking that focuses specifically on developing children's ability to question and to take responsibility for their own dialogic learning.

Collaborate in thoughtful discussion

For a successful community of enquiry a number of ground rules need to be in place. Children not only take responsibility for the agenda they set but, with assistance from the teacher, they specify the ground rules for discussion.

There is no one set of ground rules that is best for all kinds of dialogue. The following ground rules are characteristic of the kinds of intelligent behaviour (thinking skills) found in successful discussion groups. The ground rules need to be made explicit so that everyone knows what they are. They then need to be practised in small groups as well as in whole-class discussion.

Table 7.1 shows links between characteristic ground rules and relevant thinking skills:

To ensure they take responsibility for the ground rules ask the children to devise their own set of 'rules for good discussion'. Once they have discussed their rules in groups, agreed and recorded them, they can be shared. The teacher can then help the class to produce a final set of ground rules. The agreed rules may probably reflect many of the ground rules for dialogical reasoning outlined above. A suggested maximum number of rules is seven, otherwise the list will be too long to read and remember. This list should be displayed where all can see it. In succeeding lessons these rules can be referred to as 'our rules for talk'. They should be reviewed at regular intervals, and can be altered or developed by general agreement.

Teachers sometimes find it helpful when working with 'difficult' classes to appoint a pupil who finds it difficult to follow the rules as referee in charge of ensuring that others in a group keep to the rules (for example, by stopping the discussion at any point if they see a rule being infringed and reminding the group of the rule).

Research shows how important the agreeing, implementing and reviewing of ground rules is in creating the conditions for successful discussion. One study describes how teaching the

TABLE 7.1 Links between characteristic ground rules and relevant thinking skills

DIALOGIC RULES	THINKING SKILLS
All relevant information is shared	Information processing
Reasons are expected	Reasoning
Challenges are acceptable	Enquiry and reasoning
Alternatives are discussed	Creative thinking
All ideas are valued	Social and emotional learning
The group seeks better understanding	Evaluation

ground rules for effective discussion helped children do better at non-verbal reasoning test problems than control classes who had not been taught rules for discussion (Wegerif 2006). Simply learning how to discuss in reasonable and reflective ways not only develops habits of intelligent behaviour, it improves children's reasoning and problem-solving skills.

The most commonly agreed rules for successful discussion identified by children (sometimes worded differently) are:

- Only one speaks at a time.
- We all listen carefully to others.
- We think before we speak.
- We say what we mean.
- We think about what other people say.
- We give reasons for what we say.
- We can disagree and say 'Why?'.
- We show respect to others.

See p. 163 for an activity about creating ground rules for discussion.

Sessions often begin with a review of the ground rules. Children are reminded that they can stop the discussion if they see any ground rules being broken. At the end of the lesson there is a plenary in which the discussion and ground rules are reviewed, with questions such as:

- Did we have a good discussion today?
- What was good about our discussion?
- What could have been better? How?
- What do we need to remember next time?

Be critical and creative

'I have heard you are a wise man,' said a sultan to Nasruddin. 'Prove it to me. If you cannot prove that you see and know things that no one else can see, I shall have you hanged.' Nasruddin thought briefly about this and said, 'I can see a golden bird in the sky.' The sultan looked up but could not see anything. 'I can see demons within the earth,' said Nasruddin, looking down. The sultan looked down but could see nothing. 'How do you do these things, Nasruddin?' asked the sultan in wonder. 'What is that great power that enables you to see things I cannot?'

'All you need,' replied Nasruddin, 'is fear.'

Critical thinking may be described as the use of reasoning to draw inferences and make deductions (see Chapter 4). For young children it means being challenged to give reasons for opinions. Creative dialogue can be summed up as 'playful talk' which is being playful with ideas, suggesting alternative possibilities and encouraging children to be imaginative in their thinking (see Chapter 3). These dialogic habits need to be modelled by a discussion leader who probes for reasons and engages in playful speculation.

Questions calling for critical thinking include:

- *Asking for reasons*

  We need to give a reason or reasons for our puzzlement and explain what we think and why it seems strange or interesting; for example, by asking:

  - What makes you say that?
  - What reasons do you have?
  - Why do you agree or disagree with X?

- *Probing assumptions*

  Our reasons will be based on other assumptions. We can probe these, for example, by asking:

  - How do you know?
  - Why do you think that?
  - What evidence is there for believing . . .?'

- *Questions calling for judgement*

  We can help them suggest solutions to what is puzzling, to formulate and explore the judgements they make and the implications of what they have said; for example, by asking:

  - What do you conclude from that?
  - What criteria would you use to judge . . .?
  - What follows from that?

Two ways of challenging children to make critical judgements are to get them to categorise ideas and to draw careful distinctions. In creating categories we ask children to draw distinctions between things that are the same and similar in some respects but that we need to keep apart because they do not fit into that category (for a categorisation activity see p. 166). To make a distinction is to identify the property or properties within a specified category or domain in which they differ. There are also borderline cases which can provide fruitful sources of debate and discussion (see p. 167 for a task on drawing distinctions).

Questions calling for creative thinking include:

■ *Generating questions*

It is often helpful to prepare a discussion plan before a dialogue so that you have a range of stimulating questions to help children dig deeper into their thinking (see Fisher (1996) for examples of discussion plans). This also models the questions we want children to be asking.

– What question might we ask about that?

– Why . . .?

– What if . . .?

■ *Comparing and contrasting*

During a dialogue the children will often come up with several different ideas, some related, others not. These ideas need to be questioned. We need to help children see connections, make distinctions, and to clarify their thinking, for example, by asking them to compare and contrast different ideas and assumptions by asking:

– How is X similar to Y?

– Is X the same as Y?

– How is X different from Y?

■ *Hypothesising*

Hypothesising is about thinking what might be possible; for example, by asking:

– Do you have a theory why this might be?

– What does that connect with . . .?

– Supposing . . .?

George Bernard Shaw once said: 'You see things and say, "Why?" But I dream things and say, "Why not?" 'What if animals could speak? What if you woke up one morning and could not see? What if the world ran out of petrol? All these situations involve hypothetical thinking. They create a hypothesis about the world – or a possible world. One of the great abilities of the human mind is to create worlds that are only possible in the imagination. It can be fascinating to wonder what might happen if present circumstances changed in one way or another. Scientific theories begin as hypotheses about the real world. Stories and poetry begin as hypotheses about imagined worlds. Both require creative imagination.

> *Some small boys were hoping to steal Nasruddin's slippers. They pointed to a tree and said, 'Nobody could climb that tree.' 'Any of you could,' said Nasruddin, 'I shall show you.' He took off his slippers, tucked them in his belt and started to climb. 'You won't need your slippers in a tree,' said the boys. 'Oh I might,' said Nasruddin who had sensed what the boys were up to. 'You never know, I might find a road up there.'*

Exercise and expand children's imagination by encouraging them to create as many alternatives as possible (see p. 165 for a 'What if?' activity).

The use of metaphor shows the playfulness characteristic of a creative dialogue, as does the use of humour. In a discussion about wanting things, Danielle, aged 10, plays with the analogy of a ladder. What she says might also apply to the personalising of learning, the open-ended nature of dialogic enquiry and the inner purposes of education which we need to focus on and to constantly redefine:

> If you want something very much you have to think how to get it. It's like you're on a ladder. The ladder is a way of getting to it just a little bit at first and then another little bit. I want lots of things but I don't know what I want at the end of the ladder. Maybe it keeps getter longer and you never get to the end. You can give up or you can keep climbing and see.'

What philosophical enquiry offers is a tried and tested strategy for helping children to apply critical and creative reasoning to stories and other texts.

Be caring – mindful of self and of others

The two sets of attitudes or dispositions which philosophical discussion with children aims to foster are being mindful of self and of others. Both derive from the dialogical nature of the process, developing social skills through cooperative activity. Discussion in a community of enquiry requires the group to develop trust and the ability to cooperate, and to respect the views of others. Lipman calls these aspects 'caring' thinking. Caring thinking involves learning to collaborate with others in a community of enquiry, developing empathy and respect for others. It means being guided by questions such as:

- What do others think?
- Can I understand what they think?
- Can I learn from what they think?

By taking part in a community of enquiry children develop and strengthen what Goleman calls 'emotional intelligence'. Studies show that a youngster's life chances are at least as much affected by emotional intelligence as they are by other aspects of intelligence.

Emotional intelligence includes:

- *Self-awareness*: knowing how/what you are feeling and how it affects you, being realistic about one's abilities.

- *Self-regulation*: handling emotions so that they help the task in hand, being conscientious.

- *Resilience*: sustaining motivation, persevering in the face of setbacks, striving to improve.

- *Empathy*: sensing what other people are feeling, and using that information to help relate to them.

- *Social skills*: reading social situations, using skills to persuade, lead and negotiate.

Philosophical dialogue opens up a space for thinking, for sharing beliefs and fostering understanding. The following excerpt is from a discussion among a group of 9-year-olds on whether it is right for parents to smack their children:

> *Child*: I think Sophie's was a good idea, why smacking children is wrong.
> *Teacher*: What was the idea?
> *Child*: Well, she said it was wrong because smacking you doesn't tell you why it was wrong, it just tells you that if you do it you will get smacked. That means you'll do it again if you can get away with it and not be smacked. But if you are told why it is wrong . . . whatver it is . . . then you are less likely to do it again. Because you know why it is wrong. If you understand the reason . . .'

The teacher seeks the child's explanation of an idea and does not make a judgement on the correctness of the idea. The aim is to enable children to build upon their own and each others' ideas, and to take responsibility for correcting them when necessary. Children are given an arena for the free flow of their views, a space for creativity and dialogue and a voice and choice in deciding the focus and the course of the enquiry.

How does a community of enquiry work in the classroom?

Ideally the group sits in a circle or horseshoe, the aim being that everyone can see everyone else. The following are typical stages in a lesson:

- *Focusing exercise*: for example, discussing learning objectives, agreeing rules for discussion, using a thinking game or relaxation exercise to ensure alert yet relaxed attention.

- *Sharing a stimulus*: a story, poem, picture or other stimulus for creative thinking is presented.

- *Thinking time*: children think of what is strange, interesting or unusual about the stimulus and share their thoughts and questions with a partner.

- *Questioning*: children ask their own (or shared) questions; these are written on a board, then discussed, and one is chosen (or voted for by the children) to begin the enquiry.

- *Discussion*: children are asked to respond, building on each others' ideas through dialogue, with the teacher probing for reasons, examples and alternative viewpoints.

- *Plenary review*: the discussion is reviewed (e.g. using a graphic map), and children reflect on the discussion and what they have learned from it (see the next chapter for more on assessing dialogue).

- *Further activities*: children engage in follow-up activities to further explore the stimulus in creative ways in class or at home.

The following is an excerpt from a community of enquiry with 7- to 8-year-olds using as a stimulus a poem written by one of the children who was inspired by Miroslav Holub's poem 'The Door' (Fisher 2000, p.48):

> Go and open the door,
> Even if there's silence,
> Even if there's nothingness,
> Go and open the door.
> Maybe
> You
> Want to see what nothingness
> Is.
>
> Charlotte, aged 8

Teacher: So can you see nothingness?

[After posing the question the teacher asks the children to think about the question themselves for a minute, then to share their ideas with their partner before opening it up for discussion]

Charlotte: I don't think you can see nothingness – you can't see nothing!

Philip: Even if you open the door and there are no trees only white – you can still see the white.

Tara: You can see something. It may be a picture.

Chelsea: You can see it if you imagine it.

Laura: I don't think people can but maybe animals can.

Craig: Nothing is there; no, you can't see nothing.

Freddie: You mean you can't see anything.

Charlotte: You don't know what nothing is because you don't know what it looks like.

Philip: When you're dead, then in Heaven, Jesus knows what everything is.

Lauren: There's nothingness on the floor because nothing is there.

Craig: There is because there's the carpet.

Teacher: Is there always something there?

Freddie: Under the carpet is dirt – below the dirt you would fall out of the earth and end up in Heaven.

Philip: You couldn't go through the earth because there's molten stuff inside.

Tara: Nothingness means you can't see anything.

Teacher: How would you feel if you couldn't see anything?

Laura: You'd feel cold and scared – might feel scared because it's dark and lonely.

Sarah: Lonely – just on your own, completely on your own.

Craig: You'd be crying and sad. It would be blank, just white with no way out. You'd miss your family.

Charlotte: If it was just nothingness you'd just stay there and keep falling and you'd never get anywhere.

Tara: You'd feel scared.

Philip: It would be cool because you've found a place no one has been in before and you'd be famous. Maybe you could press a magic button and go back to earth.

Chelsea: I agree with what Craig said, you'd feel quite lost and sad because there'd be no one to look after you.

Charlotte: I don't agree with Philip, because what if there was no magic button – you couldn't get out and you wouldn't be famous!

Tara: It would be sad because there would be nothing to see.

Philip: What happens if you could do anything with this world [referring to the nothingness as a separate world] – put it in your pocket then you could go in and out of it when you wanted to.

Lauren: I've often thought in dreams of going into a dark place – I go through a door and there is nothing there. Then I heard a bang and the door closed and the door disappeared and I couldn't get out. Then I'd start crying in my dream and my Mum would come in and I'd wake up.

Charlotte: If you're having a dream and you're not aware you are – that could be nothingness.[1]

During a dialogue children's thinking is stimulated by two kinds of challenge – both internal and external activity of mind. To encourage internal activity of mind, 'thinking time' should be built into any philosophical enquiry, as in this example. The teacher's role is then to help extend and deepen the dialogue through questioning and other dialogic strategies.

Extend dialogue by digging for depth

The following are some teaching strategies to help children to deepen and extend their thinking:

■ *Pause for thought*

Remember 'wait time 1 and 2', by providing at least three seconds of thinking time:

- After you have asked a question, pause to allow pupils time to collect their thoughts.
- After a pupil response, pause to show you are thinking and allowing others to think.

■ *Think–pair–share*

Allow individual thinking time, ask them to discuss their ideas with a partner, then share these in class discussion.

■ *Probe*

Ask 'follow-ups' to probe their understanding (e.g. 'Why?', 'Do you agree?', 'Tell me more', 'Give an example', 'Can you elaborate?', 'How did you arrive at that answer?').

■ *Withhold judgement*

Respond to answers in a non-judgemental fashion to encourage further thinking (e.g. 'Thank you', 'That's interesting', 'Who agrees or disagrees?'). Invite a range of responses (e.g. 'There is not one right answer, think of alternatives').

■ *Play devil's advocate*

Present an alternative point of view and challenge pupils to respond to it (e.g. by saying, 'Do you agree or disagree with this view?', 'Explain why,' 'What are your reasons?').

■ *Encourage further questioning*

Invite pupils to ask questions, or to write down questions that puzzle them. Value any genuine and challenging questions. Display them to show you value them, find time to share and discuss them.

■ *Think about thinking*

Ask pupils to think about their thinking and learning (e.g. 'What thinking have you been doing?', 'What have you found hard?', 'What have you learned?'). These kinds of questions develop what many researchers now believe to be the key to higher order thinking and intelligence – metacognition (for more on metacognition see p. 178).

■ *Encourage children to extend and elaborate*

We extend our thinking through a process of elaboration. Elaboration is shown in the number and quality of different ideas used to add on to the original idea. Elaboration means extending your thinking or what others have said by building on a basic idea; for example, by asking a question that can be asked about any situation, problem or issue: 'Have we considered all factors/issues/problems/questions?', 'What more is there to add?'.

Children get better at adding more to what has been said through practice. For an activity that encourages elaboration on an idea see p. 165 for the 'Thinking chain'.

The following is part of a discussion with 7-year-old children after they had read 'The Cats and the Chapatti' (in Fisher 1999, p.8). They had chosen to answer Anna's question about the story: 'Why did they quarrel?'

Child: There were some animals quarrelling.

Teacher: What were they saying?

Child: 'No you can't', 'Yes you can' . . . that sort of thing.

Child: They were contradicting each other.

Teacher: So a quarrel is like a contradiction?

Child: [after a pause for thought] Yes.

Child: They were quarrelling with each other.

Teacher: Can you quarrel with yourself?

Child: You can't quarrel with yourself. You need to have more than one person.

Child: You can quarrel with yourself. You could punch yourself. Your brain quarrels with you . . . if you want to test yourself.

Child: I disagree with Sarah. You can't quarrel with yourself. You haven't done anything to yourself.

Child: If you punch your leg, it can't say no. Your brain says no.

Teacher: Can animals say 'yes' and 'no'?

Child: No, only people can say 'yes' and 'no'. That's how we are different from animals.

At the end of the discussion the teacher asked children to extend their thinking by discussing what they thought the moral of the story was. Here are some of their replies:

- Don't trust anyone (James).
- Don't fight and quarrel (Andrew).
- Don't be greedy or someone may take what you've got (Ryan).
- Share with other people (Conor).
- Don't fight or quarrel with your friends (Sarah).
- Be kind to everyone (Emily).

It can be useful to record a dialogue for children to discuss later or to take notes of the main ideas and themes. Asking children to take notes during a dialogue can be helpful – though sometimes they find it a distraction.

Philosophical dialogue has no fixed curriculum – it may be applied to conceptual content in any subject area. Some schools have special lessons set aside for a philosophical enquiry, as advocated by Matthew Lipman and his followers. Others try to infuse philosophical enquiry across the curriculum in subjects which naturally require conceptual exploration, such as English literature, religious education and citizenship. It may be applied to children's personal concerns, local concerns or national concerns; issues in fiction and poetry; images on the computer, on TV or film; in pictures, song and social activity. The experience of extending thinking through dialogue enables children to interrogate the world and to apply their thinking in serious and sustained ways. As Jemma, aged 10, said: 'Philosophy can help in all your lessons, no matter what you're learning.' When asked why this was so, she said: 'Because it gets you questioning and wondering why.'

Research from a wide range of studies across the world indicates that Philosophy for Children programmes, when implemented over time, can help raise intelligence and improve children's:

- achievements in academic tests;
- self-esteem and self-concept as thinkers and as learners;
- ability to engage effectively in discussion with others;
- fluency and quality of their questioning;
- the quality of their creative thinking;
- IQ and verbal reasoning.

Project evaluations confirm that students enjoy philosophical discussion and find discussion in a community of enquiry motivating. Teachers claim that philosophical discussion adds a new dimension to their teaching and the way their pupils think. The effects of philosophical discussion extend across the curriculum. Children become better at giving reasons or asking questions, exploring concepts, planning, reasoning, imagining, solving problems, making decisions and judgements the more they practise doing so. It helps children to internalise the habits of intelligent behaviour, enquiry and discussion.

The 'community of enquiry' provides an explicit model and framework for creative dialogue. As Ravi, aged 10, says: 'It can be fun playing with ideas, like thinking impossible things and wondering if they are impossible.' A good dialogue is about wrestling with ideas but also about dancing with them. As Anna, aged 10, put it: 'A good philosophical discussion is like a dance in which you have different partners . . . the music suddenly changes and you have to make up new steps.'

Extend talk for thinking in practice

The following are examples of practical activities to promote creative dialogue within a community of enquiry in the classroom. They may be adapted and developed in different ways. The activities are about helping children to develop habits of intelligent behaviour and the capacity to engage in fruitful dialogue in large groups. The tasks for developing dialogue in large groups presented here offer the following range of activities:

1 Getting children to question.

2 Philosophical questions to discuss.

3 What does it mean?

4 Thinking about telling the truth.

5 Creating the ground rules for discussion.

6 Conceptual enquiry: what is bullying?

7 The three fishes.

8 Thinking chain.

9 What if . . .?

10 Creating categories.

11 Drawing distinctions: lies, rumours and false stories.

12 Discussing borderline cases.

13 Thinking about time.

1 Getting children to question

- Write some question starters on cards, for example: Who . . .?, What . . .?, Where . . .?, When . . .?, Why . . .?, How . . .?, Could . . .?, Should . . .?, What if . . .?, What does . . . mean?

- Divide the class into small groups.

- Read a story with them.

- Ask a volunteer from each group to select a card.

- Each group must formulate a question beginning with the word on the card.

- Groups write them down on large pieces of paper so all can see.

- Discuss the questions and choose one to discuss.

Variations on this include passing the cards around so that all have a turn in asking questions using all the cards. You may well end up with a huge range of questions!

2 Philosophical questions to discuss

The following are a range of philosophical questions to discuss with children:

- Is an apple dead or alive?

- How do you know you are not dreaming at this moment?

- How do you know when something is true or not true?

- Is it right to eat animals?

- What is the difference between pretending and lying?

- What is the difference between a real person and a robot?

- Is there a difference between your mind and your brain?

- Can animals think?

- Is it ever right to tell lies?

- What are the most valuable things in your life?

- If you swapped brains with someone else would you be a different person?

- What is the difference between magic and science?

- What are the most important rights of children?

- What goes on forever? What does forever mean?

- Why did God not make us perfect?

- If you fail does it mean you are a failure? Why?

- What are thoughts? How do they affect us?

- What is evil? Are some people born evil?

- How did the world begin?

- Is it ever right to steal?

- What does it mean to be good? Is it better to be good or happy?

- What happens to you when you die?

- What is a problem? Does every problem have a solution? Why? Give an example.

- Is there only one true religion? Could many religions be true?

- Do you think there is a heaven? Why?

3 What does it mean?

Choose one or more adverts to discuss. Show the advert to children in pairs or small groups. Ask them to discuss:

- What does the advert say? (What are the words or images before them?)

- What is the advert trying to say? (What is its message?)

- What is the advert claiming? (What does it claim is true?)

- What would establish the truth of its claim(s)?

- What is strange, puzzling or misleading about the advert?

Ask students to try to find adverts that use words or pictures in misleading ways.

Ask older students to find philosophically interesting adverts (adverts that contain something puzzling or problematical in their pictures or their use of words).

4 Think about telling the truth

Key question: what is truth?

- Do you think this is a true story? Why?

- What do we mean when we say something is true?

- What do we call something that is not true? What does 'false' mean?

- What is a lie?

- What do we call a story which is not true? What is fiction/a fable/a fairy tale?

- Which character in the story was honest? What does 'honest' mean

- Which character in the story was a liar? What does 'liar' mean?

- Is it better to tell the truth or lies? Why?

- Have you ever told a lie? Can you say when or why?

- Is it ever right to tell a lie? Is it ever wrong to tell the truth?

(For the story 'Mercury and the Axe', and further questions and suggestions on ways of using the story to create a community of enquiry, see Fisher (1999, p.45) and other books in the *Stories for Thinking* series).

5 Creating the ground rules for discussion

- Discuss with children, or ask children to discuss in groups, all the 'talking' words they can think of, such as 'argument, 'discussion' and 'reason'.

- List these words.

- In groups the children then discuss and try to agree on the meaning of each word (with the help of dictionaries and thesauruses).

- They then discuss in groups 'the most important rules that people talking in groups should follow' and are asked to come up with no more than six of these.

- Discuss as a class the different sets of rules and agree on a final list to display in the class-room.

6 Conceptual enquiry: What is bullying?

Bullying

Not bullying

―――――――――――――――――― ――――――――――――――――――

―――――――――――――――――― ――――――――――――――――――

―――――――――――――――――― ――――――――――――――――――

―――――――――――――――――― ――――――――――――――――――

―――――――――――――――――― ――――――――――――――――――

―――――――――――――――――― ――――――――――――――――――

Statements

- Talking to someone
- Play fighting
- Hugging someone
- Calling someone names
- Constantly disagreeing with someone
- Passing notes about someone
- Refusing to speak to someone
- Saying someone's idea is stupid
- Shouting at someone because you are angry
- Not letting someone join in a game
- Putting a criminal in jail
- Pushing in front of someone in a line

(Activity adapted from Golding 2002)

7 The three fishes

The following is a teaching story that, according to tradition, Hussein, grandson of Muhammad, used to tell, and which has been repeated in one version or another for generations.

There were once three fishes who lived in a pond. One was a clever fish, one was a half-clever fish and one was a stupid fish. Life was happy for these fish until one day there came a man – with a net.

The clever fish remembered what he had been told, realised the danger he was in, and thought of a plan. 'There is nowhere to hide in this pool,' he thought, 'so I shall play dead.' He jumped out of the pool, lay on his side at the feet of the fisherman, and held his breath. The fisherman was surprised and, supposing him to be dead, threw the fish back into the water. The second fish asked him what happened. 'Simple,' said the clever fish, 'I played dead and he threw me back.'

So the half-clever fish thought he would do the same. He leapt out of the water at the feet of the fisherman and lay still on his side. But he forgot to hold his breath. The fisherman was surprised to see another jumping fish and threw him into his basket. But he did not close the lid. The half-clever fish summoned all his strength and was able to leap out of the basket and roll back into the water.

The third fish then wanted to know what to do. So the other fish told him exactly what they had done. The stupid fish leapt out of the pool, lay on his side, and held his breath. The fisherman, having lost two fish already, grabbed the stupid fish, not bothering to see whether he was breathing or not, put him in the basket and fastened the lid. When he got home he opened his bag, found the fish was not breathing and fed him to the cat.

- What is strange, interesting or puzzling about this story?
- What lessons do you think it teaches?
- Discuss with others what you think of the story.

8 Thinking chain

One simple way to practise generating ideas is to create a thinking chain. This is a thinking game you play with one or more other people. The rules are simple. One player starts a line of thought or a story and stops whenever they want to, the next must continue the story, stopping wherever they want to, and so on. Players who pause for too long or who cannot continue miss their turn or drop out of the game. In theory of course if we can keep adding creative ideas the story once begun could go on forever!

9 What if . . .?

Choose one of the questions below then trace the reasonable and logical consequences that would follow. You might be sure to think of good, bad and perhaps interesting consequences. Try to list or describe (in a sentence or two each) at least ten consequences.

- What if we could live forever?
- What if there was no petrol in the world?

- What if each home could use the television for only one hour a day?

- What if you woke up one morning and could not see?

- What if rats grew ten times their present size and developed a superior intelligence?

- What if exams and grades were abolished in college?

- What if our pets could talk?

- What if anyone could set up as a doctor?

- What if we never had to sleep?

- What if we could read other people's minds (and they could read ours)?

- What if everybody looked almost exactly alike?

- What if the Earth stopped revolving and the Sun did not rise?

10 Creating categories

Children can be given rules for classifying information (e.g. whether a word is being used as a noun or as a verb). The creating categories strategy, however, challenges students to categorise information by discovering the rules rather than merely memorising them. For example, students may be asked to distinguish phenomena into two categories such as animals and plants, then to research the categories and come up with proposed rules or criteria for each category. Such critical thinking approaches typically result in better understanding than more directive teaching methods.

11 Drawing distinctions: lies, rumours and false stories

Read the following story or ask children to read it in pairs:

One day a man who had been spreading rumours and false stories about Nasruddin came to him and told him he was sorry for what he had done.

'I'll never spread rumours again,' said the man. 'Tell me what I can do to make amends.'
'Nothing,' said Nasruddin.
'There must be something I can do,' insisted the man.
'All right,' said Nasruddin, 'bring me a feather pillow.'
The man soon returned with a feather pillow.
'Now stand in the middle of the street and cut it open,' said Nasruddin.
The man did as was told. The feathers came flying out of the pillow and were soon blown away by the wind. 'Now what?' asked the man.
'Collect all the feathers and put them back in the pillow' said Nasruddin.
'B-but that's impossible,' said the man. 'The feathers are everywhere.'
'So it is with the lies you have told about me,' said Nasruddin. 'They've spread so far and wide, and you cannot do anything about it now.'

- Ask the children if there is anything 'strange, interesting or puzzling' about the story. Discuss their questions or comments.

- Ask them to discuss and draw distinctions between lies, rumours and false stories. Share and list their findings.

12 Discussing borderline cases

Take a contestable concept such as 'friendship' and discuss borderline cases, drawing distinctions between 'a friend' and 'not a friend'. For example, create some statements about friendship and asked students to sort the statements into two piles, one for those they agree with and one for those they disagree with. Each group then compares their decisions with another group, and then with the whole class.

Which of these statements do you agree with and which do you disagree with?

- A friend is someone who is always there to help when things go wrong.

- A friend will always forgive you if you do something wrong.

- Friends are just the people you see every day.

- Friends are people who are the same race and religion as you.

- A friend is someone who does what you say.

- A friend is someone who will never lie to you.

- A friend is a special person you can share secrets with.

- A friend is someone who is loyal to you – no matter what.

13 Thinking about time

Time is one of your most valuable assets, but it is strictly limited. While you cannot physically re-create time, you can waste it or lose a lot of it. Time that is lost never returns, but if you take charge of your time you also take charge of your life.

> *Time is . . .*
> *too fast for those who fear,*
> *too slow for those who wait,*
> *too long for those that grieve,*
> *too short for those who rejoice,*
> *but for those who love,*
> *time is eternity.*
>
> Poem by American poet Henry van Dyke seen on display in a school in Brunei

Ask children for their thoughts, comments or questions about time. Discuss.

Ask them to discuss your own questions – for example:

- How important is 'time'?

- What is 'time' for you?

- Does time sometimes go quickly and sometimes slowly? If so, why? Give examples.

- Does everything change over time?

- Would it be possible to travel in time do you think? Why or why not?

(For more questions and activities on time see Fisher (1996, pp. 103–5.)

Footnote on Philosophy for Children

Philosophy for Children was the brainchild of Matthew Lipman. Originally a professor of philosophy at Columbia University, Lipman was unhappy at what he saw as poor thinking in his students. They seemed to have been encouraged to learn facts and to accept authoritative opinions, but not to think for themselves. He became convinced that something was wrong with the way they had been taught in school when they were younger. He therefore founded the Institute for the Advancement of Philosophy for Children (IAPC) and developed with colleagues a programme called Philosophy for Children, used in more than forty countries around the world. Lipman believes that children are natural philosophers because they view the world with curiosity and wonder. Lipman and his associates have produced a number of novels that provide a model of philosophical enquiry, in that they involve fictional children engaging in argument, debate, discussion and exploratory thinking. For more on Lipman's approach see the IAPC website (http://cehs.montclair.edu/academic/iapc/).

Many resources have been developed in recent years to adapt Matthew Lipman's approach to Philosophy for Children to the needs of children and teachers in the UK. Robert Fisher's *Stories for Thinking* (1996) is one such approach. The aim, through using stories and other kinds of stimulus for philosophical discussion, is to extend discussion and thinking in a community of enquiry in the classroom (see www.sapere.org.uk). See also Fisher 2008a and www.teachingthinking.net.

8

Dialogic Assessment

'I only took the regular course.'

'What was that?' inquired Alice.

'Reeling and Writing, of course, to begin with,' the Mock Turtle replied; 'and then the different branches of Arithmetic–Ambition, Distraction, Uglification, and Derision.'

'I never heard of 'Uglification' Alice ventured to say. 'What is it?'

The Gryphon lifted up both its paws in surprise. 'What! Never heard of uglifying!' it exclaimed. 'You know what to beautify is, I suppose?'

'Yes,' said Alice doubtfully: 'it means–to–make–anything–prettier.'

'Well, then,' the Gryphon went on, 'if you don't know what to uglify is, you ARE a simpleton.'

'What else had you to learn?'

'Well, there was Mystery,' the Mock Turtle replied, counting off the subjects on his flappers '– Mystery, ancient and modern, with Seaography: then Drawling – the Drawling-master was an old conger-eel, that used to come once a week: *he* taught us Drawling, Stretching, and Fainting in Coils.'

(From Lewis Carroll, *Alice's Adventures in Wonderland*)

This chapter explores ways of engaging children in dialogue to help improve their understanding of their learning and of themselves as learners. Children's learning is not located in their writing or other work that they do in their books. It takes place in their heads, and the best evidence of their learning is to be found in their ability to talk it through.

In the past, assessment of children's learning was thought simply to be a matter of giving them marks or grades. The teacher's role was to assess what children got right or wrong. Sometimes teachers would add a comment to their marks, such as: 'Must try harder', to which a child once responded: 'Try hard to do what?' and a friend added: 'Try hard to leave school I think.'

In recent years teachers have developed more dialogic approaches, including discussing with children what they had learnt and what they might need to do to become better learners. Research by Black and Wiliam (1998) showed that children who had these more dialogic teachers achieved greater success in future learning tasks than those who had simply been given marks or grades.

Research shows that responding to children's work with a diet of marks does not in itself improve learning. Children are best helped when they are not distracted from their work by focusing on the marks given. Teachers who replace the giving of marks with evaluative comments that focus on what is being learned often find that children value their comments and use them to help improve their work. Even better results came when teachers combined written comments with dialogue about learning. The aim of such dialogue is not just to give children critical and creative feedback on their work but to enable them to identify what they need to do to improve the outcomes of their learning. Dialogic assessment is talk about learning that seeks to move children's thinking from literal or factual levels to the evaluative and metacognitive. Table 8.1 illustrates these levels of thinking.

TABLE 8.1 Children's levels of thinking

Dialogue about learning can be:

Literal or factual – about their marks or grades, what they got right or wrong

Critical – analysing why they got their marks or grades, or their answers right or wrong

Creative – discussing what the learner might try to do to improve

Evaluative – assessing their own learning outcomes, performance and next steps

Metacognitive – developing childen's understanding of themselves as thinkers and learners

Dialogic assessment shifts the focus from competitive and summative judgements towards helping children in the formative process of learning. Children's learning is not best motivated by offering rewards, such as grades or merits. If learning is seen as a competition children soon realise that there will be losers as well as winners. Those with a track record as losers will see little point in trying. If the aim is to motivate children's effort in learning, the type of feedback they receive is crucial. It needs to be dialogic. They must be encouraged to think about and respond to comments made and be helped to understand what they need to do to improve.

Dweck's research (2000, 2006) has shown that a focus on marks and grades draws attention to children's 'ability' rather than to the importance of their effort. This damages the self-esteem of low achievers and leads high achievers to be reluctant to take risks as failure may damage their reputation. Feedback that focuses on success in learning and identifies the next steps in this process encourages children to believe that they can improve, and better motivates their efforts. When asked why he thought his dialogic teacher was good, a child said: 'My teacher wants to know what I think, not just whether I've got the right answer!'

The following are stages in a dialogic approach to assessment for learning discussed in this chapter:

1 Reviewing outcomes
2 Reflecting on progress
3 Receiving critical feedback
4 Setting learning goals
5 Assessing others
6 Self-assessment and awareness (developing metacognition)

7   Assessing dialogue

8   Dialogic assessment in practice

Children will only achieve a learning goal if they understand the objective and can assess what they need to do to reach it. So self-assessment is an essential part of dialogic learning. In practice peer assessment is important as a prerequisite to self-assessment. Peer assessment is particularly valuable because when in dialogue with each other children often explain what they say in more sharply focused language and reinforce their own learning by trying to teach and assess their peers.

Reviewing outcomes

It is not the strongest of the species that survive, nor the most intelligent, but the ones most responsive to change.

(Charles Darwin, *On the Origin of Species*)

The process of review means looking back over one's experience and thinking about what has gone well, what could have been done better and what, if anything, was learned from the experience. It is about not just reviewing actions and outcomes but about being metacognitive by helping children to think about their own thinking and learning and how they could think better and learn more.

Questions within a review can be used to explore both the plus points and the potential problems in a learning task. These include:

■   What has been achieved so far? What are the plus points, the positives, the progress made?

■   What if you are stuck? What are the obstacles to your learning and how might you overcome them?

The process of review builds in thinking time about what children have been learning, both during and after a task has been completed, and involves discussing what they are learning and what they find difficult; for example, by:

■   *Reviewing the learning objectives*: What are you trying to learn? What are you hoping to achieve? What will count as success?

■   *Reviewing what has happened or is happening*: Explain what you did/are doing. What do you intend to do next? Why?

■   *Reviewing the methods used*: What methods are you using? What problems have you found? Could your methods be improved?

■   *Reviewing the outcomes so far*: What are the outcomes so far? Are you getting the results you want? Why?

See p. 185 for an activity to encourage children to discuss the assessment of others' needs.

Children need to understand that they can fail. They also need to develop the strength and resilience to overcome failure and to recognise that some problems cannot be solved easily. If some tasks seem too much to achieve, do they know where to get help or advice? On p. 186 there is an activity that presents a famous example of someone faced with something that seemed easy but which proved impossible to do. The question it poses is one that children may sometimes need to consider: *Is this a possible or impossible task? Why?*

Reflecting on progress

Walking home one day, Nasruddin thought he would take a short cut through the woods. 'Why,' he asked himself, 'should I tread the dusty road when I could be wandering through a wood, listening to the birds and enjoying Nature? This is one of those rare days of sunshine and good fortune!' So saying he plunged into the wood. He had not gone far, however, when he fell into a large hole. He lay there, at the bottom of the hole, reflecting on his progress. 'It is not such a lucky day after all,' he thought. 'So it is just as well that I took this short cut. If things like this can happen in a beautiful setting, just think what might have befallen me on that dusty highway.'

Some people are positive about themselves. They have the attitude: 'I am good at learning, remembering and understanding things.' They are curious and have the confidence to find answers for themselves. They are able to cope with failure and frustration. They do their best when faced with challenges and this makes them successful learners. Others feel inadequate as learners. They lack confidence in themselves and in their ability to succeed. They expect to fail and to find things difficult. When they make mistakes this confirms their sense of failure. Are your children positive or negative learners?

Positive and negative learners

Being positive or negative about learning is not related to intelligence, but is a way of viewing oneself and one's ability to do things. All individuals have elements of positive and negative feelings about themselves, but these attitudes of mind can be changed. People can influence and change the way they and others feel about themselves if they are encouraged to do so.

Positive learners persist in the face of difficulties and obstacles whereas negative learners tend to avoid challenge and give up easily. Positive learners are independent and self-motivated whereas negative learners tend to rely on others for guidance and approval. Positive learners are not afraid of new and challenging experiences whereas negative learners prefer to repeat what they know they can do and will not take risks.

Table 8.2 shows some characteristics of positive and negative attitudes to learning.

Discuss this list with the children and ask them to assess what kind of learners they think they are – and what, if anything, they might do about it.

TABLE 8.2 Positive and negative attitudes to learning

POSITIVE LEARNERS	NEGATIVE LEARNERS
Are willing to try hard tasks	Are unwilling to face challenges
View problems as challenges	View problems as 'tests' of ability
Accept failure without excuses	Are quick to offer excuses for failure
Are flexible in approach, try other ways	Are rigid in their approach and give up easily
Are self-motivated to learn	Are dependent on approval from others
Want to achieve learning goals	Want to look good
Have a positive view of their competence	Are negative about themselves
Have a positive view of learning	Are negative about learning

Praise

Confidence and positive feelings grow through praise, if that praise is genuine and specific. Children need others to tell them what they have done well because they may have forgotten or not know what they have done well. They need others to help them recognise their own progress and they need to be reminded of it. However, the value of such praise has much to do with its focus.

Dweck's research found that students who received praise about their intelligence often adopted a fixed mindset. They rejected a challenging task they could learn from, instead selecting the task that would make them look clever. When they found work difficult and made errors, they lost confidence in their ability, thought they were less smart and ended up performing poorly. Students who were praised for their effort and the specifics of what made their work successful entered a growth mindset. They wanted challenge, and maintained their confidence and enjoyment in the face of difficulty. These students ended up performing far better in both academic and intelligence tests.

Praising the processes of their learning (e.g. their effort, the strategies they used, their concentration, the choices they made) and their persistence helped them to remain motivated, confident and effective. A growth mindset motivates children to engage in learning and to learn more effectively.

To ensure progress in the process of learning children need to:

■ go forward in small steps
■ set targets to achieve on the way
■ keep long-term aims in mind
■ persevere with what is important
■ review progress and end results.

Questions to review progress

Questions that children can ask themselves in reviewing their progress are given in Table 8.3.

Reviewing children's achievements, progress and future goals can be done daily, weekly, or over longer periods of time. Plenaries or mini-reviews can take place at different points during any lesson or at the end of the lesson. Many schools also set aside time each term to engage children in a long-term dialogic review, for example, in a one-to-one interview which also involves parents or carers.

TABLE 8.3 Questions for children to ask and discuss in reviewing their progress

QUESTION TO ASK	PURPOSE OF ASKING THE QUESTION IS TO
'How hard have I tried?'	assess your effort
'What have I learnt?'	assess your learning
'What have I achieved?'	focus on your achievement
'What do I feel good about/proud of?'	identify reasons to feel positive
'What do I like doing/learning?'	think about your preferences
'What do I do well?'	be aware of your strengths
'What do I find hard?'	be aware of difficulties and problems
'What don't I know/understand?'	identify any obstacles to learning
'What do I want to be able to do/improve/learn?'	plan and set targets for the future
'What help do I need?'	be aware of any help that is required
'What do I think of myself as a learner?'	assessing myself as a learner (see below)

Recording achievement

We want children to discuss and record their successes in learning because this encourages optimism and values their effort. Children can also be asked to record in writing their achievements and progress (see p. 186 for a suggested approach to this) or to keep a 'talk log'. A 'talk log' encourages children to reflect on their participation in dialogic activities by making brief notes – for example, on their contributions to discussion, the ideas of others, areas of strength and things to improve on. Talk partners can also support each other by recording each other's achievement; for example, by giving a 'first mark' to a piece of work. As Melanie, aged 10, said: 'If you are getting it wrong it is good to have a friend to put you right.'

Receiving critical feedback

Children need to have dialogic feedback from a range of partners – teachers, friends, others in the group, older peers, teaching assistants, parents and carers. Getting feedback can be a painful process, particularly for vulnerable learners, so advice on giving and receiving feedback is important. Children are often better at receiving critical, creative and evaluative feedback when they have learned how best to help and give feedback to others (see section on 'Learning partners' below).

Discuss with children the value of having 'critical friends' in learning and in life. Share with them times when critical feedback has been important to you. Discuss how best to benefit from the feedback and advice given by others. Discuss the following principles of feedback:

- Seek advice from people you trust and respect.
- Be honest and open in discussing work.
- Face-to-face feedback is best, however difficult it may be.
- Be prepared to ask questions – Who? When? Why? How? What?
- Listen carefully to the answers and comments you receive.
- Focus on specific issues you want to know about.
- Keep an open mind; don't be quick to argue or to dismiss what others say.
- Admit possible errors, avoid always making excuses, remember no one is perfect.
- Do not resent criticism; accept your shortcomings if you want to improve.
- Assess their advice, judge their evidence – accept advice but reject what is not right.

See p. 187 for a range of questions about giving and receiving feedback and advice on learning for children to discuss.

Setting learning goals

One day, Nasruddin fell asleep as he was riding along the road on his little grey donkey. Seeing the chance for a joke several boys crept up behind him and took Nasruddin's saddlebag from the donkey's back. Then they waited to see what would happen.

When Nasruddin arrived at his door he dismounted and reached for his bag. It wasn't there. He rubbed his eyes and looked again. Looking round he saw the boys staring at him. 'Boys!' he shouted, 'my saddlebag is gone. If you don't bring it back to me, I know what I'll do . . .' The boys looked at each other in dismay, wondering what Nasruddin would do. Suddenly their joke had become a serious matter. Very soon they brought the missing bag back to Nasruddin. One said, 'Now please tell us what it was you were going to do if we did not return the bag?'

'Oh,' said Nasruddin smiling, 'I have an old carpet at home. If you had not returned the saddlebag I would have made a new one.'

Successful learners set their own goals and can discuss what they want to achieve. If they find this hard to do they may need help in planning their goals. But as the pioneer of nursery education Maria Montessori used to say, we should not do for a child what they can do for themselves. A dialogic teacher will encourage children to set their own learning goals and try to find all the possibilities in a learning situation, not just the one right answer, as in this excerpt of dialogue from a maths lesson:

Teacher: Is this right?

Child: Yes, I think so.

Teacher: Are you sure?

Child: I worked it out and then I checked it.

Teacher: So it's the right answer? [Child nodded] The one and only?

Child: Yes. No. I don't know. Well, maybe there could be other right answers.
[Pause while the child thought] Yes, I can see another one.

Teacher: Is that it now?

Child: There could be more. I'll see if I can find them.

Teacher: When will you stop?

Child: When I can't find any more.

Teacher: You'll need to convince me there can't be any more!

Dialogic assessment is about helping children develop positive attitudes to learning how to learn. In so doing we help children to focus on what is important for them to think, learn and do, and to take responsibility for their own learning. Through discussion they can be helped to set long-term learning goals or targets, say for a year, five years' or ten years' time, or short-term targets for a learning day, week or month (see p. 187 for an activity that asks them to discuss their own action plan and learning targets).

Assessing others: discuss criteria and reasons for making judgements

We need to make clear the criteria by which things are judged and invite children to discuss, identify and define the criteria for judgement themselves, particularly if they are being asked to assess others. They will find it easier to assess others than to assess themselves and the skills of self-assessment are first developed by showing them how to assess others. For example, show them two pieces of work done by others (anonymous) and ask them to assess the work with a partner to decide which is better and why. Their descriptions of what is good may be used to identify the criteria which they are using to make their judgements.

Criteria are implicit in all judgements and decisions we make. What we need to do with children is to help make explicit the criteria against which they can assess others and by which to assess themselves. With primary pupils we begin by involving students in discussing the work and by constructing with them criteria by which to judge any piece of work.

Discuss with children whether they know what a criterion for judgement is (a criterion is a standard we use to assess what we have thought/done, evaluate the process and judge the outcome). Discuss different kinds of criteria, including:

■ a single criterion that is a necessary or categorical condition, for example, the objective that the words in a piece of work must be correctly spelt;

- one of a number of criteria, some or all of which may be sufficient; for example, 'these are the criteria for a successful project . . .';

- aims that we aspire to, that are desirable but are a matter of degree; for example, improving grades in a test (a comparative standard that is open to interpretation).

In other words, criteria can be single or plural, absolute or comparative standards by which we judge things. Record the criteria they identify and discuss with older children whether they are necessary, sufficient or desirable conditions. A useful tool for dialogic assessment is a 'marking ladder' used by many teachers which shows the success criteria for the task and has columns for the child's self-assessment, their partner's assessment and the teacher's evaluation.

Discuss what makes a good learning partner

Learning partners can help children assess and improve their work. Discuss with children what makes a good response partner. Discuss and agree a set of criteria by which to judge if someone is a good response partner. A class of 9-year-olds, for example, agreed on the following three golden rules for dialogic feedback with their learning partner:

- respect your partner's work, no 'put-downs'

- find good things to say about the work

- suggest how the work can be improved.

The teacher wanted the feedback from response partners to be more specifically related to learning, so she asked them how suggestions should be worded and whether the suggestions should be related to the learning objectives of the lesson. After discussion with the teacher they added to this list the criteria that:

- suggestions should be framed in positive words

- suggestions should be to do with the learning objectives.

For more on response partners see p. 190.

Help them to ask open questions

When children are helping to assess the work of others they need help in knowing what kinds of questions to ask; for example, open or Socratic questions that:

- Assess awareness of learning (What have you learnt? What have you found out? What did you find hard? What did you do well? What do you need to learn/do next?).

- Probe attitudes and feelings (What do you like doing/learning? What do you feel good/not good about . . .? What do you feel proud of?).

- Encourage target-setting (What do you need to do better? What would help you? What are your targets?).

Discuss these questions with children and invite them to suggest how best to give dialogic help to others. Here a teacher asks a 10-year-old what advice he would give to help a younger child become a good writer:

> *Teacher*: What do you think is the most important thing to make you a good writer?
>
> *Child*: Read it through and get rid of the boring bits.
>
> *Teacher*: So, what sort of bits are boring?
>
> *Child*: Well I suppose the bits where nothing happens.
>
> *Teacher*: Like what?
>
> *Child*: Well, what their names are and that.
>
> *Teacher*: So it doesn't matter if you don't know who is who?
>
> *Child*: Well it's better if you sort of find out from what's happening, you know, when people shout at them and that sort of thing, in the story.
>
> *Teacher*: Right, so finding out about the characters from what happens, instead of just being told?
>
> *Child*: Yes. And the other thing in good stories is check it all makes sense, kind of runs smoothly.
>
> *Teacher*: How do you do that?
>
> *Child*: Reading it to someone, or just telling it while you're still working on it.
>
> *Teacher*: Which is more useful?
>
> *Child*: It depends where you've got to. Telling it helps you check it's a good story. Reading it out loud tells you whether it works. Actually, someone else reading it out loud is best. Then you can hear what you've written.

In any dialogue there are key moments when the teacher chooses either to simply accept what a child says and leave it at that, or to probe further to support or challenge the child's thinking.

The test of a good dialogue with children is whether the teacher has listened to what children say and also tried to probe their thinking further. It is the probing that makes dialogue about learning better than simply writing or making a comment.

Self-assessment and awareness: developing metacognition

Self-assessment can be built into every lesson, for example, by asking after a lesson, or period of study, children to discuss and to assess:

- What they know (or understand).
- What they think they know.
- What they do not know (or confuses them) about the topic of study.

This will help them to identify what they have learnt and need to learn. It also helps to develop metacognition, that is, the awareness of themselves as thinkers and learners.

Metacognition (self-awareness) is about the ability to understand and relate to oneself. It is probably the most important aspect of human intelligence, since it is linked to the processing of all other forms of intelligence. It is the 'me' in cognition. It is the access we have to our own thoughts and emotions, to what we think and feel, and why we do things.

The following activities can help in developing metacognitive awareness:

- Keeping a personal diary or journal
- Planning how to use time
- Predicting what you will be able to do well or have difficulty with
- Discussing and understanding your feelings and moods
- Recognising who you are like or unlike (see below)
- Setting and achieving personal goals
- Reviewing and evaluating what you have done.

If we can help children bring the process of learning to a conscious level, they will be more aware of their own thought processes and have more control or mastery over the organisation of their learning.

Researchers have identified a number of metacognitive strategies that pupils should be taught if they are to become successful and independent learners. These involve the learner:

- Asking questions (e.g. 'What is the problem?').
- Planning (e.g. 'What do I need to do?').
- Monitoring (e.g. 'How am I doing?').
- Checking (e.g. 'Is it going to plan?').
- Revising (e.g. 'What do I need to change?').
- Self-testing (e.g. 'How can I test it to see if it has worked?').

These strategies are best developed through dialogue with others. It is through 'learning conversations' with teachers or with other students that such strategies are learnt and understood. These conversations are particularly effective when carried out in pairs or groups where different ways of interpreting a learning experience can be explored to mutual benefit. Adults, especially teachers, can play a key role in encouraging this metacognitive awareness in children through asking pupils to explain the successes and difficulties they have had with problems. Such discussion of the thinking and problem-solving processes that children engage in is what researchers have called 'meta-learning'.

Metacognition involves being conscious about our thinking, so that we can describe what kind of thinking or thinking skill we are using. For example, the skill being used might be to do with:

- *Checking information*: 'I am going to check whether this information is true'.
- *Being critical*: 'I am going to give reasons for what I believe'.
- *Being creative*: 'I am going to think creatively and use my imagination'.
- *Questioning*: 'I am going to question this'.

- *Decision-making*: 'I am going to think about the advantages and disadvantages before I decide'.

- *Evaluating*: 'I am going to evaluate how successful I was in achieving my goal'.

Being metacognitive means children manage their own thinking. They manage it by being thoughtful before they start, monitoring and correcting while they are doing it and reviewing what they have done when they have finished. Being in control of their thinking means being able to consciously attend to not only what they are doing but how they are thinking. They know they are exercising control over our thinking when they direct their thinking in particular ways; for example, when they say: 'I must take more care', 'I must change my plan' or 'How do I know this information is true?'

Metacognitive skills develop with age but they also develop through practice, and they show themselves in different levels of awareness.

Levels of awareness

- *Tacit use*: Children make decisions without really thinking about them.

- *Aware use*: Children become consciously aware of a strategy or decision-making process.

- *Strategic use*: Children organise their thinking by selecting strategies for decision-making.

- *Reflective use*: Children reflect on thinking before, during and after the process, pondering on progress and how to improve.

Posting a list of metacognitive questions on the wall can help to remind children of the sorts of questions they can ask themselves and discuss with others.

Teachers were encouraged to display some metacognitive prompts to thinking in every class. The questions teachers chose to display varied in each class. Questions on display included:

- What have you learnt today?

- What have you found hard today?

- How can you apply what you have learnt?

- What could you have done better?

- What do you want to learn tomorrow?

- What helps you to learn?

Think books: creating a space for thinking about learning

Many teachers encourage their students to keep journals, learning logs or 'think books' as learning diaries in which to record their questions, observations and feelings about what has been taught, learnt or discussed. Children need help in keeping and learning from such journals. Questions such as those above can help to focus their responses. Their journals can be made interactive, with the teacher or a chosen response partner making a written response to journal entries. Or children may prefer their journals to be private, so that they can feel free to record their true feelings and observations about what they have learnt and about themselves as learners.

The following is an example of the guidance offered to a primary class by a teacher when introducing 'think books' for the first time:[1]

Think books help us to think about:

■ How we think.

■ How we learn.

■ Why we don't understand and what we are doing about it.

■ And explain our thinking – why do we think this. . . .

Think books help us to remember that:

■ We are thinking and learning people.

■ We need to be honest about our successes.

■ We don't need to get stressed if we get it wrong or it is hard – we need to think 'why?' and do something about it!

I can write in my think book:

■ What I have learnt that is new.

■ What I have learnt better.

■ Something I am learning about explained in my own words to show that I understand.

■ New words and what they mean.

■ My best thinking of the day and why I think it is my best thinking.

■ How I could improve my thinking.

I can also write about my:

■ Thoughts.

■ Feelings.

■ Questions.

■ Confusions.

■ Worries.

■ And 'WOW – GOT IT' moments in my thinking and learning.

Figure 8.1 is a page from a 'think book' by a special needs child reflecting on himself as a learner, which provided a useful basis for further discussion with the teacher.

The process of dialogic assessment is an ideal means for developing these important metacognitive functions related to learning:

■ *Inner meaning*: Having a sense of purpose about learning, and knowing the reasons, the value and significance of learning activities.

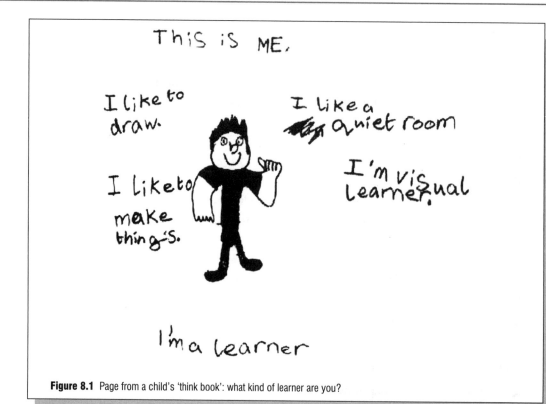

Figure 8.1 Page from a child's 'think book': what kind of learner are you?

- *Self-regulation*: Developing the need to think about and plan their work, encouraging self-control and personal responsibility in learning.

- *Feelings of competence*: Feeling confident about learning, knowing what you can do and how to get help.

- *Feelings of challenge*: Being self-aware, knowing how to deal with challenge, difficulty and failure.

- *Communicating*: Developing the ability to communicate, to share thoughts through dialogue, writing and creative expression.

- *Setting targets*: Setting personal goals or learning objectives to aim for, having high but realistic expectations.

- *Being aware of self-change*: Knowing that you can change, gaining feedback on learning and identifying achievements.

Assessing dialogue

A good discussion is more than just talking and listening . . . it's when you learn something.

(Paul, aged 10)

Involve children in assessing the quality of dialogue in the classroom. Ask them to identify success criteria by which to judge the qualities of a dialogue. For example, if dialogue is to be possible, the people involved need to listen and respond. For dialogue to be sustained, engagement and participation are needed. When dialogue is good, the participants will show dialogic skills and gains in understanding, and evidence through what they say and do that dialogic learning is happening.

The framework for assessing dialogue shown in Table 8.4 lists success criteria with a description of evidence of these different levels of engagement. The framework can form the basis of an assessment record or as a stimulus for discussion with children.

TABLE 8.4 A framework for assessing dialogue

SUCCESS CRITERIA	EVIDENCE	LEARNING BEHAVIOURS
Listening	Focuses and pays attention to what is said	Listening to each other and looking at who is speaking
Responding	Responds to the dialogue by speaking and listening	Some spoken contribution or active listening with use of facial expression or movement, such as nodding, in response to other speakers
Engagement	Shows consistent attention and interest in the dialogue	Consistently responding to others' contributions and showing interest in the dialogue, though not necessarily saying much
Participation	Engages in sharing, turn-taking and contributing to dialogue	Makes extended contributions, elaborating on what others say or putting other points of view, and giving more than one-word answers
Dialogic skills	Displays ability to actively listen, question, communicate, reason, extend ideas and collaborate in dialogue with others	Includes making eye contact, taking turns, speaking audibly and fluently, making good use of language, asking relevant questions, using persuasive argument, presenting exploratory ideas, giving good reasons and evidence, challenging others, building on ideas and sustaining the dialogue
Understanding	Develops knowledge, concepts or understanding through dialogue, is able to judge and assess the quality of dialogue	Able to identify how knowledge, ideas and concepts have been developed by dialogue, able to judge and assess quality of dialogue and their contributions to it, and identify how it could be improved

Dialogic assessment should be integrated with other records and feature in day-to-day lesson planning. It is about listening to, thinking about and responding to what individual children are doing, saying and learning.

Summary of key principles

The key messages of this chapter which reflect the main messages of research into effective assessment for learning are:

1　Make thinking about learning explicit.

2　Engage learners in dialogue about their learning.

3　Help learners to be clear about what successful learning means.

4　Involve learners in peer and self-assessment.

5　Develop learners' self-awareness through dialogue and assessment of learning.

The crucial indicator of success in dialogic assessment is the quality of the pupils' contributions. If children are to be helped to progress as learners they must participate in sustained and reasoned discussion about their learning, which means that they should be expressing themselves in fully formed sentences using such words as 'think' and 'because', not merely giving answers as short phrases or single words. The following strategies aim to help children to practise putting their thoughts on learning into words they can share with others.

Dialogic assessment in practice

The following are examples of activities that may be used to develop practice in dialogic assessment. The activities are about helping children engage in dialogue about their own learning in order to improve their ability to learn. It is about helping them to take responsibility for their own learning and to build confidence in their capacity to learn and assess learning through dialogue with others.

The dialogic assessment tasks presented here offer ways to stimulate dialogue through the following strategies:

1　Discuss assessments given by others.

2　Is this a possible or impossible task?

3　Record achievement.

4　Discuss your success.

5　Discuss how to advise others.

6　Discuss action plan and targets.

7　Discuss goals, intended outcomes and criteria for success.

8　Discuss thinking and learning vocabulary.

9 Discuss the purpose and value of study.

10 Discuss how you have learned.

1 Discuss assessments given by others

Share and discuss examples of people assessing the needs of others, as in the following story:

One day, when Nasruddin emerged form the mosque after prayers, a beggar stopped him and ask for alms. Nasruddin asked, 'Are you extravagant?'

'Yes,' replied the beggar.

'Do you like sitting around drinking coffee and smoking?' asked Nasruddin.

'Yes,' replied the beggar.

'I suppose you like to go to the baths everyday?' asked Nasruddin.

'Yes,' replied the beggar.

'. . . And maybe amuse yourself, even, by drinking with friends?' asked Nasruddin.

'Yes I like all those things,' replied the beggar.

'Tut, tut,' said Nasruddin, and gave him a gold piece.

A few yards further on another beggar who had overheard the conversation begged for alms also.

'Are you extravagant?' asked Nasruddin.

'No,' replied second beggar.

'Do you like sitting around drinking coffee and smoking?' asked Nasruddin.

'No,' replied second beggar.

'I suppose you like to go to the baths everyday?' asked Nasruddin.

'No,' replied second beggar.

'. . . And maybe amuse yourself, even, by drinking with friends?' asked Nasruddin.

'No, I want to only live simply and to pray,' replied second beggar. Whereupon the Nasruddin gave him a small copper coin.

'But why,' wailed second beggar, 'do you give me, an economical and pious man, a penny, when you give that extravagant fellow a gold coin?'

'Ah, my friend,' replied Nasruddin, 'his needs are greater than yours.'

Share this story with the children and discuss questions that arise from it, such as:

■ Was Nasruddin right or wrong in what he said or did?

■ How is it best to assess what other people need?

■ How should people assess what you need?

2 Is this a possible or impossible task?

This story of 'Sissa and the Chessboard' was first recorded by the writer Ibn Kallikan in 1256 CE.

> *According to an old tradition the first person to invent chess was an Indian named Sissa ben Dahir. He presented the game to King Shirhan as an excellent means to train people in thinking about strategies for winning wars. The king was so pleased with the game that he asked Sissa what reward he would like for inventing chess.*
>
> *'Your Majesty,' said Sissa. 'All I ask is one grain of wheat to be placed on the first square of the chessboard, two grains of wheat on the second square, four grains on the third square, eight on the fourth and so on. All I want are the grains of wheat that will cover all sixty-four squares of the board, with each square having twice the number of grains as the previous one.'*
>
> *'Is that all you wish, Sissa, you fool?' exclaimed the astonished king.*

Discuss with the children:

- How many grains of wheat did Sissa require?[2]

- Was it an impossible task? Could the king have provided that much grain?

- This is an old teaching story. What moral or lesson do you think it is trying to teach?

3 Record achievement

Ask children to discuss with a partner and complete a record of achievement, to help them to be a positive learner and identify important elements in their progress as learners. Ask them to review their achievements over a day, week, or a longer period of time.

When they have discussed and completed their record they should sign and date it and keep it for future reference and review.

1   *What things are you pleased about?*

2   *What have you done well?*

3   *What have you worked hard on to improve?*

4   *Who or what has helped you?*

5   *What is your next target or goal?*

Signed . . . .   Date . . . .

4 Discuss your success

Think about and discuss answers to these questions with your partner. Keep this list and look at it or add to it from time to time. Practise being a positive thinker.

My greatest success was when . . . .

I am good at . . . .

I have helped others by ....

The best decision I ever made was ....

What I like learning most was ....

Something I recently learnt to do was ....

My proudest moment was when ....

The most difficult thing I have ever done is ....

The bravest thing I have ever done is ....

5 Discuss how to advise others

Discuss with children, or ask children to discuss the following questions about the best way to help and advise others and give them dialogic feedback on their work:

- Do you need to trust and respect people giving advice to others? What does this mean?
- Should you always be honest and open with them about their work?
- Is face-to-face discussion, or written comments on work, the best way to help others?
- What questions should you ask others about their work?
- Does someone who helps others need to be a good listener? What does this mean?
- Is it best to focus on specific issues in a piece of work you want to help with or just give a general comment?
- Is it good to encourage the other person to say things? Why?
- Is it easy to admit errors? Should you? What helps with this?
- Is any piece of work perfect?
- Is advice always good? What is good advice?

6 Discuss action plan and targets

Ask children to think about and discuss plans and targets with their partner, trying to answer questions like:

1 *What are my plans for the future?*

2 *What do I want to try to achieve?*

3 *What do I want to try hard to improve?*

4 *What help will I need?*

5 *What are my next targets?*

Signed .... Date ....

Setting targets or goals for the future is an important part of success in learning and in life. But setting targets and goals is not easy. Ask the children to try to make them:

- simple
- specific
- short-term.

Ask the children to discuss what they want to achieve today, tomorrow, by the end of the week. When they have decided what their achievements might be ask them to write them down to keep and review again sometime in the future.

What I want to achieve today is . . . .

What I want to achieve tomorrow is . . . .

What I want to achieve by the end of the week is . . . .

7 Discuss goals, intended outcomes and criteria for success

In any learning task the students can be invited to review what they want to achieve.
Choose a topic of study and ask students to identify the task and goals (aims) of learning. Ask them also to discuss the goal, intended outcome(s) and to specify criteria for success. The following chart is one way of recording a review of personal goals:

- *Topic*:
- *Task*:
- *Goals*: What am I trying to achieve?
- *Outcomes*: What am I going to do?
- *Criteria*: How will I know if I am successful?

8 Discuss thinking and learning vocabulary

We need to engage students in dialogue about their thinking and learning. Invite them to discuss keywords and concepts related to their study with their learning partners. Introduce them to the vocabulary to talk about thinking and learning. Table 8.5 lists some thinking words to discuss with students aged between 5 and 14.

9 Discuss the purpose and value of study

Whatever your children are studying, ask them to think about the possible reasons for studying this subject or topic and to discuss what purpose and value it has with their partners. They should record what they and others think, as in the chart below:

TABLE 8.5 Thinking words

abstract – concrete
accept – reject
agree – disagree
analogy – metaphor
analysis – classification
argue – persuade
argument – quarrel
assess – evaluate
assumption (implicit) –
   assertion
authority – plausibility of
   evidence
brain – mind
cause – effect
cause/effect relationships
claim – suggest
clarify – confuse
classify – category
clear – ambiguous
   (vague/imprecise)
compare – contrast
concepts (clear/fuzzy)
consistent – circular argument
consistent – inconsistent
content – context
criteria (criterion) – judgement
data – information
dilemma – compromise
distinctions – similarities
empathy – emotional
   intelligence
evidence – example
example – counter-example
explain – justify
explicit – implicit
fact – opinion
fair – unfair
fallacy – fallacious argument
hypothesis – statement of fact
identical – contradictory

imagine – imagination
implications – consequences
infer – imply – entail
inference – deduction
interpretation – point of view
justified – unjustified
know – believe
listening – speaking
logic/logical – illogical
logical certainty – logical
   impossibility
meaning – definition
mystery – philosophy
necessary – sufficient
   conditions
objective – subjective
observation – interpretation
qualifying – refuting
paraphrase – summarise
plausibile – implausible
possible – probable – certain
predict – assess
prejudice (bias) – balanced
   view
premise – conclusion
principle – grounds for belief
problem – solution
prove – disprove
prove (proof) – guess(work)
question/s – answer/s
questions (open and closed)
rational – irrational
real – not real
reason – explain
reason – faith – intuition
reasons – supporting
   arguments
relevant – irrelevant
right – wrong
rule – exceptions

rule – rules
similar – different
simplified – over-simplified
talking – discussing
thinking – thoughts – ideas
true – untrue (truth/lies)
view/s – opinion/s
weak/strong argument –
   criticism

**Add your own 'thinking and
learning words' to this list:**

Subject of study	*Purpose and value for studying it*
_____	_____
_____	_____
_____	_____
_____	_____
_____	_____
_____	_____

10 Discuss how you have learned

Ask children to think back to something they have learnt in the past and discuss with a partner what they learnt, and how they learned it. Ask them, for example, to discuss and note their answers to these questions:

- ■ What did you learn?
- ■ How did you learn?
- ■ Did others help you to learn? How?
- ■ Did you help yourself to learn? How?
- ■ What, if anything, might have helped you to learn better or faster?

9

The Dialogic Future

Nasruddin and a friend were walking down a road.
 'If you had a wish for the future what would you wish for, Nasruddin?' asked the friend.
 'A pile of gold', said Nasruddin.
 'That would make you a rich man,' said his friend. 'Would you share your gold with me?'
 'No,' said Nasruddin.
 'No,' exclaimed his friend. 'We have been friends for so long and we have shared so many joys and sorrows, and you won't share your gold with me?!'
 'Look,' said Nasruddin. 'Imagine a pile of gold for yourself and leave mine alone!'

To succeed in an uncertain future young people will need to be flexible, adaptable and creative. Children can expect to work in jobs that do not yet exist and to use technology not yet invented. They are likely to have to change jobs several times and to cope with information that is doubling every few years. What they need therefore is an education that equips them for uncertainty and a long future – hopefully for eighty years or more of active life.

We are preparing them for many possible future worlds. For this they need the skills of 'possibility thinking', including the ability to ask questions such as: 'What if . . .?'; 'Perhaps if . . .?'; 'Why?' and 'Why not?' They need to engage in dialogue about these questions, and to reflect on what concerns them all – the problems and opportunities of their future world.

How do we help to prepare them for this changing world? One way is to try to engage them in 'futures thinking' – thinking ahead. Ask them to imagine what it might be like in a future world, for example, to think about how things might change – what sort of jobs they might do, the types of houses they might live in, how the environment might change, what inventions and new forms of travel there might be, what holidays or what the schools of the future might be like.

One of the disquieting features of recent research into children's attitudes is the apparent growth in their fears about the future. How do we instil in them the confidence that they can make a difference? One way might be to ask them to imagine their ideal future world and ways in which this world might be realised. What world do they want? What sorts of people do they want to be?

This chapter on the dialogic future for children will include a focus on the following ways of encouraging dialogue with and between children about the future.

1 Thinking ahead: focusing on creative futures.

2 Green thinking: facing environmental challenges.

3 Possibility thinking: creating possible and better worlds.

4 Dialogue and technology: developing dialogue in a techno-world.

5 Future thinking in practice.

Thinking ahead: focusing on creative futures

If we don't look after the world who will?

(Daniel, aged 9)

Unlike animals that have no language in which to predict the future or describe the past, human beings have the capacity to construct in their imaginations many possible futures. Every human life is a kind of experiment where future outcomes are uncertain, and different possibilities can be imagined. Although much of the future remains unknown through the use of imagination children can envisage what it might be like. Thinking ahead invites students to think along a time scale into the future, to ask '*What might be?*' and to think creatively of what may be to come.

Thinking ahead can occur along a time scale which is immediate, short-term, medium-term or long-term. Choose a time scale as a focus for dialogic enquiry and refer to concepts of possibility, probability and certainty in discussing questions such as:

■ What outcome are you sure about?

■ Will it always turn out like this?

■ What else could it be like?

■ Do we know what will happen?

■ What do you think will happen? Why?

Part of assessing possible consequences is working out not only what will happen, but also the risks involved – factors that might upset our predictions and alter the consequences:

■ What are the opportunities? What is the ideal (best) outcome?

■ What are the dangers?

■ What might go wrong?

■ What is the worst thing that could go wrong?

■ What is the most likely outcome?

Thinking ahead offers good starting points for creative dialogue. A question like '*What do you think will happen next?*' could refer to the next page, episode, book, picture, design, action or idea. Begin a thought or a story and invite the student to discuss it with a partner. What might the sequel be? An understanding of the concepts of past, present and future is a gradual process in young children but it is a powerful tool for grasping how things change and how we change too.

Dialogic assessment provides good opportunities to focus on thinking ahead (see p. 197 for some more activities to encourage creative dialogue about thinking ahead).

Green thinking: facing environmental challenges

'Green thinking' means thinking about ways to preserve and enhance the environment. It is stimulated by engagement with real problems and lived experience, and involves using our knowledge and skills for practical purposes to improve the environment. Any local environment can offer starters for investigation, problem-solving and 'green thinking'. Questions to discuss about any environment include:

- *What*: What are the problems? What do we need to find out? What should we do?
- *Where*: Where do the problems occur?
- *Why*: Why is it a problem?
- *When*: When do problems occur?
- *Who*: Who is involved?
- *How*: How can we improve/make safer/better preserved/more beautiful the environment?

Issues in the local environment that might be worth thinking about and discussing include:

- *Green spaces*: How to use, improve, design a play area for children.
- *Keeping the neighbourhood tidy*: How to discourage litter/encourage tidiness, design litter bins, where should they best be put?
- *Local routes*: To places of interest – quickest, safest, most interesting.
- *Local transport*: How it could be improved –≠transport of the future using road, rail, sea or air; consider speed, safety, payment and pollution factors.
- *Local issues*: What is the main local problem – causes, possible cures and what can we do about it?
- *Conservation*: What should be conserved – why, how, where, when?
- *Old people*: How to help them, how they can help us, problems of old age.
- *Leisure facilities*: Discuss a range of activities that would appeal to local people in creating a leisure complex.
- *Recycling*: What needs recycling, why and how?
- *Campaign*: Plan how to advertise, fundraise or make something to help the local environment.

Find information on conservation and green issues in local newspapers or organisations to share and discuss with children. Focus on local needs and how they can be met, helping children to see where they can make a difference in a small way; for example, by discussing with a community police officer ways to ensure the environment is safe as well as green (see p. 198 for some starters for discussion on green issues).

Possibility thinking: creating possible and better worlds

Progress is impossible without change, and those who cannot change their minds cannot change anything.

(George Bernard Shaw)

Children need to know how things are, but also how they might be different. Imagination can enable them to think about how things might be different in ways that are not restricted to the possible and practicable. They can dream the impossible and the impracticable and try experimenting with thoughts and ideas, speculating on how things might be different. They can create new worlds for themselves and for others, see things in new ways, go where they want to go, and create thoughts that no one has imagined before.

What if animals could speak? What if you woke up one morning and could not see? What if the world ran out of petrol? All these situations involve hypothetical thinking. With these hypotheses they are creating a possible world. Scientific theories begin as hypotheses about the real world, and stories and poetry begin as hypotheses about imagined worlds. The creative imagination required is fuelled by creative dialogue.

Do not allow children to be trapped into thinking that there is always only one way of doing something. Help them see that there may be many uses for any object or experience. They might adapt things in different ways for different purposes. They might change their habits. The world might be changed. Encourage them to think – 'How else might this be?' And, 'How else might we be?' Are they the person they want to be? How else might they act? What else might they do?

Is the world the place they want it to be? How else might it be? How else could we or others act to make a better world?

See p. 198 for some dialogic activities to encourage possibility thinking.

Dialogue and technology: developing dialogue in a techno-world

A computer is like a slave, not a friend.

(Carl, aged 10)

Children today are awash with information in a world of information pollution and overload. They increasingly live in a cyber-culture where the image reigns supreme and information comes pre-digested. For years technology advocates have claimed that access to information is 'power' – but 'information' by itself doesn't mean anything. Knowledge on its own is inert, in the sense that it does not explain itself. Information by itself does not help children solve problems, analyse or understand the 'facts' presented to them. Downloading knowledge from the Internet may not activate their minds, but it can make them dependent on a techno-world created and controlled by the minds of others.

Better than being locked into a world of chat, texts and computer games is to encourage children to engage in human interaction and dialogue, and to stimulate their minds through books rather than images, real experience rather than the virtual reality of techno- and televisual worlds.

Children live in a 'soundbite' society. In many homes there is a dearth of dialogue and in some classrooms research shows that the average answer expected of children is five words or fewer. Children can be rich in computer facilities, but dialogue-deprived. Computers in the classroom may have no positive effect on children's educational performance and heavy computer use at home can be detrimental to children's learning. 'Students perform significantly worse if they have computers at home,' the authors of a recent report conclude (see the Alliance for Childhood's critical reports *Tech Tonic: Towards A New Literacy* and *Fools Gold: A Critical Look at Computers in Childhood*, at www.allianceforchildhood.org). By contrast, research shows that children with access to around 500 books in their homes perform better. The negative correlation, researchers claim, is because children with computers neglect their homework more and have less time for reading. In addition, heavy computer use limits their opportunities for dialogue and other forms of social interaction.

Computers at home are not so much used by children for running educational software, exploring the Internet for useful data or composing better homework assignments, all things that would have a positive impact on performance, but rather for playing games, chatting with friends and being otherwise entertained. Computer use can displace other activities, like dialogue with parents or peers, which are more conducive to thinking and learning.

The availability of computers at school does not necessarily lead to better student performance either. Research shows the following correlation between computer use and educational performance:

- Little computer use = poor performance.
- Moderate computer use = higher performance.
- Frequent computer use = poor performance.

The important issue is *what* you do with the computer, not just its availability. E-mail use, website accessibility and educational software can all facilitate dialogic interaction, both at home and at school. Teachers should use technology as a stimulus for and not an alternative to dialogue with and between children. Technology is useful only so far as it helps children develop the habits of mind, feeling and action that over time help develop their capacities for dialogue, thinking and moral understanding.

Children need to be taught how to make technological choices that serve human needs. This will require a move from a passive attachment to screen-based entertainment to one in which the development of dialogic learning is at the heart of new and developing technologies, to help support democracy, ecological sustainability and a just society. Teachers and parents need to develop their own technology literacy to help support dialogue in the home and at school.

Children are immersed in a virtual, high-tech world that they are often expected to navigate with little guidance and few boundaries. Technology needs to be used to support educational and family habits that are healthy both for children and for the survival of the Earth. It is within the context of dialogic relationships that children learn best. As we shift more towards the impersonal use of high technology as a major tool for teaching young children, the danger is that we will lose the creative context of dialogic relationships that reinforces learning at all ages.

The ways in which teachers can use technology to further dialogic learning include:

- ensuring that dialogic homework features on the school's learning platform technology;
- using a child's personalised online learning space or e-portfolio as a focus for dialogic assessment;
- recording on a digital recorder the first draft of a child's writing or learning activity, to discuss with a partner, response group or class;
- recording a dialogue on a digital recorder, then transcribing it, or for the child to listen and discuss and evaluate or to extend the dialogue;
- using the digital video cam to record a dialogue and using this to reflect on or evaluate the process as well as the content;
- using a digital camera to record a visit, to discuss and create captions for a website, wall display or thinking journal;
- creating with a partner a powerpoint presentation of joint research or context for learning.

To sum up, the key messages of future thinking should be:

- Make dialogue and human relationships a top priority at home and school.
- Engage children in green thinking to focus them on their relationships with the living world.
- Foster creative dialogue every day, and make it feature in every lesson.
- Use technology to enhance opportunities for dialogue.
- Promote creative dialogue with and among children engaged in future thinking.

The best education does not require high-tech products in the classroom. It needs to focus on basic human needs which includes the regular practice of creative dialogue to enhance teaching and learning through heart, hand and head.

Future thinking in practice

There is never a last word because there can always be another word.

(Paul, aged 8)

Creative dialogue leaves room for the unexpected, an adventure in thinking without endings or boundaries, reflecting a future full of possibility. The following sections discuss possible dialogic activities that focus on future thinking:

1 Thinking ahead.

2 Should we be optimistic or pessimistic about the future?

3 Thinking about the environment.

4 Possibility thinking.

5 Space pioneers.

6 Survival kit criteria.

7 How are you similar to or different from a computer?

1 Thinking ahead

Do some forward thinking about the topics below. Specify a time scale for your forward thinking (e.g. less than a year, one to five years, five to fifteen years, or twenty-five-plus years). Discuss with a partner, for example:

■ a classroom or school of the future;

■ the development of computer technology;

■ what will happen when the world runs out of oil;

■ the effects of continued global warming;

■ what living in a house of the future would be like;

■ one or more things that would improve the human body;

■ how a robot of the future might work and what it might do;

■ the forms that transport for the future might take and the problems it needs to solve;

■ what three wishes you have for the future of the world;

■ what a time capsule might contain for someone in the future to find.

2 Should we be optimistic or pessimistic about the future?

A recent newspaper report on a survey of people's attitudes to the future bore the headline: 'People are more pessimistic about the future.' Ask children to discuss whether they are optimistic or pessimistic about the future. Winston Churchill, Britain's leader during the Second World War, advised: 'Be an optimist. There is not much use being anything else.' What he did not say was why we should be optimistic.

■ Ask children to discuss with a partner reasons for thinking we should be optimists; that is, being cheerful, hopeful and believing things will turn out well in the future.

■ There are two sides to every viewpoint. Ask children to discuss with a partner the reasons for being pessimistic. Explain that to be pessimistic is to be fearful about ways in which things will get worse in the future. What might be the reasons for being pessimistic?

■ Discuss which of these views it is better to take. Why? Do others agree?

3 Thinking about the environment

Discuss with a partner:

- What is pollution? What are the dangers of pollution?
- What are your views about graffiti?
- How would you improve a local park or green space?
- What a safe but interesting play area for children might look like.
- What are the problems with litter? How can we help? Design a litter bin that would help improve the environment.
- What problems do birds face? How can we help? Design a bird-table that would help feed birds in winter.
- How could local transport be improved?
- Design a leisure complex to include activities that would appeal to local people.

4 Possibility thinking

Choose one of the questions below and then trace the reasonable and logical consequences that would follow. You might be sure to think of both good, bad and perhaps interesting consequences. Try to list or describe (in a sentence or two each) at least ten consequences.

- What if we could live forever?
- What if there was no petrol in the world?
- What if you woke up one morning and could not see?
- What if rats grew ten times their present size and developed a superior intelligence?
- What if our pets could talk?
- What if anyone could set up as a doctor?
- What if we never had to sleep?
- What if we could read other people's minds (and they could read ours)?
- What if everybody looked almost exactly alike?
- What if the Earth stopped revolving and the Sun did not rise in the morning?

5 Space pioneers

Imagine that a new planet has been discovered in our solar system. This planet resembles the Earth in every way except that there are no human beings living there. You have been chosen to lead the fist pioneers to settle on the newly discovered planet. You can select five advisers to go with you who you think will be most valuable on the new planet. Select five from the following list of ten people:

- Pat, aged 45, schoolteacher
- Bob, aged 56, builder
- Gary, aged 34, cook
- Fleur, aged 27, botanist
- Simon, aged 43, farmer
- Mary, aged 32, engineer
- John, aged 51, priest
- Omar, aged 40, architect
- Ben, aged 36, sports coach
- Nadine, aged 30, doctor

When you have chosen five advisers to join you as space pioneers, put them in order of preference. What do you think the possible benefits and drawbacks (pros and cons) would be of choosing these people? Ask others to choose their list. Compare your list and reasons for making choices with theirs.

6 Survival kit criteria

Ask children to imagine you are about to set out on a journey of exploration to unknown lands, like the great travellers and explorers of the past such as Ibn Battutah or Marco Polo. What supplies, equipment and personal possessions would they take with them? Discuss and list the ten portable items that you think they would most want on such a journey.

ITEM: WHAT I WOULD TAKE	CRITERION: REASON WHY I WOULD TAKE IT
1	
2	
3	

7 How are you similar to and different from a computer?

'What is a person?' is a fundamental question for educators and for learners. One way to engage children in responding to this question is to ask them to discuss in what ways they think they are similar to and different from a computer (or any other physical object). These could be noted on a chart and then shared with other groups.

How are you similar to and different from a computer?

SIMILAR	DIFFERENT

If there are differences between human beings and computers then children should be educated as persons with these qualities and not treated as objects like computers. What, then, should their education include?

Conclusion

Creative dialogue is no mere conversation. It is not just about speaking and listening but about thinking together. In a world beset by problems and strife caused by the failure of communication there can be no task more important than teaching children how to engage in productive discussion. Their happiness in human relations and their future success will depend in large part on their ability to think, talk and listen. Creative dialogue is the heart of education and should be part of all teaching and learning.

Dialogue is not always easy to achieve. It can be a real challenge, for adults as well as for children, to listen carefully and to talk in depth about issues that matter. It can be tiring to sustain and may not always work. It will often involve much tacking from side to side, like a yacht sailing against the tide. When it works there will be a forward movement, sometimes in odd directions and with unexpected outcomes. As one child said after a philosophical discussion: 'Wow, I never knew we could have so many thoughts!'

All human dialogue must in a sense be incomplete (unless the talk is about a closed question, problem or topic for which there is only one right answer). A creative dialogue has no final end because there is always something more that might be said. What sustains it is sensitive listening and talk that builds upon ideas and provokes and assesses new thinking. It builds intelligence, expands consciousness and provides a model for productive human relationships. Through creative dialogue children learn how to become co-constructors of new ideas, new meanings and better worlds. Many teachers find that creative dialogue with children is the most rewarding part of teaching. It enables any encounter with children to become an adventure in thinking.

Notes

3 Creative Talk for Thinking

1 The poem may be found in *Poems for Thinking* (Fisher 1997b, p.104).
2 A version of this story may be found in *Stories for Thinking* (Fisher 1996, p.33).

4 Critical Talk: Developing Verbal Reasoning

1 Reason 1: *Smoking in the street is not illegal.* Reason 2: *People who smoke get a lot of pleasure from it.* Conclusion: *People should be allowed to smoke where they want to.*
2 The claim that a horse was brought to court is a factual claim, that it was 'magnificent' is a judgement or opinion. The claim that none could ride it is a factual claim. 'None except me' was claimed by Nasruddin to be a fact, but it turned out to be a false opinion.
3 We might want to challenge the claim that 'most parents would prefer to have sons' by asking for evidence.

   If the first claim is true it would justify arguing that 'if people can choose the sex of their child it is likely there would be many more boys than girls'. The first statement supports this conclusion. However, the claim that 'this would lead to serious social problems' is not here supported by argument or evidence. To accept this as true we would need to know more, since it may or may not be true.
4 An argument is made here where the claims, if they are true, support the conclusion. However, there may be other relevant arguments to consider before making a judgement on this issue.
5 The first reason, 'many people claim that watching violence on TV makes people more violent', is a factual claim. It may be making one of two claims. It may refer to *all* people or to *some* people. We need to know this since it may affect the argument. We may also want to know what evidence supports this claim. The second part of the argument, 'this is not true since I watch violence on TV and this has not made me more violent', is also a factual claim. How do we know it is true? If the first reason refers to only *some* people then the second reason does not justify saying 'this is not true'. The conclusion 'you should be free to watch whatever you want' is a value claim. We need to consider what this means. What does 'being free' mean? Does 'to watch whatever you want' refer only to violent programmes (i.e. some) or to any (i.e. all) kinds of programme? We would also need to consider the consequences of such a principle to accept the argument.
6 1. Not valid – no premise in this argument connects 'my turn' with 'my ball'. 2. Not valid – we do not know what will happen if you do not eat an apple. 3. Valid. 4. Valid. 5. Not valid – nothing proves the air from the pine woods was the cure.

7   Mencius argued that the only thing to do was to arrest his father. Shun should not interfere with the judge who was acting within the law. However, Mencius continues, Shun would then have abdicated the throne and fled with his father to the safety of the distant sea coast.

5 Talking to Learn Across the Curriculum

1   Nasruddin replied, 'Donkeys.'

6 Talking Together: Talk to Think in Groups

1   'Oh great king, would you kindly draw up your knees?' said Birbal. The emperor drew up his knees. Birbal then threw the cloak over him and it covered him from head to toe. The courtiers, realising that they had failed the test, quietly left the room.
2   Hobbits and Orcs solution: 1. Initial situation hhhooo ⇔; 2. Two orcs cross hhho ⇔ oo; 3. An orc comes back hhhoo ⇔ o; 4. Two orcs cross hhh ⇔ ooo; 5. An orc comes back hhho ⇔ oo; 6. Two hobbits cross ho ⇔ hhoo; 7. An orc and hobbit come back hhoo ⇔ ho; 8. Two hobbits cross oo ⇔ hhho; 9. An orc comes back ooo ⇔ hhh; 10. Two orcs cross o ⇔ hhhoo; 11. An orc comes back oo ⇔ hhho; 12. Two orcs cross ⇔ hhhooo. Notice on step 7: an orc and hobbit who have already crossed must return to ensure the orcs do not outnumber the hobbits on either side.
3   Answer: 7 + 49 + 343 + 2401 + 16,807 = 19,607.
4   Answer uses the same method, but adds an extra stage: 7 + 49 + 343 + 2401 + 16,807 + 117,649 = 137,256.

7 Extending Talk for Thinking

1   The author is grateful to Julie Winyard for this excerpt of classroom discussion.

8 Dialogic Assessment

1   I am grateful to Julie Winyard for this example of guidance and the 'think book' page shown in Figure 8.1.
2   Sissa required 2 to the power of 64 −1= 18,446,744,073,709,551,615 grains of wheat. The king could never provide that amount of wheat from his kingdom since it was more than the whole world could produce in many years.

Further Reading

Alexander, R.J. (2006) *Towards Dialogic Teaching* (3rd edn). Cambridge: Cambridge University Faculty of Education: Dialogos.

Bakhtin, M. (1981) *The Dialogic Imagination.* Austin: University of Texas Press.

Bakhtin, M. (1986) *Speech Genres and Other Late Essays.* Austin: University of Texas Press.

Black, P. and Wiliam, D. (1998) *Inside the Black Box: Raising Standards Through Classroom Assessment.* London: NFER Nelson.

Black, P., Harrison, C., Lee, C., Marshall, B. and Wiliam, D. (2002) *Working Inside the Black Box: Assessment for Learning in the Classroom.* London: NFER Nelson.

Black, P., Harrison, C., Lee, C., Marshall, B. and Wiliam, D. (2003) *Assessment for Learning: Putting it into Practice.* Buckingham: Open University Press.

Buber, M. (1923/1958) *I and Thou* (2nd edn). Edinburgh: T. & T. Clark. Translation: R. Gregory Smith.

Cam, P. (2006) *20 Thinking Tools.* Australian Council for Educational Research.

Dweck, C.S. (2000) *Self-theories: Their Role in Motivation, Personality and Development.* London: Taylor & Francis.

Dweck, C.S. (2006) *Mindset.* New York: Random House.

Fisher, R. (1996) *Stories for Thinking.* Oxford: Nash Pollock.

Fisher, R. (1997a) *Games for Thinking.* Oxford: Nash Pollock.

Fisher, R. (1997b) *Poems for Thinking.* Oxford: Nash Pollock.

Fisher, R. (1998) 'Thinking about thinking: developing metacognition in children.' *Early Child Development and Care* 14, pp. 1–15.

Fisher, R. (1999) *First Stories for Thinking.* Oxford: Nash Pollock.

Fisher, R. (2000) *First Poems for Thinking.* Oxford: Nash Pollock.

Fisher, R. (2001) *Values for Thinking.* Oxford: Nash Pollock.

Fisher, R. (2005a) *Teaching Children to Learn* (2nd edn). Cheltenham: Nelson Thornes.

Fisher, R. (2005b) *Teaching Children to Think* (2nd edn). Cheltenham: Nelson Thornes.

Fisher, R. (2006a) *Starters for Thinking.* Oxford: Nash Pollock.

Fisher, R. (2006b) 'Still thinking: the case for meditation with children.' *Thinking Skills and Creativity International Journal*, pp. 146–51.

Fisher, R. (2007a) 'Dialogic teaching: developing thinking and metacognition through philosophical discussion'. *Early Child Development and Care* 177(6), pp. 615–31.

Fisher, R. (2007b) 'Dancing minds: the use of Socratic and Menippean dialogue in philosophical enquiry'. *Gifted Education International Journal* 22 (2 and 3), pp. 148–59.

Fisher, R. (2008a) *Teaching Thinking: Philosophical Enquiry in the Classroom* (3rd edn). London: Continuum.

Fisher, R. (2008b) 'Educating for enquiry: personalising learning through dialogic teaching', in *The Routledge International Companion to Gifted Education*, ed. T. Balchin, B. Hymer and D. Matthews. London: Routledge.

Fisher, R. (2008c) 'Philosophical intelligence: why philosophical discussion is important in educating the mind', in *Philosophy in Schools*, ed. G. Hand and C. Winstanley. London: Continuum.

Gardner, H. (1993) *Creating Minds*. New York: Basic Books.

Golding, C. (2002) *Connecting Concepts: Thinking Activities for Students*. Australian Council for Educational Research.

Habermas, J. (1990) *Moral Consciousness and Communicative Action*. Cambridge: Polity Press.

Habermas, J. (1991) *The Theory of Communicative Action. Vol. 1*. Cambridge: Polity Press.

Hattie, J. (2008) *Visible Learning: A Synthesis of Over 800 Meta-analyses Relating to Achievement*. London: Routledge.

Haynes, J. (2008) *Children as Philosophers: Learning Through Enquiry and Dialogue in the Primary Classroom*. Abingdon: Routledge.

Hobson, P. (2000) *The Cradle of Thought: Exploring the Origins of Thinking*. Basingstoke: Macmillan.

Jones, D. and Hodson, P. (eds) (2006) *Unlocking Speaking and Listening*. London: Fulton.

Lipman, M. (1991) *Thinking in Education*. Cambridge: Cambridge University Press.

Pope, R. (2005) *Creativity, Theory, History, Practice*. London: Routledge.

Robinson, K. (2001) *Out of Our Minds: Learning to be Creative*. Oxford: Capstone.

Topping, K.J. and Trickey, S. (2007) Collaborative philosophical enquiry for school children: cognitive gains. *British Journal of Educational Psychology*, 77(4), pp. 786–796.

Trickey, S. and Topping, K.J. (2006) 'Collaborative philosophical enquiry for school children: socio-emotional effects at 10–12 years.' *School Psychology International*, 27(5), pp. 599–614.

Vygotsky, L. (1991) 'The genesis of higher mental functions', in *Learning to Think*, ed. P. Light, S. Sheldon and B. Woodhead. London: Routledge.

Wegerif, R. (2006) 'Dialogic education: what is it and why do we need it?' *Education Review*, 19(2), pp. 58–67.

Index